Creole Renegades

UNIVERSITY PRESS OF FLORIDA

Florida A&M University, Tallahassee
Florida Atlantic University, Boca Raton
Florida Gulf Coast University, Ft. Myers
Florida International University, Miami
Florida State University, Tallahassee
New College of Florida, Sarasota
University of Central Florida, Orlando
University of Florida, Gainesville
University of North Florida, Jacksonville
University of South Florida, Tampa
University of West Florida, Pensacola

# Creole Renegades

Rhetoric of Betrayal and Guilt in the Caribbean Diaspora

BÉNÉDICTE BOISSERON

UNIVERSITY PRESS OF FLORIDA

Gainesville/Tallahassee/Tampa/Boca Raton

Pensacola/Orlando/Miami/Jacksonville/Ft. Myers/Sarasota

Publication of this paperback edition made possible by a Sustaining the Humanities through the American Rescue Plan grant from the National Endowment for the Humanities.

The publication of this book is made possible in part by a grant from the Office of the Vice President of Research and Creative Scholarship at the University of Montana.

Published in the United States of America

First cloth printing, 2014
First paperback printing, 2022

27  26  25  24  23  22    6  5  4  3  2  1

Library of Congress Cataloging-in-Publication Data
Boisseron, Bénédicte. author.
Creole renegades : rhetoric of betrayal and guilt in the Caribbean diaspora / Bénédicte Boisseron.
pages cm
Includes bibliographical references and index.
ISBN 978-0-8130-4979-3 (cloth) | ISBN 978-0-8130-6879-4 (pbk.)
1. Creoles—Caribbean Area. 2. Creole literature—North America. 3. Caribbean Area—Emigration and immigration. 4. West Indians—Migrations. 5. Ethnicity—Caribbean Area. 6. Nationalism—Caribbean Area. 7. Broyard, Anatole. 8. Condé, Maryse. 9. Danticat, Edwidge, 1969– 10. Laferriére, Dany. 11. Naipaul, V. S. (Vidiadhar Surajprasad), 1932– 12. Kincaid, Jamaica. I. Title.
PM7834.C37B65 2014
417'.2209729—dc23    2013051136

The University Press of Florida is the scholarly publishing agency for the State University System of Florida, comprising Florida A&M University, Florida Atlantic University, Florida Gulf Coast University, Florida International University, Florida State University, New College of Florida, University of Central Florida, University of Florida, University of North Florida, University of South Florida, and University of West Florida.

University Press of Florida
2046 NE Waldo Road
Suite 2100
Gainesville, FL 32609
http://upress.ufl.edu

To Ulrich, Armand, and Pierre, and in loving memory of my mother

It should give you not only comfort, but a sense of cultural obligation,
to feel that you are an important part of the Caribbean as external frontier.

GEORGE LAMMING, "CONCEPTS OF THE CARIBBEAN"

# Contents

# Acknowledgments

In 1999, after forty years in the French *métropole*, my father, a *négropolitain*, and my mother, a French *métropolitaine*, took the entire family to Guadeloupe for a visit. In the streets of Pointe-à-Pitre, a stranger hailed my father: "Hey, you are not from Guadeloupe, right?" "Not for a while," my father admitted. "How did you know?" I, the half-*negzagonale*, asked the stranger. "I can see it just from the way your father walks." This project began on that day, in the streets of Pointe-à-Pitre, as I learned my first lesson on the complex choreography of the idiosyncratic Antillanity in my father's footsteps. I would like to thank my parents, Luc and Brigitte Boisseron, for their love and encouragement. *Kenbé rèd pa moli: oui maman.*

•

I would like to express my deepest gratitude to Frieda Ekotto for her intellectual expertise, her precious guidance at every step of this long process, and the countless hours of stimulating discussions. I am also extremely grateful to colleagues and friends for their editing contributions: Ione Crummy, Anny Curtius, Yvonne Gritzner, Katie Kane, Danielle LaVaque-Manty, Naomi Shin, and Miriam Ticktin. I owe a debt of gratitude to Jarrod Hayes and Mamadou Diouf for their unwavering support over the years. Special thanks are extended to Anja Bandau for hosting me at the Institute for Latin American Studies, the Freie Universität Berlin, Germany. I gratefully acknowledge the Alexander von Humboldt Foundation, the Office of Research and Creative Scholarship at the University of Montana, and the Summerfield Baldridge Book Subvention Fund in the University of Montana College of Arts and Sciences for financial support to carry out this project.

The kindness of my colleagues in the Department of Modern Languages and Literatures at the University of Montana is also greatly appreciated. I am grateful to the reviewers at University Press of Florida for their insightful comments and suggestions. I thank my family, Papoteuse, Patrick, Thomas, Guillaume, Clothilde, Armand, and Pierre, for their patience and encouragement, and Sophie my guardian angel. And finally, thank you to my husband Ulrich, my companion in arms in Cuccuma (Berlin) and Zootown (Missoula), without whom this book could not have been written.

# Note on Translations

Any translation without a page reference is my own. The original version, along with the appropriate page reference, is provided in the footnotes.

# The Second-Generation Caribbean Diaspora

In a 1985 public lecture in Toronto, Canada, the Barbadian-born George Lamming told the crowd, "Wherever you are, outside of the Caribbean, it should give you not only comfort, but a sense of cultural obligation, to feel that you are an important part of the Caribbean as external frontier."[1] Lamming's off-center Caribbean, this extendable Caribbean frontier resulting from a postcolonial and global era of geographical porousness, is today not a new concept. Suffice it to say that Little Haiti in Miami, the Antillean Sarcelles in the Parisian suburbs, and the Haitian diasporic community of Flatbush in Brooklyn attest to the viability of a Caribbean world outside of the archipelago. This book, however, does not address the external frontier of the Caribbean diasporic community of, let us say, Paule Marshall's *Brown Girl, Brownstones* or of Sandra Cisneros's *The House on Mango Street*. The goal of this study is rather to bring attention to a new, more controversial voice from the Caribbean diaspora: that of the Caribbean *individual* writing outside of both the internal and external Caribbean frontiers. *Creole Renegades* looks at immigrant writers who had to—more or less controversially—leave their native environment and, as a consequence, relate to their community from a questionable distance as they reassessed the assumed cultural obligation imposed by their Caribbean, and more broadly, black diasporic cultural background.

The concept of diaspora, in the context of the black diaspora, suggests today a sense of diffraction, which goes against the ancestral use of the word evoking a centripetal compulsion through a desire for reunification. *Diaspora*, the Greek for "scattering," initially referred to Hellenistic Jews severed from Palestine and living in exile. In the seventeenth century, the word extended to the exiled condition of the Huguenots, the Armenians, and the Palestinians. From the late sixteenth to the early nineteenth centuries, the Middle Passage initiated the black African diaspora, which consisted of Africans involuntarily shipped to the New World as part of the triangular slave trade. *Diaspora* traditionally implied a binary perspective: the land of asylum on the one hand and the home left behind on the other. The longing to return "home," which is inherent in most initial diasporas, offered a teleological and homogeneous perception of migration. But with time, in the case of the black African diaspora, the first (transatlantic) wave of migration gave way to a second wave primarily located in the United States, and the result is a stratified diasporic community. As Jana Evans Braziel and Anita Mannur point out:

> This early transatlantic African diaspora resulted in numerous fractured diasporas in the late nineteenth and throughout the twentieth century, as black Africans migrated from south to north in North America and across the Western hemisphere—from Port au Prince to Montréal, from Kingston to London and elsewhere.[2]

In the 1990s, scholars started to focus on the exponential growth of the black diaspora, "scattering" gradually becoming synonymous with "seeding." In much the same process, diaspora has grown—to use Gilles Deleuze and Felix Guattari's terminology—"molecular," engaged as it is in a process of becoming and heterogeneity. Stuart Hall draws attention to the fact that diaspora must be defined, not as "an essence of purity," but rather as "the recognition of a necessary heterogeneity and diversity."[3] As diasporic phenomena become increasingly scattered, the idea of unity in spite of, and certainly because of, primal uprootedness turns out to be obsolete. To put it simply, in its newly perceived diffractive nature, diaspora is, paradigmatically, tantamount to creolization. As Gilroy says, diaspora means "like a number of other key concepts that have been deployed to do parallel work—hybrid, border, creolization, *mestizaje*, and even locality."[4] More recently, Jana Evans Braziel and Anita Mannur have confirmed Gilroy's view writing that "like the critical terms *rhizome, créole, creolization, hybridity, heterogeneity, métis*, and *métissage*, then, diaspora has emerged as an internal critique of . . . binarisms."[5] The emergence of an ever-growing second-generation diaspora—what Braziel and Mannur refer to as "fractured diasporas"—complicates the idea of home. In his 1994 article "Diasporas," James Clifford viewed the erosion of memory as a contributory factor to the loss of a sense of connection to the past home. "This sense of connection must be strong enough to resist erasure through the normalizing processes of forgetting, assimilating, and distancing."[6] But the connection to the homeland and the pressure of not forgetting the original home are antiquated assets when the diasporic home itself is said to be diffractive, unsettling, and creolized. Initially severed from Africa, and more recently moving toward northern destinations in America, the modern black diaspora in the New World necessarily holds a stratified perception of the "prior home."

Though arguably diffractive, the Caribbean diaspora has also been engaged, paradoxically enough, in a slow process of territorialization over the course of the twentieth century, which has grounded once dispersed peoples into rooted communities in spite of the lingering effect of colonization. The second-generation Caribbean diaspora works as a counterforce to the reterritorialization of the prior generation. The second-generation diaspora, as it needs to be understood within the context of this book, is the one that is currently molecular; it *always already* pushes delineated—both interior and external—frontiers. The traditional sense of diaspora is connected to *minority*, two concepts that presuppose the idea of people from a common background sticking together in a situation of geographical and cultural estrangement. Hannah Arendt, who coined the word *minority* back in the 1950s, wrote that post–World War II European minorities "never reached the stage of national freedom and self-determination to which colonial peoples already aspired and which was being held out to them."[7] And indeed, unlike minorities in nation-states, the first-generation Caribbean diaspora today evokes some sense of national freedom, self-determination, and territorialization. As the Barbadian Edward Brathwaite says, "Creolization (despite its attendant imitations and conformities) provided the conditions for and possibility of local residence."[8] Even when it comes to the islands of Martinique and Guadeloupe, despite an enduring sense of alienation initiated by their departmentalization (1946), the two islands have reached a relative sense of archipelagic domiciliation.[9] No doubt, the Caribbean identity is still deeply shaped by the slavery that initiated its diasporic history, but it is safe to say that it has become, on some islands more than others, a domiciliated diasporic identity. Uprootedness is still a pertinent topic today, particularly in literature, but it applies more accurately to the second-generation Caribbean diasporic subject who lives alone, both outside the archipelago and outside Europe. When it comes to Caribbean literature, one tends to overlook the fact that Frantz Fanon and Aimé Césaire chose to reside neither in the Caribbean nor in the *métropole* while writing their monumental political testaments. Fanon's 1961 *Les damnés de la terre* (*The Wretched of the Earth*, 2001) was written in Tunisia, while Césaire drafted his 1939 epic poem *Cahier d'un retour au pays natal* (*Notebook of a Return to the Native Land*, 2001) in Dalmatia, Croatia. The writers at the center of *Creole*

*Renegades* have made similar choices in their context of enunciation. From a decentered location, they write against new types of binarisms: neither the Caribbean nor Europe, neither the ex-colony nor the *métropole*, neither the periphery nor the center. This book gathers writers who share a similar intention to speak outside of any sedimented diasporic frontiers.

Maryse Condé was born in 1937 in Pointe-à-Pitre, Guadeloupe, a French island located in the Lesser Antilles. She studied in Paris, worked in then soon-to-be-independent West Africa, and then moved to the United States, where she has been living on and off for more than thirty-five years. She is currently professor emerita at Columbia University and the author of numerous novels, essays, and plays. Dany Laferrière was born in 1953 in Port-au-Prince, Haiti, in the Greater Antilles. He left Haiti at the age of twenty-four during the Duvalier regime and found a new home in Montreal. Since arriving in North America, Laferrière has lived in both Miami and Montreal. He is today the author of close to twenty books, all of which were published in North America.[10] Edwidge Danticat was born in 1969, also in Port-au-Prince. She left Haiti at the age of twelve to join her parents in Brooklyn. She attended Barnard College in New York and earned an MFA in creative writing from Brown University. She currently lives in Miami and is the recipient of various awards, including the prestigious MacArthur Foundation Genius Award. Jamaica Kincaid was born in 1949 in Antigua, in the Lesser Antilles. She moved to the United States at the age of seventeen and worked various jobs before becoming a full-time writer. Most of her books deal with the colonial past of her native island, as well as her conflicted relationship with her family in Antigua. Her main residence is in Vermont, but she also lives in California, where she teaches at Claremont McKenna College. Anatole Broyard was born in 1920 in New Orleans. He is the offspring of a Louisiana Creole family whose ancestors came from France and Haiti (formerly Saint-Domingue). As a young child, Broyard moved to Brooklyn with his family. He held a number of teaching positions, including at the New School for Social Research, New York University, and Columbia University. He is mostly known today for having been one of the most acclaimed literary critics for the *New York Times*. During his lifetime, he was often said to be working on an autobiographically inspired book, which he never completed. After his death, others wrote the story of his life.

Though all these Creole figures have received international acclaim for their work, they also all share a noticeably ambivalent relationship with their background, which, literally speaking, is the ground on which they allegedly turned their backs. Their communities (broadly defined) have accused them, in one way or another, of being traitors, sellouts, or simply opportunistic writers who are oblivious to their origins. In Edouard Glissant's theory of the Caribbean cultural rhizome stretching out to the world, Patrick Chamoiseau's praise of Creole heterogeneity encompassing cultural diversity, and Benítez-Rojo's "cultural meta-archipelago without center and without limits,"[11] it may be surprising to realize that the expatriate, this decentered figure living outside of the native Caribbean, is not necessarily a welcome figure in the Caribbean. The modern Caribbean diasporic author is a ragamuffin of a sort, a street renegade no longer fitting within a traditional and surprisingly sedentary ideology of Caribbeanness. With its tradition of postcolonial deconstruction and its important "contribution to the deconstruction of old systems of thought,"[12] the Caribbean diasporic culture is in need of fracture in order to create oppositional molecules that can deconstruct its totality.

## Creole Renegades and *Isolatoes*

Antilleans use a subtle taxonomy of cultural categorizations to identify one another. In the Antilles, there is a special way to walk, to talk, and to laugh. This is the reason why Antilleans have recourse to a specific terminology to identify those who do not belong. *Négropolitain, negzagonal, débarqué*—the French Antilles are not at a loss for words when it comes to pinpointing those who do not belong. *Négropolitain* is a combination of *nègre* (Negro) and *métropolitain* (from metropolitan France) and refers to black Antilleans who show French genotypical characteristics due to having lived a long time (presumably too long) in the French *métropole*. *Negzagonal* is similar in its neological construction, made up as it is of the words *nègre* and *hexagonal* (the hexagonally shaped metropolitan France) and describes black Antilleans from France. The *negzagonal* is usually born of Antillean parents, but, unlike the *négropolitain,* is born in the *métropole.* As for *débarqué,* it is an old version of *négropolitain.* Frantz Fanon, in *Peau noire, masques blancs* (*Black Skin, White Masks,* 1967), devotes a whole section to this unpopular cultural figure. The Martinican author describes the *débarqué* as an Antillean-born subject who, after some time spent in France, has freshly landed back in Martinique or Guadeloupe and flaunts disgraceful signs of French acculturation. All these words that originate from a sedentary Antillean perspective carry unpleasant undertones. They convey an uncanny sense of *Entfremdung*, a particular feeling of estrangement with the native land after an extended geographical separation.[13] *Entfremdung* is a current phenomenon in French overseas departments known for their commuting cultures, but this condition of defamiliarization is a double-edged sword: the Antillean-in-residence may be just as critical about the *débarqué*'s acculturation as the *débarqué* may be about the Antillean-in-residence's infallible permanence.

Given the controversial departmentalization of Martinique and Guadeloupe in 1946, it is not that surprising to find lingering anti-French assimilation semantics in the French Antilles. Again, the negative connotation brings us back to the concerns that Fanon raised in *Peau noire, masques blancs* about the pathological alienation of (post)colonial Antilleans having lived in France. The mistrust toward the hybrid condition of being both *métropolitain* and Antillean is understandable, even though its legitimacy is admittedly more contestable today than it was in the 1950s. Since the mid-1990s, there has been a growing interest in hybrid literature in both French and English. Gisèle Pineau (Guadeloupe), Suzanne Dracius (Martinique), Fabienne Kanor (Martinique), Caryl Phillips (St. Kitts), and Andrea Levy (British born to Jamaican parents), to name a few, have produced remarkable works addressing cultural in-betweenness. Yet, this literature, albeit groundbreaking in its bicultural scope, is predicated on the old binary metropolitan center / Empire. The limitation of this literature lies in its presupposition of not necessarily a Eurocentric but at least and definitely a Euro-inclusive enunciative framework.

Up to the early 1990s, the field of Caribbean Studies remained ideologically accountable to Europe, even and particularly so in its discourse of resistance. This postcolonial discourse, while aiming to defy European subordination, somehow kept Europe at the center of its preoccupations. As Françoise Lionnet and Shumai Shi point out, when "critiquing the center . . . , the center remains the focus and the main object of study."[14] This scholarly trend reached its peak in 1989 with the simultaneous publication of, for the English, *The Empire Writes Back* by Bill Ashcroft, Gareth Griffiths, and Helen Tiffin, and for the French, *Eloge de la Créolité* (*In Praise of Creoleness*, 1990) by Jean Bernabé, Patrick Chamoiseau, and Raphaël Confiant. In his 1982 piece from the *Times of London* entitled "The Empire Writes Back with a Vengeance" (the op-ed that inspired Ashcroft and his coauthors to write *The Empire Writes Back*), Salman Rushdie argues:

> In the rich, powerful societies of the West, it is possible to exclude politics from fiction; to treat public affairs as peripheral and faintly disreputable. From outside the West, this looks like the sort of position one can only take up inside a cocoon of privilege. There are very few writers in

the new English literatures who do not place politics at the very centre of their art.[15]

Whether in French or in English, it is undeniable that the Caribbean literature of the 1980s was politically engaged, as writers felt compelled to put politics at the center of their art. This postcolonial literature was engaged in "writing back with a vengeance" to the center, eager as it was to present the archipelagic culture of *métissage* as the New World order. The consequence is that, as the authors of *The Empire Writes Back* convincingly argue, the overall Empire-writing-back rhetoric successfully challenged "the world-view that can polarize center and periphery in the first place."[16] There is no doubt that the world perspective has been largely decentered in a rhizomatic poetics of *tout-monde* (Edouard Glissant) and archipelagic chaos (Antonio Benítez-Rojo). That said, Rushdie's main idea that writers outside the West are in consensus in seeing apolitical fiction as the exclusive privilege of the West has become more contestable today. In the area of African Studies, Evan Mwangi has recently brought attention to what the author names African "self-reflexive fiction."[17] Instead of writing back to an imaginary center, Mwangi posits that a theoretically unaccounted for African literature, starting in the mid-1980s, has been mainly preoccupied with local and personal issues. Odile Cazenave and Patricia Célérier proposed the same type of argument in their 2011 publication *Contemporary Francophone African Writers and the Burden of Commitment*. The two argue that many modern African writers have grown to privilege personal concerns over political engagements, consequently putting the tradition of a postcolonial discourse of resistance to rest.

In the same vein, *Creole Renegades* seeks to challenge "the writing back to the center" consensus in postcolonial studies. Yet, the book does not offer a local or native focus as an alternative, nor does it emphasize national self-reflexiveness. *Creole Renegades* seeks to complicate the issue of postcolonial decentralizing, arguing instead that, in a Caribbean context, local literary production has incidentally become the new center from which individual diasporic voices are breaking free. The project therefore proceeds past the *writing back to the (local) self* model in order to question the very meaning of *center*, no longer simply in terms of the metropolis but also today in terms of the native colonial place. In a Caribbean diasporic context, decentering is therefore double, taking place both outside of the metropolis and outside of the native Caribbean. Again, it needs to be stressed that decentering has recently grown, literally speaking, more diffractive. Caribbean-born writers have ceased to write either from or to the metropolitan center; they have also ceased to write at home in the restricted sense of "home" as a native place; and they even have ceased to write within the collective consciousness of the external frontier of the Caribbean. Rather, they have started producing within a Pan-American context for themselves and about their individual selves. Those writers are neither *négropolitain* nor *negzagonal*; we shall call them, for the purpose of echoing C.L.R. James, *Renegades*.

The Trinidadian Cyril Lionel Robert James was born in 1901. He is known for his political activism in London and America, his writings on the Haitian Revolution and cricket, and his seminal study of Herman Melville's *Moby-Dick*, entitled *Mariners, Renegades, and Castaways*. James wrote *Mariners, Renegades, and Castaways* in 1953 while being detained on Ellis Island awaiting deportation for a visa violation. As it happened, James produced his most influential work in what can be seen as the epitome of transient land: Ellis Island, the terra incognita of independent creativity. The title, *Mariners, Renegades, and Castaways*, alludes to Ahab's crew in *Moby-Dick*, a bunch of castaways and renegades set on a dark mission in the middle of the ocean. In this book, James draws attention to the oft-overlooked crewmembers on Ahab's boat who happen to be nearly all islanders. Each member is said to represent a nation of the globe. "*Isolatoes*, Melville called them,"—James explains—"not acknowledging the common continent of men, but each *isolato* living on a separate continent of his own."[18] The analogy is obvious: James, isolated, or rather in isolation on Ellis Island, is an extension of Melville's *isolato*. The writer is marooned in American waters to get his own sublimated version of *Moby-Dick*. Yet, like Melville's *isolato*, the Trinidadian writer is so unique and alone in his transience because he embraces singlehandedly "a separate continent of his own."[19] Out of those particular writing conditions, James the renegade writer comes across as a Melville-like figure, caught in his search for "the whale's white hump" in the name of "his whole race from Adam down,"[20] and yet first and foremost driven by his purely individualistic monomania, like a tragic hero taken by his own identity quest.

The renegade writers discussed in this book come after the author of *Mariners, Renegades, and Castaways*. Most of them evolve in a Pan-American radius, stranded in their own Ellis Island of isolation in Northern America while pressured to represent their entire nation of Caribbeanness. In *The Other America*, J. Michael Dash persuasively argues that, even though "New World" as in "New World Studies" ignores the Amerindian civilization, the term, in comparison with the more restricted "American Studies," efficiently translates a Pan-American perspective inclusive of the Americas and the Caribbean. The renegade writer, as presented in this book, is a New World subject connecting the Caribbean and North America and creating a literary relation between those two American axes. Maryse Condé (Guadeloupe–North America), Dany Laferrière (Haiti–Canada), Edwidge Danticat (Haiti–North America), Anatole Broyard (New Orleans–New York), and Jamaica Kincaid (Antigua–North America) comprise the renegade figures at the heart of this study. V. S. Naipaul is the only Caribbean migrant writer addressed in the book who did not migrate to America. But it is precisely his renegade status that highlights the difference between the "old" model from Europe and the "new" model of renegade from America. Because of political or economic reasons, education or the need to emancipate from the family, or simply because of the washed-out color of their skin after generations of Afro-American miscegenation, Condé, Laferrière, Danticat, Broyard, and Kincaid have all ended up leaving the south for a northern destination. Producing outside the Caribbean archipelago or New Orleans, those writers have dared to question their cultural obligation of *Caribbeanness* or *Creoleness*, a questioning that has left them prey to accusations of betrayal back home. The first-generation Caribbean diaspora as a location of primal residence, parental figure, and territorialization presents itself as the new center, the center to which diasporic writers need to talk back—like a defiant offspring insubordinately asserting his personality against authority; an expatriate who finally answers the native community's call after a deafening absence; or the immigrant writer desperately trying to reach back to a community that disowned her.

As Stuart Hall argued, all cultural identities raise questions of positioning and context of enunciation.[21] Yet, no matter the intended ideological context of enunciation, the context of reception remains the defining quality of the Caribbean diasporic voice, for better or for worse. Even though they aim at individual contexts of enunciation, Caribbean migrant writers are often recalled by their community and brought back to their cultural obligations as unwilling national spokespersons. Their ambivalent enunciative context is somehow reminiscent of C.L.R. James and Ahab's crewmembers: an *isolato* committed to a personal cause, yet at the same time fully aware of the weight of representing alone his or her entire continent. This vision of the modern Caribbean diaspora challenges Stuart Hall's further description of the diaspora as "this oneness," "common," "shared," being "the truth, the essence, of Caribbeanness."[22]

Return and Detour

As Geneviève Fabre and Klaus Benesch point out, "the myth of origin, of homeland and return . . . had always been an essential component of African diasporic consciousness."[23] But after the Pan-African and Negritude movements, the black diaspora has, on many occasions, shown its nonallegiance to the myth of origin, particularly so in Martinique. Glissant's *Antillanité*[24] initiated what the critic Ronnie Scharfman calls a "resistance-as-residence," a resistance "domiciliée."[25] Bernabé, Chamoiseau, and Confiant, inspired by Glissant's *Antillanité*, opened their manifesto *Eloge de la Créolité* with "Ni Européens, ni Africains, ni Asiatiques, nous nous proclamons Créoles" (Neither Europeans, nor Africans, nor Asians, we proclaim ourselves Creoles),[26] hereby rejecting the Pan-African consciousness of the Négritude poet Aimé Césaire. In diasporic cultures, the fantasy and impossibility of return traditionally keep the community together through an ever-postponed materialization of the return. The modern possibility of commuting, on the other hand, has changed the diasporic subject's geographic and temporal horizon. No longer impossible, the option of return has made the common fantasy of the diasporic community obsolete. As return gets technically easier, dispersion subsequently becomes more mobile, transient, and less permanent. In that regard, James Clifford says:

> Dispersed peoples, once separated from homelands by vast oceans and
> political barriers, increasingly find themselves in border relations with
> the old country thanks to a to-and-fro made possible by modern tech-
> nologies of transport, communication, and labor migration."[27]

Clifford's emphasis on the ease of commuting erases the line between the home state and the adopted land, thus turning immigration into a border diaspora, a kind of diaspora of which to-and-fro mobility weakens the inclination toward settlement. How one relates to the community back home becomes a personal matter, given that the potential for return is now a matter of individual choice.

The Haitian Creole *dyaspora*, a word that specifically applies to Haitians living outside of Haiti, is a good illustration of Clifford's vision. *Dyaspora* is a condition created by the other's gaze, and more particularly the gaze of the community back home. Edwidge Danticat's 2010 book-length essay *Create Dangerously: The Immigrant Artist at Work* gives an astounding description of the *dyaspora*:

I meant in that essay to list my own personal experiences as an immigrant and a writer, of being called *dyaspora* when expressing an opposing
political point of view in discussions with friends and family members
living in Haiti, who knew that they could easily silence me by saying,
"What do you know? You're living outside. You're *dyaspora*." I meant to
recall some lighter experiences of being startled in the Haitian capital
or in the provinces when a stranger who wanted to catch my attention
would call out, "Dyaspora!" as though it were a title like *Miss, Ms., Ma-
demoiselle,* or *Madame.* I meant to recall conversations or debates in
restaurants, at parties, or at public gatherings where members of the
*dyaspora* would be classified—justifiably or not—as arrogant, insensi-
tive, overbearing, and pretentious people who were eager to reap the
benefits of good jobs and political positions in times of stability in a
country that they'd fled and stayed away from during difficult times.
Shamefacedly, I'd bow my head and accept these judgments when they
were expressed, feeling guilty about my own physical distance from a
country that I had left at the age of twelve during a dictatorship that had
forced thousands to choose between exile and death.[28]

The Caribbean diasporic writer is forced to feel shame for living and writing
outside of her native island. As an expatriate, she is accused of opportunism
for writing about the island while presumably living "comfortably" in the land
of freedom and opportunity. Not just Danticat's but also Laferrière's Haitian
migrant writing is imbued with a pervasive sense of personal guilt, which
translates into a need on their part to justify why they chose not to die for their
country but to make a living from writing about that country instead. From a
cynical perspective, it could be said, as it will be argued at times in the book,
that the guilt of the immigrant writer is exacerbated by a situation of reverse
remittance. Instead of giving back to the community, the said economy of return in the border diaspora allows the immigrant writer to capitalize on a visit,
allowing new writing material acquired during the visit to be brought back
to the adopted land. "Return" indicates, in this context, the capital gained *in
return* for investment as the writer invests efforts in a transnational commute.
In truth, Danticat and Laferrière make it clear in their work that the reality is
much grimmer than a simple question of economics and added value. Writing
about home is indeed a means of subsistence, but it is not *only* that—and certainly not primarily that. Writing is before all a means of survival, surviving
the separation and the distance. They write not to die, figuratively speaking,

in the adopted land, just as they left home not to die, literally, in their home country. Clinging to figurative survival is the lot of many diasporic writers, no matter the nature of the sociopolitical situation in their home country. Jamaica Kincaid writes about her brother dying of AIDS in Antigua: "I knew instinctively, that to understand it, or to make an attempt at understanding his dying, and not to die with him, I would write about it."[29] The more the reality of home dies out, the more pressing it is for the writer to recapture the lost origin in order to avoid dying along with the fading memory.

Despite occasional visits home, second-generation diasporic writers undoubtedly suffer from their geographical distance from their homelands. As Michael J. Dash says, for those who decided not to return, "the burden of guilt is one of the defining features of the 'tired ghosts' of the Haitian diaspora. Guilt at having survived while others were massacred."[30] Laferrière and Danticat's writing is haunted by the specters of Jacques-Stephen Alexis, Marcel Numa, Louis Drouin, Jean Dominique, and all the others who eventually left their temporary exile in America for Haiti (except for Alexis, who left Paris for Haiti). All those people ended up dying in their fight for their country once they returned to Haiti. In the mid-1980s, the fall of the Duvalier regime turned the "tenth department" into a commuting diaspora. The tenth department refers to Haitians living abroad; together they form an extra department, since Haiti officially comprises nine departments. Wyclef Jean, the Haitian-born musician who initially played in the Haitian-American band the Fugees, epitomizes the concept of *commuting diaspora*. In spite of keeping his main residence in the United States, and because he goes regularly back to Haiti, Wyclef Jean felt entitled to run for the 2010 Haitian presidential election. Eventually, the Electoral Commission ruled his candidacy ineligible due to a lack of a permanent residency status. It remains true that, for many like Jean, Haitianness is perceived as a commuting identity. Today, Haiti is not only in the Caribbean (the geographical frontier) or only abroad (the external frontier), but it is also in the to-and-fro movement between Haiti and the adopted land of America. Diasporic perception is today not about where the diasporic subjects no longer are or where they are. It is also about, as Patricia Noxolo and Marika Preziuso put it, "where they could have been or might have been."[31] This new currency includes the flexibility and mobility of the diasporic subject, while addressing the moral pressure and personal accountability attached to the absence.

In his novel *L'énigme du retour* (*The Return*, 2011), Dany Laferrière reveals that the new possibility of visiting home is more a curse than a blessing. The visit cruelly allows the well-fed (*fed in America*) to witness a country ravaged by hunger, poverty, and social instability. As Danticat says in *Create Dangerously*, there is not much to do to combat the misery at home besides writing about it once back in North America. Why face the devastation left behind when the land of asylum now feels more like home than the birthplace? In some way, the impossible return feels safer than its materialization given that limited movements offer the unsuspected comfort of powerlessness, especially when the exile can hide behind an attitude of *if only I could go back home and help. . . .* Losing touch with one's kin portends the unavowed bliss of ignorance. And indeed, according to Milan Kundera in *L'ignorance* (*Ignorance*, 2000), the pain of exile is partially due to the sweet-and-sour phenomenon of nostalgia, which etymologically refers to the condition of ignorance. Nostalgia—in Spanish *añoranza*, from the Latin *ignorare*—is initiated by the pain of being ignorant of the state of the people left behind. Now, the possible return suddenly offers a personal choice—in some cases an unwelcome one coming at the price of guilt and a sense of betrayal. While the *fantasy* of return is a commonly discussed aspect of the traditional diasporic experience, the *possibility* of return is an unexplored side of the modern border diaspora that deserves scholarly attention. In moving from Caribbean diasporic subject to Caribbean diasporic commuter, migrants gained some benefits but also lost some in the new accessibility of the native land. *Creole*, from the Spanish *criollo*, refers to "one native to the settlement, though not ancestrally indigenous to it."[32] The Creole community is the result of a primal severance, and therefore it is diasporic by nature. As aforementioned, the modern Caribbean diasporic subject should be defined, more accurately, as second-generation diaspora. No longer of a collective nature, this second rupture carries a personal agency, and along with it a personal responsibility for which the migrant subject will have to account when he or she returns home for a visit.

Edouard Glissant argues, "La première pulsion d'une population transplantée . . . est le Retour" (The first compulsion of a transplanted people is . . . the Return).[33] Soon after, the fantasy of return turns into a reality of detour. Detour, for Glissant, represents the impossible demand of becoming one again with what was left behind. Detour is like Benítez-Rojo's chaos "that returns, a detour without a purpose, a continual flow of paradoxes,"[34] or Derrida's *différance* as *différence*;[35] it is never the same twice, and, more importantly, it is never a final return. Within the grand meta-archipelagic spiral of difference lie other microscopic movements of difference, which are fractured and mo-lecular diasporas. Those smaller movements are performed by the second-generation diaspora going back and forth and never returning to the same point, which brings to mind James Clifford's famous phrase "roots always precede routes."[36] Once territorialization starts its process, a new embryonic deterritorialization takes over, somewhere else, differently. In other words, the diasporic commuter will deterritorialize endlessly the slow domiciliation of the archipelagic identity in a systematic countermovement. The diasporic commuter is the nomad par excellence.

## The Maroon

*Voyage aux îles* (Travel to the islands of America), by the French missionary Jean-Baptiste Labat, gives a rather unflattering portrait of the maroon. In his travel diary, the priest finds only two main reasons why the slave would run away from the plantation: either out of laziness ("pour ne pas travailler" [to avoid work][37]) or out of culpability and cowardice ("pour éviter le châtiment de quelque faute qu'ils ont faite" [to avoid punishment for misconduct][38]). But more importantly, Labat depicts the isolated maroon as a thief feeding off oth-ers' labor: "ils ne sortent que la nuit pour aller arracher du manioc, des patates, ou autres fruits, et voler quand ils peuvent des bestiaux et des volailles" (they go out only at night to get manioc, potatoes, or other fruits, and to steal, when-ever they can, animals and poultry).[39] Labat's depiction admittedly comes from a colonial perspective, the perspective readily available at the end of the seventeenth century and beginning of the eighteenth century. That said, the maroon has always been historiographically a controversial figure, at times seen as a hero for his bold escape and at other times as a renegade for sacrific-ing his peers in his determination to protect his own freedom. The main bone of contention has to do with the treaties signed, in various locations, between the maroons and the planters, in which the former agreed to return future runaway slaves to planters in return for the guarantee of their own freedom. In Jamaica, for example, a pact sealed the fate of maroons and the English to-gether: the maroons agreed to tell on slave fugitives in return for the usufruct of the northern part of the island. Kamau Brathwaite, in *The Development of Creole Society in Jamaica*, describes the important role of maroons as slave-catchers in eighteenth century Jamaica, detailing their collaboration with the whites—a collaboration that was necessary if the maroons wanted to maintain the independence they had gained in 1740.[40] Richard Price, venturing into the less-trodden historical path of the maroons in *Maroon Societies*, points out that the post-treaty Jamaican maroons—who "bought, sold, and owned substantial numbers of slaves [and] hunted new runaways for a price"—were nicknamed "the King's Negroes."[41] Despite the compromising role of those slave-catchers, however, the historian Michael Craton raises an important point in defense of the maroons. As Craton argues, for maroons, compromising their kin was part of the Faustian bargain meant to stabilize their society, as a simple act of survival. Indeed, maroon societies had to define their identity, "without which they would have remained amorphous and unfixed."[42] For that reason, as Craton claims, "by hunting runaways rather than acting as a focus for slave resistance, maroons preserved their communities from further dilution and reduced the threat of competition for the backlands."[43] The survival strategies of the maroons boil down to a simple question of whether the end justifies the means. Rarely is it mentioned that not only runaways but also slave women from the plantation captured by the maroons became collateral damage in the bigger plan of creating a sustainable maroon society. Because of the low ratio of men to women in maroon communities, captured slave women, what Craton refers to as "female recruits,"[44] were often shared among men in a form of sexual and domestic commodification.[45] But again, as many historians would admit, maroons were people at war who sought to survive—by whatever means.

The anthropologist Kenneth Bilby, who researched the artistic expressions, song lyrics, and stories of Winward maroons—descendants of free maroons from Jamaica—points out in *True-Born Maroons* that stories of maroon betrayals abound in both written and oral traditions, which suggests that ancestral maroon betrayal is still an unresolved issue in maroon consciousness. In the French Antilles, the maroon's negative reputation lingered for many generations, so much so that, in the 1980s, Glissant took it upon himself to rehabilitate the maroon's image. Edouard Glissant blames historians for focusing too much on the maroons' infamous acts while ignoring their heroism. According to Glissant, this biased historiography has deeply influenced the Antillean collective consciousness, the proof of which is that the *nèg maroon* has often been used in the Antilles as a device to threaten bad children. For Glissant, even though maroons committed reprehensible acts, this figure is still "le seul héros populaire des Antilles" (the only popular hero in the Antilles)[46] who showed courage and determination. The maroon holds a special place in Glissant's poetics, which explains why his favored diegetic landscape is the forest, the space of the fugitive slave. Besides Edouard Glissant, Raphaël Confiant and Patrick Chamoiseau have also used marooning as a token of Caribbean heroism in their work. But their rehabilitation omits that the maroon is neither an unredeemable rogue nor a spotless hero. In her historical saga *Ségou: les murailles de terre* (*Segu*, 1987), Maryse Condé explains the consequences of the pact between maroons and slaveholders in some detail.[47] When Françoise Pfaff, in *Entretiens avec Maryse Condé* (*Conversations with Maryse Condé*, 1996), asks Condé why she chose to revive this darker side of Jamaican history, the author explains that even though most historians and people choose to ignore the dubious role of the maroons, they prefer mentioning heroic acts of rebellion. Even though, as Glissant would agree, breaking away from the master and starting a new life in hostile territories constitute acts of heroism, this unfortunate pact shows that fighting for survival does not always go hand in hand with heroic resistance. As Condé says, the history of the maroons in Jamaica offers an interesting lesson on freedom in that it shows that people who fought to get freedom are, at times, willing to do anything, "prêts à sacrifier les autres" (even sacrificing others),[48] as she says, in order to guarantee it for themselves.

The maroon exemplifies how a departing subject can equally be seen as a hero and a traitor in the history of the Caribbean. As such, the maroon appears as the ultimate Creole renegade. It is undeniable, as Paul Butel points out, that runaway slaves, in both the French and English Caribbean, infamously joined gangs of maroons and ransacked plantations, "volant les Négresses et les vivres" (stealing slave women and food)[49] in order to survive in isolation. They fed off others' labor in order to maintain their settlement and stay alive in those "high and rather barren reservations."[50] In *L'invention du quotidien* (*The Practice of Everyday Life*, 1984), Michel De Certeau argues that any act of resistance involves leaving the system of oppression in order to look at it from a distance and better assess the kind of rebellion needed to overthrow it. In *Le roman marron* (*The Maroon Novel*), Richard Burton applies De Certeau's notion of *resistance* to Caribbean marooning, arguing that marooning was a preliminary tactic of rebellion. Yet, we know now that the maroon's actions did not always fit Burton and De Certeau's heroic picture, which means that the maroon's outward escape was not always a strategic step toward future retaliation. Those heroic stories have too often overshadowed what Dash calls "small-scale marooning,"[51] meaning periodic absenteeism from the plantation. Realistically speaking, it is obvious that in the Creole economy of survival, a clear break with the plantation system was not always feasible: deals, thefts, pillaging, and occasional returns were also part of Caribbean history. Granted, it was a less glamorous part, but nonetheless a deeply human part. But again, should this aspect of history obliterate the fact that runaway slaves showed courage, determination, and defiance against the 1685 *Code noir* (the Black Code) that promised to mutilate or kill them upon their capture? Admittedly, not all maroons were heroes like the *Mulâtresse Solitude* (Guadeloupe), Leonard Parkinson (Jamaica), or François Mackandal (Saint-Domingue). But should this lack of heroic altruism lead us to conclude that the human-all-too-human maroon had no redeemable qualities?

The history of Jamaican marooning breaks the myth of an invincible Creole community. It puts an end to the presumption that, in suffering, people naturally stick together; that in a diasporic context, the members of a community stay together at all costs; and most of all, that the departure of one can only mean remittance for all. Condé was ostracized by Guadeloupeans for speaking publicly against them, chastised by the Martinican literary intelligentsia for standing apart from the Creolist community. Broyard was posthumously maligned by the African-American scholar Henry Louis Gates for choosing to ignore his black Creole background in order to make it as a white man in North America. Danticat has been anathemized by the Haitian community for being a "parasite," exploiting her "culture for money and what passes for fame."[52] Laferrière has faced criticisms for leaving Haiti in the midst of the 2010 earthquake devastation. As for Kincaid, she has been subject to much criticism for deprecating her island in her infamous essay *A Small Place*. All of these authors have been held accountable for their individual positions of enunciation, for allegedly thinking about themselves first, their freedom, their survival, and their autonomy. Their works, lives, or actions have occasionally been characterized as unsympathetic to their islands, individualistic, or plainly selfish and opportunistic. On the other hand, all have also been critically praised for their beautiful work and for addressing, in an international forum, important issues related to their island and their Creole condition. All in all, they are perceived as renegades with redeeming qualities or heroes with debatable motives, an ambiguous position not that different from the maroon's.

In *L'esclave vieil homme et le molosse* (*The Old Man Slave and the Mastiff*), Patrick Chamoiseau depicts the breathless flight of an elderly slave who, after a life of submission in a plantation, decides to run away to the mountains. The tired old man chases alone the mirage of a belated freedom. Chamoiseau offers no specific reasons why the slave would suddenly run off, except for the beauty of "Marronnage!"[53] There is immense poetic beauty in the old slave's aimless flight, a man in a single line of flight, to paraphrase Gilles Deleuze and Félix Guattari, running alone to the end of life. If Maryse Condé tried to break the myth of the honorable maroon in *Ségou*, it is precisely because Condé is a kind of maverick herself, like the weary slave. Alone against all, Condé has always rejected the myth of an indivisible Creole community. As a consequence, she has been chastised in her native island and criticized by her literary peers in Martinique for following her own course. Condé resisted the *Créolité* trend in the 1990s and rejected Césaire's Négritude. She compared the two literary movements to the "theory of social realism,"[54] blaming French Antillean literature for ignoring individual expression in favor of a Pan-African or Antillean ideology of communitarianism. Talking about the Antillean pressure to conform to one Creole model, Condé vehemently rejected the assumption that if all Antilleans were the same, it would be better for society. "Mais ce n'est pas du tout la vérité. Nous sommes 400,000 Guadeloupéens, c'est-à-dire 400,000 personnes avec des identités différentes" (But it's not true at all. There are 400,000 Guadeloupeans and therefore 400,000 people with different identities).[55] In that sense, Condé is very much like Laferrière, since both writers are vocal about their right to individual expression. As Laferrière repeatedly said, "Je n'écris pas, dois-je le répéter, pour défendre et illustrer la créolité, le métissage ou la francophonie" (I don't write, I repeat, to defend and illustrate Créolité, métissage, or francophonie).[56] And like Condé, Laferrière has repeatedly criticized writers who use myths (like that of the honorable maroon) to galvanize Caribbean communities. This kind of literature, he says, bores him to death.[57] If Condé and Laferrière come across as very determined in their rejection of francophone literary movements, it is because, as French-speaking Caribbean writers, they come from a tradition of literary movements that are very much community-based. They need therefore to forcefully distance themselves from the weight and breadth of those movements. Dash has pointed out that Haiti and Martinique represent two extreme alternatives, "caught as they are between the poles of impoverished isolation and chronic dependency." The Republic of Haiti was "the first Caribbean state to declare itself other," while the department of Martinique "never had the opportunity to declare itself other."[58] It remains the case that, despite their extreme differences, writers from both islands end up fighting the same fight, desperately clinging to individual expression against the voice of an overpowering Creole community.

Finally, the Anatole Broyard case offers an interesting reflection on Creoleness and renegadism, as it shows how the two are inherently linked. Broyard was born in New Orleans to black Creole parents whose ancestors came from France and Saint-Domingue. As a child, he moved to New York with his family. There, the racial configuration was different from that of New Orleans, a city used to Creole-produced racial subtleties. It should be noted that New Orleans should be seen—particularly in the context of this study—as a Caribbean city outside of the strictly speaking "Caribbean." Due to its unique Saint-Domingue–initiated Creole composition, New Orleans is an external frontier of the Caribbean. As pointed out earlier, Anatole Broyard became infamous after his death for having passed for white his entire adult life in the United States. What made it possible for him to do so was the generations of African–white American "miscegenation" that resulted in erasing most of his black genotype. Soon after his death, two main protagonists, his daughter Bliss Broyard and Harvard professor Henry Louis Gates, competed over the privilege to reveal the *true story* of Anatole Broyard. Both ended up publishing their own versions of the story, but both seem to have equally struggled with trying to make sense of Broyard's racial passing. As *Creole Renegades* argues, it is difficult to grasp the full extent of the Broyard case without a meticulous semantic exploration of the word *Creole*. The semantic history of the word shows that it refers to white, black, both, or neither. *Creole* mainly means acclimation to the land and, by extension, adaptation to new circumstances. In essence, *Creole* is essentially chameleon-like and opportunistic. Whether black or white or both, the Creole identity means a state of almost native yet not quite, almost like you, yet so imperceptibly different. One should look at a picture of Anatole Broyard to understand the full extent of Creole ambiguity. In other words, Creoleness is the epitome of evasiveness, just like the runaway slave who is both adored and despised. Creole renegades are at their best when they are uprooted and transplanted into a non-Creole environment. We can see then to what extent they are able to adapt and readjust their Creoleness to fit new circumstances. Anatole Broyard puts into an explicit narrative what is at stake in the subtly displaced Creoleness of Kincaid, Condé, Laferrière, and Danticat.

## America

Though born and partially raised in Haiti, Danticat, unlike Laferrière, writes exclusively in English. It seems that, because of this, the writer needs to distance herself from francophone literary movements. She has lived in the United States since the age of twelve and has preserved her Haitian culture thanks to her family in Brooklyn. Danticat has gradually lost her ability to speak French due to a lack of practice (she speaks Creole when she is with her family). Frantz Fanon's well-known statement "parler, c'est . . . surtout assumer une culture, supporter le poids d'une civilisation" (to speak, means . . . to assume a culture and bearing the weight of a civilization)[59] refers to the alienating language of colonization. For Fanon, the alienating language was French, but for Danticat, French is not an issue, since she does not write in the language of the long-gone master. By her own admission, she has even lost the ability to read a book written in French without the help of a dictionary. American English is for Danticat growing up the language of emancipation. This new language, which she refers to as her "stepmother" tongue, has allowed her to find unity between the written and the spoken word. "So I wrote," she says, "in a language I didn't speak regularly [French] and spoke a language I couldn't write [Creole]. When I came here and learned English, it was the first time I could write and speak the same language."[60] Danticat's experience with English in the United States provides us with a unique case of linguistic emancipation. Even though some French-speaking Antilleans, like the Haitian René Depestre, consider French a language of freedom (*Le métier à métisser*), others, like the Martinicans Confiant and Chamoiseau, carry a more conflictual relationship with the language of their citizenship. Danticat herself admits to having mixed feelings toward the French language.[61] With American English, Danticat stays away from the French, which allows her to avoid—what Celia Britton terms—the potential "ambivalent identification" that she could have had "with the white Other's speech."[62]

As an expression of subjection and a tool for emancipation, language is an important context of enunciation that has been heavily discussed in scholarly works (Fanon, Glissant, Walcott, Deleuze, Guattari, Spivak). This book, however, goes beyond the linguistic trend as it seeks to embrace a Pan-American perspective oriented not so much in the *language* of production as in the *location* of production. Over the last two decades, the relation between identity and language has been a predominant question in Postcolonial Studies. Today, the question of positioning has grown to be the main concern of the second-generation Caribbean diasporic writers. Danticat receives criticism not so much for writing in English about her native island as for writing about them in North America. In "Cultural Identity and Diaspora," Hall enunciates three different phases of positioning in the Caribbean cultural identity that he calls—after Léopold Sédar Senghor and Aimé Césaire—*présence*. They are the *Présence Africaine*, which is evocative of the Negritude movement (see Alioune Diop's journal of the same title); the *Présence Européenne*, which "is about exclusion, imposition and expropriation";[63] and the *Présence Améric-aine*: "the 'New World' presence—America, *Terra Incognita*—is therefore it-self the beginning of diaspora, of diversity, of hybridity and difference, what makes Afro-Caribbean people already people of a diaspora."[64] The last is often overlooked by Caribbean people and North Americans alike because the Ca-ribbean is rarely said to be American, a word that usually exclusively applies to the people from the north. Yet, as Laferrière argues, Caribbean people *are* Americans:

> The Caribbean is a region of America. I detest the word "Antilles," which alludes to France. When I say that I am an American, I do it in order to place myself and to say that I am not an Antillean (*Antillais*)—not a French subject. I belong to this continent that the United States has wanted to keep simply for itself.[65]

America, for Laferrière, has quickly become more than a continent, more than a mere geographical delineation; it is first and foremost an ideology, the ideol-ogy of the third continent, neither Africa nor Europe, but the place where one can attempt to stay out of a postcolonial polarity: "Then there is our attitude in regard to the French culture. Everything was done against or for France. But I am in America."[66] Condé shares the same view as Laferrière. She also chose America as a third alternative, the only one that seemed to work for her. She says in an interview:

> Je me suis dit l'Europe ce n'est pas l'endroit dont je rêvais pour vivre et créer, l'Afrique non plus, c'est où alors? L'Amérique??? Essayons! On se rend compte que les frontières ne veulent plus rien dire, et où on le peut, où on se sent bien, enfin, pas trop mal, on se fixe et on se construit.
>
> (I told myself, Europe is not the place that I dreamed of to live and write, Africa neither, where is it then? America? Let's try! One realizes that frontiers no longer mean much, wherever one feels good, or at least, not too bad, is where one settles down.)[67]

America offers a tabula rasa for Caribbean writers who are no longer inter-ested in shaping their voice according to the African or European presence, whether to embrace or reject those presences. A noticeable number of Caribbean diasporic writers look to North America as the land of emancipation. Condé, Laferrière, Danticat, and Kincaid have all chosen to write back—not to the colonial center but to their archipelagic origins—from North America.

A turn of the century paradigm for this geographical blank slate can be found in the experience of Bahamian Bert Williams (1874–1922), a black comedian whose "coon" routine made him famous throughout North America. Caryl Phillips, Williams' biographer, argues that his iconic status could not have flowered in his homeland but only in the "big country to the north" where "anything is possible."[68] But for Williams, the cost of realizing his artistic possibilities in North America was that he became the proverbial stranger in his own land, regarded by many of his black peers as a sellout. Phillips, a professor of English at Columbia University, is like his subject, a man of Caribbean descent (St. Kitts) living in the United States. Through telling the life of Williams as he imagines it, Phillips offers reflection, and probably also self-reflection, on what it means for a Caribbean subject to move to North America. Phillips presents the country to the north as the land of the Faustian bargain—namely, a land of opportunity and perdition. With the exception of Naipaul, *Creole Renegades* focuses on Caribbean (Creole) American writers who have admitted one way or another that had they not moved to the north, they might never have produced what they did. Kincaid, in an interview rightly titled "Jamaica Kincaid: From Antigua to America," addresses the importance to her of living in America instead of living in England. As she says, in America she does not have "to please an English audience, or an English colonial audience."[69] But more importantly, the writer argues that she can only write the way she does because she left Antigua: "One of the things I noticed about writers who live there, and one of the reasons why I do not live there, is that you become very involved in politics, and you no longer write."[70] Looking back on her career, Condé makes a similar comment, describing Guadeloupe as "a colony with no room for creativity, a place where, during my twenty-two years there, I didn't do anything interesting. When I think of what I have accomplished at Columbia and at other American universities, I think it is sad."[71] In *Create Dangerously*, Danticat quotes Laferrière's *L'énigme du retour*: "'What is certain,' writes the novelist narrator, 'is that I wouldn't have written like this if I had stayed there / maybe I would not have written at all.'"[72] Like it was for Bert Williams, the country to the north has been the land of great creative production for a significant number of Caribbean-born writers. That said, North America has also been the platform from which the native Caribbean community has gotten a better look at those writers, their lives, their work, and their choices, for better or for worse.

Laferrière has pushed the envelope more than any other diasporic writer when it comes to presenting America as the land of not only creative opportunities but also, and more importantly, opportunism. When he published *Comment faire l'amour avec un nègre sans se fatiguer* (*How to Make Love to a Negro without Getting Tired*, 1987), his first novel and the one that brought him instant fame, Laferrière made a career choice somehow similar to that of Bert Williams. Laferrière launched his career by capitalizing on the Negro stereotype. In the book, Laferrière presents the black as a hypersexual man involved with various white women in Montreal. Laferrière's main plot arches back to the old racial cliché of the black male slave preying on the master's wife. One could be tempted to read the interracial sexual plot in Laferrière's book as a vengeful Schoelcherian cry of victory in a master-slave dialectic as a reenactment of "Vive Schoelcher!" (Hail to Schoelcher!),[73] as the black man ejaculates inside the white woman's vagina (Fanon). Given that Victor Schoelcher was credited with the abolition of slavery in Martinique and Guadeloupe, the Schoelcher tribute is often used to signal victory over the white master. What Fanon suggests in *Peau noire, masques blancs* is that the tribute can be used to signal victory over the white master at the moment of ejaculation when the black man has sexual intercourse with a white woman.[74] However, there is definitely no Schoelcher or Dessalines-like heroic dimension in Laferrière's book. Or at least this is not the official message that Laferrière tries to convey in this book. We know that Laferrière has always made a point in his career of staying away from racial, postcolonial, or simply Haitian politics. He has greatly emphasized his apolitical stand as a Haitian-born writer. This is the reason why Laferrière's provocative intention in *Comment faire l'amour avec un nègre sans se fatiguer* was to sell the novel using the same ideological framework as Bert Willams's black makeup. Both used a performance that capitalized on the Negro caricature and gave a special treat to the white audience in return for their money. This is not to say that Laferrière is truly a sellout. His Bert Williams type of persona could be a subversive literary strategy meant to deconstruct the insidious racial stereotypes that the writer skillfully feigns to embrace. Nonetheless, once in North America, Laferrière has chosen to come across as an ambiguous subject whose work blurs the frontier between opportunities and opportunism. It is admittedly a daring choice but one that definitely made him stand out from other writers of Haitian descent in America. All this is to say that the "country to the north," as Phillips calls it, is emblematic of both the terra incognita of endless creative possibilities and the Faustian land of overachievement. This ambivalence is what makes the performance of those writers, either in a book or as a life to live, truly unique yet controversial.

•

Chapter 1, "Anatole Broyard: Racial Betrayal and the Art of Being Creole," looks in detail at the connection between the notion of betrayal and the concept of Creoleness. It proposes a theory of racial passing as a quintessential expression of Creoleness in which discrepancies, shifts, slippages, and alterations, which are often misconceived as calculated expressions of betrayal and duplicity, are in fact defining components of both racial passing and the history of Creoleness. The chapter follows the life of Anatole Broyard (1920–90), an American writer and literary critic of Creole descent from New Orleans who controversially hid his black origins in New York in the hopes of making it as an American—as opposed to an "African-American"—writer. Racial passing, a concept pertaining to the Jim Crow–impacted America, initially refers to legally black albeit visually white people who chose to pass for white in spite of the one-drop rule. Based on the semantic history of the word *Creole* in the Caribbean and New Orleans, the study challenges scholarly readings that fix racial identity, arguing instead that race, as racial passing and Creoleness attest, is by nature equivocal and mostly determined by the variable context of reception. Several texts on racial passing—Henry Louis Gates's "The Passing of Anatole Broyard," Nella Larsen's *Passing*, Boris Vian's *J'irai cracher sur vos tombes* (*I Spit on Your Graves*, 1948), and Phillip Roth's *The Human Stain*—complement the study of Anatole Broyard.

Chapter 2, "Maryse Condé's *Histoire de la femme cannibale*: Coming Out in the French Antilles," is based on a reading of the work and life of the Guadeloupean writer Maryse Condé. The chapter proposes a reflection on the culture of departure and return in the islands of Martinique and Guadeloupe. For generations, islanders have moved to continental France for economic or social reasons, and most of them have chosen to return on a regular or permanent basis. The Antillean community has notoriously been brutal toward those returnees for showing signs of cultural denaturalization. More extreme cases of Antillean commuters are those living outside both metropolitan France and the Antilles. After some thirty years in North America, Maryse Condé is today the epitome of the renegade for the Antillean community. This chapter seeks to demonstrate that Condé's work bears the marks of its expatriate context of production, which are traceable through the recurrent presence of homosexuality in her writing, an otherwise very rare occurrence in Antillean literature. Relying heavily on the social study of the Martinican Frantz Fanon (*Peau noire, masques blancs*), this section draws an unprecedented parallel between the *makoumé* (homosexual in Creole) and the *débarqué* (returnee). It proposes a theory of homosexuality as the symbolic site of denied access to return. Fanon has famously contended that the homosexual exists elsewhere but not in the Antilles. Fanon's old view, as the chapter argues, applies today to the *departee*: after coming out, there is no way back for the one who left the Antilles. Ultimately, it shows how a sedimented diasporic nation deals with individual displacement by making the stray Antillean accountable for the unredeemable personal act of severance.

Is writing about home a cultural obligation or an act of opportunism for the expatriate writer? Testimonial work by two Haitian American writers living in North America, Edwidge Danticat and Dany Laferrière, allows us to explore this sensitive question in depth in chapter 3, "Edwidge Danticat and Dany Laferrière: Parasitic and Remittance Diaspora." The motivation behind the decision to write testimonials about Haiti is a major subject of dispute between Haitian diasporic writers and their native community. This chapter explores the culturally perceived impertinence of testimonials in cases where the author happens not to live at home. Writing testimonials requires that the immigrant use the experiences of people who live at home or capitalize on the timeliness of a visit home at the precise moment of a tragedy. Keeping in mind that Haiti carries an important journalistic culture where the role of the writer is often mixed with that of the journalist, Haitian diasporic writers are often pressured to give back to the community through a journalistic duty of memory, even in absentia. On the other hand, what is remittance to some is parasitism to others, particularly to those in the Haitian community who ascribe a negative connotation to *dyaspora* (Creole spelling). *Dyaspora*, for some locals, is an expatriate feeding off Haiti's resources when the time is right, including exploiting marketable stories from abroad. Is the Haitian diasporic writer feeding Haiti or feeding off Haiti? Given that survivor's guilt is one of the main features of the Haitian diaspora, the moral conflict between writing as remittance or subsistence adds a crucial layer to the already complex question of diasporic betrayal and guilt in the modern Haitian context.

Chapter 4, "V. S. Naipaul and Jamaica Kincaid: Rhetoric of National Dis-Allegiance," questions the assumed duty of loyalty that befalls immigrants in regards to their native postcolonial nations. Should publicly criticizing home be necessarily viewed as an act of treason in Caribbean diasporic writing? To answer this question, the text turns to Antiguan-American Jamaica Kincaid's body of work, with special emphasis on *A Small Place*, a book perceived to be highly detrimental to the image of the Caribbean and for which Kincaid has been anathematized. Kincaid, who wrote *A Small Place* in North America, proposes a vision of America as a site of creative freedom where criticizing home is a personal affair and not necessarily a postcolonial historicized endeavor. Kincaid's criticism of the Caribbean differs from that of the Trinidadian-English V. S. Naipaul's in *Middle Passage*, given that the latter, in contrast to Kincaid's North American viewpoint, offers a European perspective on the Caribbean. The chapter juxtaposes Kincaid with Naipaul in order to show both the similarities between the two provocative renegade writers as well as the importance of the geographical context of production that eventually sets them apart. Yet, no matter the intended ideological context of production, postcolonial writers, wherever they write, are inevitably recalled by their communities and brought back to their unwilling role of national spokespersons. For Kincaid, Naipaul, and all the other writers addressed in the previous chapters, the context of reception, even more than that of production, remains the defining quality of the Caribbean diasporic voice.

Chapter 5, "Creole versus *Bossale* Renegade: 'Turfism' in the Black Diaspora of the Americas," explores the *bossale* roots of the Creole renegade, using the Middle Passage as a symbolic background to address the question of individualism in black diasporic literature. Unlike the Creole born in the Americas, a *bossale* is an African slave shipped to the New World in the triangular trade. The *bossale* roots of the Creole subject arc back to the survival instinct of the African captive in the slave ship. The *bossale* image, which calls upon the importance of basic individualism and Darwinism in the context of the black diaspora, sheds light on the tradition of literary "turfism" traditionally at play in Caribbean and African-American communities. The slave ship chronotope is not used in this chapter the way Paul Gilroy understood it in *The Black Atlantic*—namely, as a token of black transatlanticism and antiessentialism. Rather, it refers to the exiguity and suppressive nature of the Caribbean and African-American literary space. This chapter looks at the reasons behind black diasporic writers' infamous antagonism toward one another, arguing that the lack of individual space is the contributing factor for those writers' need for emancipation. "Turfism" is a consequence of the slave ship dynamic that historically forced the blacks to make it on their own in spite of the suppressive state and exiguity of the locale. The tradition of black Pan-American turfism helps us understand why some writers, like Maryse Condé, have pitched their voice far from their local residence. In so doing, they have created more room for themselves and a more autonomous kind of literature, yet a literature that is often perceived by the community back home as too individualistic and disengaged.

1

# Anatole Broyard

## Racial Betrayal and the Art of Being Creole

> Their mixed and split origin is what decides their fate.
>
> SIGMUND FREUD, "THE UNCONSCIOUS"

*Racial passing*, a concept that derives from the context of Jim Crow America, initially refers to people who are legally black but visually identified as white, who choose to pass for white in spite of the one-drop rule. The anthropologist Marvin Harris coined the term for the taxonomical practice of the one-drop rule: *hypodescent*. Its logic stipulates that someone with both black and white ancestors will be assigned the "lowest" racial caste, no matter how infinitesimal his or her percentage of black blood. The reason behind the practice of hypodescent reaches back to slavery, when slaveholders sought to protect their interests by ensuring that their illegitimate black offspring would add to their growing slave capital and be deprived of genealogical and property rights. The segregated Jim Crow era cemented the legal and economic viability of the hypodescent rule by drawing a clear line between blacks and whites. In the 1960s, Harris somewhat bluntly explained, "The reason for this absurd bit of folk taxonomy is simply that the great blundering machinery of segregation cannot easily adjust itself to degrees of whiteness and darkness."[1] As William Javier Nelson rightfully observes, the result of this racial definition has been a racial anomaly in its "inclusion in the African-American group of individuals of mostly European ancestry."[2] Though of European descent, the oxymoronic "white blacks" are the result of an American idiosyncratic practice of looking at blackness as a "monolithic identity,"[3] leaving no room for anything other than blackness. In other words, the role of the hypodescent rule is to indefinitely set the limits of racial dilution, thereby reaffirming the compulsion of drawing the "color line" (W.E.B. Du Bois) continuously.

Racial passing came as a response to the one-drop rule. In her memoir *One Drop: My Father's Hidden Life—A Story of Race and Family Secrets*, Bliss Broyard recounts the life of her French Creole father, Anatole Broyard, who was born in New Orleans and moved to New York with his family as a child. Anatole Broyard was also a renowned literary critic who, though legally black according to the one-drop rule, passed for white his entire adult life on the East Coast and was "outed" by black scholar Henry Louis Gates after his death. Though an act of defiance against the logic of hypodescent, racial passing is also often perceived as a betrayal of the black community, given that to jump over the racial fence is obviously a controversial choice for blacks. Although the passing subject is not necessarily Creole in the strict Spanish sense of *criollo* (of European or African descent but native of and raised in the Americas, including New Orleans), there is arguably something quintessentially and alluringly Creole about passing—namely, the noncommittal nature of the act. Like passing, Creole is a concept that stands on both sides of the fence, which is why the Creole subject holds the potential to come across as a misleading figure. This chapter proposes a theory of Creoleness in which discrepancies, shifts, and slippages, which are often misconceived as calculated expressions of betrayal, are in fact defining and natural components of the Creole identity. The passing paradigm contributes to a better understanding of Creole's unreliability because, like passing, Creoleness results from racial and sexual (miscegenation) promiscuity and thus bears the signs of deviance and astray-ness (*deviare*). The passing story of Broyard is a platform that allows us to understand Creoleness as fundamentally unpredictable, seeing the Creole subject as always "in situation"[4] and therefore permanently unfixed. Also, the story of Broyard—and here literally meaning "Broyard as a narrative"—can illustrate how both race and sexuality question the unreliable semantics of the word *Creole*. What if the Creole subject, as a natural-born noncommittal subject, were the quintessence of the renegade figure? What if Broyard, by passing, was only being true to his treacherous Creole self?

## Anatole Broyard: A Creole Story

Anatole Broyard was a highly respected literary critic best known for his influential position at the *New York Times*. He was born in the New Orleans French Quarter to Paul Anatole Broyard and Edna Miller. His birth certificate identified his race as black, but when he died in 1990 from prostate cancer, his death certificate identified him as white. After his death, Anatole Broyard became famous and infamous for passing for white during his entire adult life. While he was a child, his family moved from Louisiana to a mixed-raced neighborhood in Brooklyn; this early move was a turning point in the boy's life. Obviously, in New York, the racial configuration was different from that in New Orleans, a city that was used to Creole-produced racial subtleties. To obtain employment, Broyard's parents were forced to pass for white, but they would revert to their black identity when they returned home at the end of the workday. Anatole, however, was raised as a black boy, and on several occasions, he had to pay the violent price of looking too white for the taste of black bullies. As an adult, he capitalized on what was once a predicament. During the years he was a student at Brooklyn College, served in the navy in World War II (as a white officer overseeing a black crew), and worked as an intellectual bohemian and bookshop owner in Greenwich Village, Broyard never revealed his black racial status. Broyard married a Puerto Rican woman, and they had a daughter. After the war, Broyard left his wife and child for a life of physical and intellectual pleasures in Manhattan. Much later, at forty-one years old, he married a woman of Norwegian descent; they had a son and a daughter, who both looked white. After their birth, Broyard left his Village Bohemian life behind and brought his family to Connecticut, where his children attended an all-white private school, and the family enjoyed a country club lifestyle that was very different from his modest black origins in New Orleans. To complete the racial passing, Broyard had to make the ultimate sacrifice of cutting ties with his family, which he did to a great extent, especially with his sister Shirley, who was the most dark-skinned member of the family. Even though his wife, Sandy Nelson, was aware of his black ancestry (one of Anatole's friends told her when she and Anatole got engaged), his children never knew. When he was on his deathbed, Sandy insisted that Anatole tell the children. The physically weakened father argued that he could not muster the physical strength to engage in the draining discussion that the shared secret would have entailed. Finally, Sandy broke the news to Todd and Bliss shortly before Anatole died. It seemed that his secret was always about to be revealed and yet forever postponed.

In 2007, seventeen years after Broyard's death, Bliss, who had become a literary critic and writer, released the story of her father's passing in *One Drop: My Father's Hidden Life—A Story of Race and Family Secrets*. In addition to retracing the life of her father and his ancestors, Bliss described her painstaking journey to racial and Creole consciousness as she slowly came to terms with her newfound heritage. In the book, she describes the moment when her mother revealed the family secret outside the hospital where her father lay dying. She explains that her mother used the word *Creole*, a word that Broyard did not fully grasp at the time. Her mother said that her father "had 'mixed-blood,' and his parents were both light-skinned Creoles from New Orleans, where race-mixing had been common."[5] *Creole* is also the word that Anatole had used as a young man to describe himself to Harold Chenven, a white classmate at Brooklyn High School. Years later, when Bliss was working on her book, Chenven told her that when Anatole had used the word *Creole*, he was "worldy enough" to understand that it meant "of mixed race," even though he "thought to himself that Bud Broyard didn't look like a Negro. His skin was as pale as, or even paler than, his own."[6] Like Bliss's mother, Chenven automatically associated *Creole* with mixed race. But Bliss, who by then had spent years researching Louisiana Creoles, was well acquainted with *Creole*'s elusive and ambiguous nature. For her, Anatole chose that word precisely for the sake of its double-edged connotation: "By describing himself that way, my father could avoid the black/white question and let people draw their own conclusions."[7]

Broyard was, according to Henry Louis Gates's 1996 *New Yorker* article "The Passing of Anatole Broyard," some kind of a trickster. The word *Creole* requires rigorous semantic handling. Just as New Orleans became the home of French, Arcadian, and Haitian refugees, the very word *Creole* carries an underlying sense of evasion, a connotation of which Broyard clearly took advantage. Broyard's *Creole* was an evasion in the same way that "he'd mostly *evaded* [my italics] the question, saying something vague about 'island influences'"[8] when Bliss's mother had once asked her husband about his racial background. The word *Creole* could have indeed meant "mixed race" for a worldly person like Cheven, but the mixed-race connotation in *Creole* carries an added value: the mixing of races is not necessarily in a given person, but it can also occur in a given environment between blacks and whites living in the same space and sharing a common history and culture. In other words, Creole can be either black *or* white, and not necessarily black *and* white.

After her mother used the word, Bliss Broyard looked up the meaning in a dictionary and included the full definition in her book. The dictionary is a recurrent preliminary step in texts dealing with Creole, given that the meaning of the word needs constant semantic reassurance. Nevertheless, because the word *Creole* is of a chameleonic nature, the dictionary fails to provide a clear, unequivocal, and—as usually expected from a dictionary—fixed definition.

The *American Heritage Dictionary* that Bliss used gave the following definition—which consists of two categories divided into the first two (white) and the last two (black and mixed race):

- Any person of European descent born in the West Indies or Spanish Harlem.
- Any person descended from or culturally related to the original French settlers of the southern United States, especially Louisiana.
- Any person of Negro descent born in the Western Hemisphere, as a Negro brought from Africa.
- Any person of mixed European and Negro ancestry who speaks with a Creole dialect.

The organization of the list may be reflective of the hypodescent taxonomical logic: hierarchically, white is superior to black, so it comes first in the listing. Alternatively, it could point to the dictionary's inclination to see *Creole* as a label that first applied to whites, which is incorrect because historically the word did not originally carry a distinct racial orientation. The extensiveness of the list gives an obvious clue as to the confusion surrounding the word *Creole*.

Quite understandably, the spectrum of possibilities, based on either/or both, offers a freedom of choice that can easily lead to misunderstandings. As the Martinicans Bernabé, Chamoiseau, and Confiant point out in their essay *Eloge de la Créolité*, the word *Creole* has not always carried the official connotation of mixed race:

> Le mot "créole" viendrait de l'espagnol "criollo" lui-même découlant du verbe latin "criare," qui signifie "élever, éduquer." Le Créole est celui qui est né et a été élevé aux Amériques sans en être originaire, comme les Amérindiens. Assez vite, ce terme a désigné toutes les races humaines, tous les animaux et toutes les plantes qui ont été transportés en Amérique à partir de 1492. Il s'est donc glissé une erreur dans les dictionnaires français à compter du début du dix-neuvième siècle, lesquels ont réservé le terme "Créole" aux seuls blancs créoles (ou Békés).

> (The word *Creole* would come from *criollo*, which itself derives from the Latin verb *criare*, meaning "to raise, to educate." The Creole, born and raised in the Americas, is not a native, unlike the native Indians. Soon enough, the term came to designate all the races, as well as all the animals and the plants shipped to America after 1492. An error therefore

found its way into French dictionaries from the nineteenth century on, as they restricted the word *Creole* for the white Creoles only [*Békés*].)[9]

Basically, *criollo* makes no racial distinction; its main function is to distinguish the natives from those born in the colonies of European or African descent. As Doris Garraway points out in *The Libertine Colony*, "The colonial missionary writers Du Tertre and Labat used the term to mean simply 'born on the colonies,' a designation used for both the master and servile classes."[10]

Far from being, as the Creolists suggest, a fortuitous "error" in French dictionaries, the white exclusive label is in fact the product of an intentional historiographic maneuver by white Creoles who, for political reasons, needed this semantic slippage. In Latin America, as Gwendolyn Midlo Hall explains in *Africans in Colonial Louisiana*, *Creole* was indeed first used to distinguish American-born from African-born slaves, but in the Spanish and French colonies of the late eighteenth and early nineteenth centuries, during American struggles for independence, the Creole elite reconfigured the definition of *Creole* to mean only people of "European descent born in the Americas."[11] The relabeling came as a response to the American Anglophones' accusation that white Creoles were incapable of self-rule because of their "racially mixed heritage."[12] As the white Creoles were forced to look at themselves through the other's (the Anglophone's) gaze, this sudden examination forced them to point the finger at the Other within their own Creole group. This raciopolitical shift accounts for the gradual appearance of *Creole*'s white exclusive label in dictionaries; it also explains the inconsistencies in successive dictionaries pressured to one stance or the other. As a result—as Sylvie Dubois and Megan Melançon explain in "Creole Is, Creole Ain't"—the 1869 edition of the *Larousse* dictionary defines *Creole* as those native to the local populace, but the 1929 edition depicts *Creole* as only "Caucasian." The 1929 edition relies on grammatical intricacies to explain the semantic slip: used as a noun, Creole is strictly Caucasian, but as an adjective, it can by way of analogy apply to non-Caucasian peoples of the colonies. Also, as Virginia Domínguez points out in *White by Definition*, the 1929 *Larousse* argues that the word *Creole* could indeed apply to blacks as long as the word *Negro* followed the word *Creole*; "thus, Haitian Creoles, for example, were 'really' Creole Negroes and not simply Creoles."[13]

The semantic evolution of the word *Creole* attests to the white Creoles' ambivalent position toward the Creole label. The racial connotation of *Creole* in New Orleans was mostly motivated by power, money, and politics. As long as the free people of color, meaning the colored Creoles, had money and were of use, the white Creoles did not mind sharing the label with them. For example, during the Spanish Regime, the colored Creoles became wealthy through Spanish land-tenure policies. At that point, the label *Creole* was extended to encompass white and colored Creoles. As Dubois and Melançon write, "Although the WCrs (white Creoles) insisted that Creoles were by definition white, they allowed the CCrs (colored Creoles) to identify themselves as Creoles too, claiming with a certain pride that 'New Orleans has had an unusually superior class of black.'"[14] Furthermore, during the Haitian Revolution, as a massive immigration from Haiti (formerly Saint-Domingue) to New Orleans took place, the Haitian Creole immigrant aristocracy, which was both white and black, further collaborated, without much resistance from the New Orleans white Creoles, in tainting the usage of the word *Creole*. Domìnguez points out, "Practically all the refugees from Saint-Domingue qualified as Creoles, regardless of physical appearance or the racial characteristics of all their ancestors."[15] However, the purchase of Louisiana by the United States in 1803 clearly redefined the history of Creole semantics. As locally born Anglo-Americans started to outnumber the Creole population in Louisiana, the Creole label was felt to be threatened, but, as Domínguez explains, it was mainly a cultural and linguistic concern and not a racial one:

> Language became crucial, and crucial customs were frequently mentioned and compared. Southern Louisiana society was polarized into Creoles and Americans. Classification as Creole or as American soon became, for sociopolitical purposes, more significant than classification by economic status. *Gens de couleur* were not excluded from the Creole category.[16]

It was therefore by the Civil War era, when Anglo-Americans started accusing the white Creoles of not being able to govern themselves because of their "touch of the tar brush" that the fight over the Creole label took a clearly racial turn. The economically and politically weakened white Creoles had no choice but to ostentatiously impose a white-only restriction on the Creole label. Then, stimulated by the post–Civil War crisis and the beginning of the Jim Crow racial polarization, "a near-obsession with metasemantics [about Creole as only white] ruled much of the 1880s and 1890s,"[17] which consolidated Creole's white-only label up to the civil rights movement and even beyond.

All this is to show that semantic discrepancies, shifts, slippages, and alterations are inherent components of the Creole concept and history. The racialization of the Creole has, in sum, been negotiated based on a question of convenience. Creole is that which will adjust and adapt to circumstances and, like a chameleon, will *pass* in a chosen environment. Its chameleonic feature arches back to the very etymology of the word *Creole*, meaning acclimation to a new environment. Creoles are those whose ancestors came from Europe or Africa but were themselves born in the Americas and have *adapted* to their new land. Yet, like racial passing, Creole involves acclimation with a value added: there is always something unaccounted for in the acclimation that defies the endemism and the indigenousness of the situation, which is something essentially Creole. Again, from the Spanish *criollo*, Creole means someone born, raised, and educated in the new land but not native to the land.[18] Not native to the land is an inherent part of the Creole definition, the reason why the Creole identity will always bear the signs of its uprootedness and acclimation. For that matter, when Jean Bernabé defines *creolization* as a "processus d'*autochtonisation*,"[19] the Martinican linguist brings out a fundamental contradiction inherent in the Creole concept. *Autochtone*, from the Greek *autos* (itself) and *kthôn* (land), refers to someone coming from that land. However, Bernabé's process of "autochtonisation" leads to an unavoidable and essential oxymoron as he states that the Creole—though from that land—comes from somewhere else.

But while Creoles have acclimated to their environment—so much so that they come across as originating from that very land—the difference with the "real" native persists. For example, as David Buisseret points out, the Creoles and the Europeans are cousins with irreconcilable differences:

> Creolization . . . was not a voluntary activity. The adaptive pressures were omnipresent and irresistible, even if a person or group tried to resist them. In the Spanish world it was thus impossible for a *criollo*, however well placed, to take on all the characteristics of the *peninsulares*. A seventeenth-century gentleman of Virginia might wish and think himself still to be an English gentleman, but in fact he would speak slightly differently, eat differently, dress differently, and in short be different from those cousins who had stayed in England. It goes without saying that Franco-Canadians rapidly became different from those who continued to speak the French of Touraine.[20]

These differences account for the almost but not quite unfathomable ambiguity in the Creole identity. The Creole is still quite like the European mainlander, yet not completely so. Creole is a syncretic expression that retains an extra something of its heterogeneous union. Ralph Bauer and José Antonio Mazzotti pointed out that Juan Lopes de Velasco was the first author to use the word *criollo* in his *Geografía y descripción universal de las Indias* (1570). The author used it pejoratively, claiming that the Spaniards born in the Indies, "who are called creoles, turn out like the natives even though they are not mixed with them [by] declining to the disposition of the land."[21] Creole was initially made to denote approximation: someone who is "like" but is not a native, and someone who grows to be estranged from the homeland. The condition of in-betweenness is clearly highlighted here, which may be the reason for the negative light. The resentment originates from a sense of uneasiness at the Creole's unstable position of being neither Spaniard nor native but a mutant in the strict sense of "in the process of alteration."

Coming back to Anatole Broyard, his claim of Creoleness resonates differently when seen in a larger scope. Creole, not unlike passing, carries the sense of adapting to one's environment, and for Broyard, it means more precisely rejecting any fixity and racial sedentarism, whether black, white, or biracial. Broyard did not actively deny the rumors of blackness floating around him. As Gates says, "Broyard responded with X-Acto knives and evasions, with distance and denials and half-denials and cunning half-truths. Over the years, he became a virtuoso of *ambiguity and equivocation* [my italics]."[22] Broyard had not only the power to stand on one side or the other of the spectrum but he could just as well stay in the middle and capitalize on his flexibility. In the following subway image that Gates borrows from the scholar W. F. Lucas, Broyard sounds like a racial *passe-muraille*, someone able to freely walk through racial walls: "He was black when he got into the subway in Brooklyn, but as soon as he got out at West Fourth Street he became white."[23] His all-purpose status also meant that, if need be, Broyard could go home and revert to being black again, just as his parents did on a daily basis after work.

And indeed, we see a compulsion to go back home with Broyard, to haunt what is left behind. Going home for Broyard, however, is not literal or geographical but mainly creative. The editor at the *Book Review* (1965–85) says about Broyard's writing, "What I found fascinating was his ability to take the strict academic or intellectual approach that at the time was presumed to be a part of white culture and combine it with the looseness, vividness, and spontaneity of black culture."[24] The editor's comment is of course to be taken with a grain of salt. Is there indeed such a thing as "writing black," or is the perceived black idiosyncrasy a genre that the editor retrospectively ascribes to Broyard once he finds out that Broyard was a black man passing for white? The question of "black style" aside, there is no denying that Broyard openly enjoyed and regularly wrote about black culture. His inclination for black-related topics undeniably lent a black cultural touch in a white literary world. As Bliss Broyard says:

> Yet my father persisted in acting as a bridge between the uptown (black) world and the (white intellectual) Village. He started to bring a group of disciples up to Spanish Harlem every Thursday night. He continued to write about the jazz world, Afro-Cuban music, and the sexuality of dancing—none of which were typical subject matter for the average white intellectual. And my father didn't shy away from "primitive" pastimes, even working out with George Brown, the boxing coach who was reputed to have trained Hemingway.[25]

Broyard engaging in hobbies characteristic of African-American culture is the extra something that vernacularizes his white identity and make his passing undeniably subversive. In *The Signifying Monkey*, Henry Louis Gates looks at vernacularism as a tactic of quiet opposition: "Whereas black writers most certainly revise texts in the Western tradition, they often seek to do so 'authentically,' with a black difference, a compelling sense of difference based on the black vernacular."[26] This black difference is a form of evasion because Gates uses the word *vernacular* in its etymologically literal sense: *verna* meaning "slave born in his master's house."[27] This is not just any kind of evasion, however; the black alteration of the white word refers to an inner evasion—what Michel De Certeau calls "la tactique" (the tactic), which is a technique of opposition "à l'intérieur du champ de vision de l'ennemi" (within the enemy's field of vision).[28] Blacks make the master's house theirs, surreptitiously adding a black difference that allows them to leave the master's house in a discreet escape that echoes the marooning tradition in the Americas. In other words, by adding a unique black difference to the *Book Review* or the *New York Times*, Anatole Broyard vernacularizes the white text as a way to bring it home. Broyard did not escape but instead brought his New York white intelligentsia world of literature back to his black New Orleans slave-impacted origins.

The critic Sybil Kein offers an interesting etymological source for the word *Creole*:

> The *Harvard Encyclopedia of American Ethnic Groups* explains that the word "refers to people, culture, to food, and music, and to language." Originally from the Portuguese *crioulo*, the word for a *slave brought up*

*in the owner's household* [my italics], which in turn probably derived from the Latin *creare* ("create"), it became *criollo* in Spanish and *créole* in French.[29]

Kein's etymology of *Creole* as a slave brought up in the owner's household is almost identical to Gates's take on the word *vernacular* as a slave born in the master's house. Because, for Gates, *vernacular* involves a spirit of inner opposition, Kein's *Creole* should by extension hold a similar contestatory nature. More importantly, it is assumed that this call involves a dispute over so-called "home ownership." Kein's take on *Creole* as etymologically a slave who is brought up in the master's house, combined with the pervasive idea throughout various dictionaries that the word initially only applied to whites, creates a metafictional intrigue. It all comes down to a story of *jus soli* (the law relating to the land). The master's house is white, but because the slave was born in the master's house, he or she can claim birthrights and dual ownership of the house. In return, the master will dispute the slave's claim of dual ownership. The *Creole* label is yanked back and forth as dictionaries will not settle the case, the word remains a floating racial signifier. Anatole Broyard is a product and a beneficiary of Creole's unsettled racial matters. Not only can he apply the label according to his own needs, but he can also reenact at leisure the *jus soli* claim by vernacularizing the white text with his special black difference—this extra something that brings the white text home. Broyard is admittedly, to some extent, a traitor for conveniently jumping over the fence and leaving his people behind. Yet, Broyard's passing can also be read as an oppositional tactic that allows him to insidiously reclaim a property right from which blacks were divested under the hypodescent regime. Ironically enough, the very nature of Creoleness prevents us from putting a fixed label on Broyard's own passing.

## The Passing Genre: Racial Defiance and Sexual Deviance

Given that the light-skinned passing subject is the result, at one point in the lineage, of a sexual encounter between a black and a white, it is undeniable that racial passing somehow exposes the (historically marked as "controversial") practice of miscegenation. In *The Libertine Colony*, Doris Garraway calls attention to the fact that, when addressing the issues of *métissage* (mixed race) and Creolization, Francophone writers tend to obliterate the sexual dimension inherent in those concepts. Garraway laments the fact that Edouard

Glissant and the Creolists Raphaël Confiant, Patrick Chamoiseau, and Jean Bernabé "are far less explicit about the roles of gender and sexuality, tending to invoke *métissage* only to pass immediately to its metaphorical rather than literal meaning."[30] And yet, Creolization, as Edward Brathwaite defines it, is a "cultural action or social process"[31] that forced racial and cultural conjoining through the meeting, and mating, of distinct cultures. Brathwaite writes, "It was in the intimate area of sexual relationships that the most significant— and lasting—intercultural Creolization took place."[32] Interracial sexuality is, to some extent, the backbone of Creolization. As such, Creolization and its subsequent *métissage* should technically be treated as a sexually initiated deviation from the initial course of cultural homogeneousness. As a result, the black who passes for white carries more often than not the seal of deviance (deviation), not only because she or he is a so-called traitor of the black community but also because his or her passing was enabled by the sexual "deviance" of miscegenation. There is a cause-and-effect connection between racial passing and miscegenation that, as we shall see, accounts for the tendency to treat racial defiance within the realm of sexual deviance.

*Passing*, the Harlem Renaissance novel by Nella Larsen about racial passing, offers a good example of defiance as deviance. Larsen's story revolves around two light-skinned female characters, Irene and Clare, old childhood friends who lost touch after one chose to "go native" (a Harlem Renaissance colloquialism for "passing"). Irene, who lives as a black woman, is married and has a child in Harlem. Clare, whose name sounds like the French word *claire*, as in *claire de peau* (light-skinned), has chosen to pass for white. She lives in Manhattan with her white husband, who is unaware that she is legally considered black. The story is narrated through Irene's third-person eagle-eye narrative that closely studies, reads, and interprets the specifics of her friend's passing for white:

> Her lips, painted a brilliant geranium-red, were sweet and a little obstinate. A tempting mouth. The face across the forehead and cheeks was a trifle too wide, but the ivory skin had a peculiar soft luster. And the eyes were magnificent! Dark, sometimes absolutely black, always luminous, and set in long, black lashes. Arresting eyes, slow and mesmeric, and with, for all their warmth, something withdrawn and secret about them.[33]

First comes the screening, then the crack:

Ah! Surely! They were Negro eyes! Mysterious and concealing. And set
in that ivory face under that bright hair, there was about them something
exotic.[34]

The "Ah! Surely! They were Negro eyes!" points to a crack in the otherwise
perfect picture. The glance behind the scene is made possible by a close reading of the subject. Irene's scrutiny is so meticulous that it sounds as if she
wished to live Clare's life vicariously:

She [Irene] wished to find out about this hazardous business of "passing," this breaking away from all that was familiar and friendly to take
one's chance in another environment, not entirely strange, perhaps, but
certainly not entirely friendly.[35]

By the end of the sentence, one can no longer ascertain whether Irene is still
referring to Clare's racial passing or to her own repressed wish to pass for
Clare. Her chosen words—"familiar," "not entirely friendly," "not entirely
strange"—assume a multifaceted ambivalence—to be quite white but not entirely so (both "familiar" and "strange" in color), to be friends ("friendly") but
not quite entirely so ("strange"), to be Clare but not quite entirely her, to be
familiar and strange, I and other. The Narcissus-like Irene gradually falls into
her own reflection in her close-up reading of Clare.

The visible crack, the "ah ha moment" described above, provides Irene with
a cathartic moment of clarity after the *unheimlich* pressure of unwavering ambivalence.[36] The sine qua non condition of the passing narrative lies precisely
in the alluring promise made by the text to crack the ambivalence. The passing
narrative therefore builds on the imminence of the "Ah! Surely! They were Negro eyes!" epiphany. This literary genre calls to mind Henry James's "The Figure in the Carpet,"[37] the secret to be unraveled yet ever postponed.[38] Larsen's
novel offers a variation on James's story in that the "eureka moment" occurs
at the beginning, in full diegetic sight. The already exposed secret is a reverse
leap of faith meant to discredit, from the start, the feasibility of the representation of whiteness. That said, the early outing of the white-black subject will
not entail an interruption of the scrutiny. On the contrary, Irene's study of her
subject grows so obsessively close that Irene will eventually push Clare off a
balcony to her death, as if there were no more space for Clare to step away
from Irene's snooping.[39]

We could call such a thing an "Irene syndrome"—an obsessive desire to out
the passing subject, both "out" in the figurative sense of racial outing and in

the literal sense of pushing the passing subject to his death due to excessive scrutiny. Anatole Broyard was racially outed several times. Chandler Brossard, who had previously been one of Broyard's best friends, used Broyard's passing as an inspiration for his main character in his 1952 novel *Who Walk in Darkness*. Before the release of the novel, however, Broyard threatened to sue Brossard if the latter did not readjust his story. Brossard's character ended up not being black but illegitimate. Then came the 1996 article in the *New Yorker* by Henry Louis Gates, titled "White Like Me,"[40] a reference to John Howard Griffin's 1961 memoir *Black Like Me*, about his experiences when he altered his appearance to look black. In his piece, Gates, who was at the time the head of the Department of African and African-American Studies at Harvard, announced to all that "Broyard was born black and became white."[41] In 2007, Broyard's daughter, Bliss Broyard, published the most anticipated book about her father, *One Drop: My Father's Hidden Life—A Story of Race and Family Secrets*. It took her more than a decade to complete it. She thoroughly combed through genealogical archives and researched the complex history of African-Americans and Creoles in Louisiana, all the way back to January 13, 1753, when Etienne Broyard from La Rochelle, France, moved to New Orleans. Bliss Broyard did not beat Henry Louis Gates to the revelation about Anatole Broyard, a situation that, as she recounts in her book, she resented. In 1996, Gates contacted Bliss Broyard to ask her private questions about Anatole Broyard's passing. Bliss was not aware that, as an academic and scholar of African-American studies, Gates was interested in the story from a personal standpoint as well as a professional one. After several friendly and laid-back conversations over the phone, Broyard was taken aback when Gates broke the news that his article about her father passing would appear in the *New Yorker*. "Isn't that great," Gates says to her. She writes:

> No, I told him. It wasn't great. Not at all. *I* was planning on writing about my father. "As you know." I added pointedly. Gates sharply replies: "Well, why haven't you, then? . . . You've known for over five years now."[42]

Henry Louis Gates—the distinguished scholar with an erudite understanding of black issues in America—and Bliss Broyard—sheltered her entire childhood to the point of racial oblivion but with an intimate knowledge of her father—argued over the legitimate authorship of the story to be told. The secret was undoubtedly meant to be revealed; it was just a matter of who, after Brossard's failed 1952 attempt, would break the story.

The passing narrative was essentially caught between being repeatedly postponed and itching to be told. Gates and Bliss Broyard's anticipation builds upon the "eureka moment" of what should have remained concealed but that they will inevitably bring to light. Their feud reenacts the outing endlessly deferred (Bliss B.) and yet already told (Gates). Bliss Broyard recounts the incident in her book years later, which allows her to discredit Gates's article while giving her a chance to tell the story that was never really told (properly). In spite of Gates, Bliss Broyard recreates for readers the virgin context of an outing yet to be committed. As she mentions in her book, some of the things that Gates wrote about Anatole Broyard were incorrect. Yet again, how could he have gotten it completely right, since he had never even met Anatole Broyard?[43] As compensation for releasing the scoop first, Gates offered to make an arrangement with Tina Brown so that Broyard's daughter could write a piece about her father in an upcoming "black issue"[44] of the magazine—as if Gates did not understand, even though he mentioned it in his article,[45] that her father passed for white precisely to avoid being branded as a "black author."

Henry Louis Gates and Bliss Broyard found themselves in a chiasmic position: black knowledge with no intimate experience on the one hand and intimate experience with no black knowledge on the other—two positions that both complement and mutually reject each other. From their opposite and opposing positions, neither one can see the whole figure in the carpet. With his critical distance, Gates easily redefines Broyard as black, just like on Broyard's birth certificate. With her intimate proximity, Bliss Broyard can convincingly recapture what brought Anatole Broyard to pass for white up to his death certificate. Yet, what the two cannot manage to do together is account for the irrepressible desire to tell the story first, to elbow their way into first place in the race to out and unveil Anatole Broyard's secret passing. The history of Anatole Broyard's outing reads like the juicy sexual outing of a public figure. Tina Brown, the queen of New York's glossy multimedia intelligentsia; Henry Louis Gates, the academic "celebrity" from Harvard; and Bliss Broyard who benefited from an impressive number of fellowships and grants (listed in her thank you note) to write her version of the story: all three create a hype around the recounting of Anatole Broyard's passing. The *New Yorker* released Gates's anticipated article in June 1996, a day that Bliss describes as follows:

> I flew to Boston the day the issue was released. A row of *New Yorkers* lined the glass window of a Logan Airport newsstand. The white

wrapper advertising highlights from the magazine read in black letters: WHITE LIKE ME. THE PASSING OF ANATOLE BROYARD. I had a wild impulse to charge inside the store and rip all the magazines down. *I wasn't ready yet.*[46]

The description carries undertones of tabloid sex scandals; Anatole's dirty little secret is incestuously and brazenly thrown in the daughter's blushing face. In Bliss's recounting of the experience, race and sexuality hold hands between brackets: "I read about what people had thought and said about my dad—his racial and romantic career—behind his back."[47] "The glare of the spotlight"[48] not only made Anatole—with his bare skin so shamelessly flaunted—racially naked to the public eye, but it also left him sexually exposed. "But my family and I stood stiff with anger, blinded under the glare of this sudden spotlight. The characterization of my father as an obsessive seducer of women particularly upset my mother."[49]

The story of Anatole's passing is introduced here through an amalgam of sexuality and race. The combination makes it sound as if passing for white were not an enticing enough story, as if the unveiling of his black blood were only the tip of a more insidious iceberg; as if, finally, racial treachery needed to be articulated within a sexually suggestive syntactic framework in order to hold meaning. But what needs to be pointed out here is that the palpable sexual tension in the story of Broyard's passing is not ignited by the passing itself but by the act of reading the passing subject, the sexualizing of Irene's scrutiny. Both the critics Deborah E. McDowell and Judith Butler have argued that, in Larsen's *Passing*, Irene's obsessive search for more clues of passing, more signs of betrayal in Clare, carried lesbian tendencies. The two have posited that Clare's racial passing was only the *manifest* text that aimed to hide Irene's lesbian passing, which was the true *latent* message in Larsen's story. This assumption was partially based on Irene's supposedly paranoid tendencies, corroborated by the fact that she suspected her husband Brian of having an affair with Clare as a transference of her own desire for Clare. However, in "Paranoid Interpretation, Desire's Nonobject, and Nella Larsen's *Passing*," Brian Carr argues that the transference is actually on the side of the two critics. McDowell and Butler transfer onto Irene their own wish to sexualize the passing subject. For Carr, the two critics act upon a paranoid compulsion to overinterpret (and let us add "sexualize"), the same kind of compulsion that they claim to have detected in Irene's behavior. Carr further asserts that McDowell and Butler's paranoid homosexual subtext holds a Freudian twist given that "for Freud, paranoia is virtually unthinkable without homosexuality."[50] Looking for Irene's purported homosexuality has led McDowell and Butler to take an active role in Irene's supposed paranoia: they paranoically look for the repressed sexual message in Irene's own supposedly paranoid reading.

In his convincing critical demonstration, Carr falls one step short of coming to two necessary conclusions: first, that this overreading compulsion is an inherent component of the passing narrative genre, both within and outside the text, and second, that this compulsion reveals a more insidious tendency to equate hidden blackness with hidden sexuality, an equation that presents the "deviant" race as a familiar channel for "deviant" (as in "not straight") sexuality. The compulsion of overinterpretation is easy to comprehend. Because passing means betraying an invisible secret, one is drawn to fruitlessly look for the visibility of a secret, a secret that cannot be seen because the passing narrative hides a nonvisible blackness. The awkwardness of the situation thus compels one to indefinitely look for the something behind the nothing in order to find what should have remained secret, whether it is an affair (Irene's overreading) or a repressed homosexuality (McDowell and Butler's overreading). The critic fabricates a setting of closeted homosexuality that will validate the compulsory need to out the passing subject. As to the question of homosexuality, the situation is more complicated. When McDowell suggests that underneath the story of Clare's passing looms a hidden account "of Irene's awakening sexual desire for Clare,"[51] her assertions are grounded in the specific context of the black 1920s. As she explains, in the predominantly male Black Renaissance context, black women felt pressured to speak about their sexuality "obliquely"[52] and "indirectly"[53] for fear of either fitting the black female exotic stereotype or displeasing the black intelligentsia that disapproved of sexual promiscuity in black narratives. McDowell hypothesizes that Larsen conveniently displaced the sexual narrative onto the supposedly cheating Brian in order to hide Irene's reprimandable fantasies.[54] Irene would therefore have used Brian as a convenient outlet to express her own sexual desires for Clare. The interesting aspect of McDowell's argument is that, because Larsen must address black female sexuality obliquely, the sexuality itself becomes "oblique," nonstraight, and "deviant" in the sense of not conformist—in other words, "queer."

Judith Butler, who probably picked up on the amalgam between queering the sexual message and queering Irene's sexuality, wrote a follow-up to McDowell's article that she titled "Passing, Queering: Nella Larsen's Psychoanalytic Challenge." In it, she expatiates on McDowell's theory of sexual passing and reiterates the assertion that Brian is an unbeknownst cover for Irene's hidden sexual desire. She writes:

> Brian carries that repudiated homosexuality, and Irene's jealousy, then, can be understood as not only a rivalry with him for Clare, but the painful consequence of a sacrifice of passion that she repeatedly makes, a sacrifice that entails the displacement or rerouting of her desire through Brian.[55]

But we see here that the "rerouting" and "displacement" take place not only in the love triangle, from Clare to Brian, but also from McDowell to Butler. Butler takes on McDowell's theory and further displaces it to make language the real queer manifestation in Larsen's story: "As a term for betraying what ought to have remained concealed, *queering* works as the exposure within language—and exposure that disrupts the repressive surface of language—of both sexuality and race."[56] Queerness is not sexuality but its exposure in language, not race but its verbal exposure that ought to have remained secret. Here, Butler's definition of queering is an unannounced paraphrasing of Freud's aforementioned *unheimlich* (himself paraphrasing Schelling) as "everything that ought to have remained . . . secret and hidden but has come to light."[57] "Everything that ought to have remained secret but has come to light" is incidentally the work of the scrutinizer and the critic, the one who compulsively reracializes and, by the same token, sexualizes the passing subject. The telling on the passing subject is the scarlet letter of betrayal, since its very function is to show the visible signs of the undue telling. Butler compensates for the invisible nature of the (racial) secret by overstressing the question of its exposure. Yet, for Butler, the exposure is not meant to expose the secret but its *indirect*, hence nonstraight/deviant, expression in sexuality.

McDowell and Butler's repressed homosexuality theory says more about the one who tells about the passing than the one being unveiled. The alleged (homo-)sexuality here is the pure *jouissance* that feeds on the quest, on the desire to know what cannot be revealed, or what is not. As Carr explains:

> The novel allows us to focus on the ways knowledge and desire are sustained by their lack of nonobject that would complete or satisfy them, on how routine understandings of race and sexuality tend toward paranoid interpretive closure and on why we want to substantialize everything as if there were no nothing.[58]

Carr's theory lays stress on the critic's *desire* for the truth, a desire that contagiously invests the passing subject with a libidinal drive. What Clare's story reveals is that, once on the other side, the passing subject becomes an object of desire that the scrutinizer or the reader yearns to possess. Clare is a cryptic narrative that Irene wants to decode or, more literally, unveil—hence the pervasive sense of lust and scandalous sexuality surrounding the passing subject. Henry Louis Gates is, in that sense, very much like Irene, McDowell, and Butler, because his scrutinizing goes hand in hand with sexualizing Broyard.

Anatole Broyard, or rather his later ego, has been sexualized many times before. Boris Vian's 1946 crime novel *J'irai cracher sur vos tombes* (*I Spit on Your Graves*, 1948) and Philip Roth's *The Human Stain* (2000), two classics about racial passing, are eerily close to Broyard's story. Both books use sexuality as a subplot to introduce the topic of passing. Chronology-wise, it is unlikely that Vian was inspired by Anatole Broyard's passing when he wrote his novel, given that in 1946, when Vian wrote the manuscript, Broyard was still an unknown figure who had freshly made it to Greenwich Village. Yet, Vian wrote his manuscript about a black man who passed for white and worked in a bookstore in a southern town at about the same time that Broyard, who was already passing for white, opened a bookstore on Cornelia Street in Greenwich Village. Also, Vian's character is portrayed as a ladies' man just like Broyard, although, unlike Broyard, the protagonist used his sexual drive in the service of activism. Vian's story revolves around a man named Lee Sullivan who turns his penis into a deadly weapon against white southern belles as a revenge for the murder of his brother. When Sullivan's murderous rampage catches up with him, he is publicly hung, but his penis does not totally surrender. Vian chooses the following sentence to close the novel: "Sous son pantalon, son bas-ventre faisait encore une bosse dérisoire" (Under his pants, there was still a pathetic bulge in his lower abdomen).[59] Sullivan was a sexual magnet for women. He had a little something in his voice—"Il y a quelque chose en vous qu'on ne comprend pas bien. Votre voix" (There is something in you that we do not totally understand. Your voice)[60]—and in his build— "Vous avez les épaules tombantes comme un boxeur noir" (You have slouching shoulders like a black boxer)[61]—which made him sexually irresistible to women unaware of his racial ambiguity. Sexuality empowered Sullivan as a *passé blanc* (the name used in Louisiana for the passing subject), but sexuality also brought about his downfall.

As for Philip Roth, the author denies that *The Human Stain* is based on the life of Anatole Broyard, even though his main character Coleman Silk, like Broyard, passed for white his entire adult life, enlisted in the navy during World War II, practiced boxing, aspired to live in bohemian Greenwich Village, taught literature at a university (Broyard taught at New York University), chose to pass for white in a small New England white community, and ended up married with children who were unaware of his black lineage. Roth claims that he read Gates's *New Yorker* article after he had started working on *The Human Stain*. Whether or not the similarities between Coleman Silk and Anatole Broyard are fortuitous, what is particularly interesting in Roth's novel is the explicit sexual undertone ascribed to racial passing. The novel begins with a semantic displacement meant to echo the racial displacement of the main character passing for white. Coleman, a classics professor, quits his job at Athena College after a rift over a misunderstanding on the word *spooks*, referring to unknown students on the attendance list. Unbeknownst to him, the unassiduous students were black. Because of their complexion, his use of "spooks" to mean "ghostlike" was misinterpreted as the racial slur for blacks. The irony of the story is that Coleman is himself a black passing for white. Appropriately, the first chapter of Roth's novel is entitled "Everyone Knows," but the title does not refer to everyone knowing about Coleman's passing but about his affair with Faunia, a thirty-four-year-old janitor on campus. The affair is particularly scandalous given that Coleman is a seventy-one-year-old ex-dean of the college where Faunia is now a janitor. "Everyone Knows" comes from the anonymous letter presumably sent by Delphine Roux, a young professor of languages and literatures, to Coleman:

Everyone knows you're
sexually exploiting an
abused, illiterate
woman half your
age.[62]

Because "everyone knows" plays on a double-entendre, the narrative builds on a metonymical shift from racial passing to dirty sexual secret. The salaciousness of the sexual affair ("she's turned sex into a vice again"[63]) splatters the other (racial) secret that, though revealed to readers, is not told to the intradiegetic "everyone" mentioned by Delphine Roux. Everyone except Coleman knew the absent students were black, and nobody except Coleman knew he was black. Yet, Coleman is outed and chastised for sexual, not racial, misconduct. Because racial outing relies on a chimerical presupposition of blackness unverifiable to the eye, it calls for a substitution that sexualizes the dirty secret, making it visible, provable, and then condemnable. Roth conveniently contextualizes Coleman's sexual passing with a sexual repressed affair that has become the talk of the town. Reversing McDowell and Butler's paranoid compulsion, the author suggests that a sexual *manifest* text hides a *latent* message of racial passing. And like McDowell and Butler, Roth leads us to conclude that there is always a compelling need, in critics and writers alike, to dig out the sexual secret behind the story of racial passing.

Returning to Henry Louis Gates and his *New Yorker* article on Broyard, Roth had supposedly not read Gates's article before writing *The Human Stain*, and yet Gates's work, just like Roth's, pointedly highlights the symbolic importance of the sexual anecdote in the story of racial passing. Like for Roth, "everyone knows" is a favored hearsay mode of exposure Gates uses to address both Broyard's racial passing and his sexuality. In his article, Gates emphasizes greatly and unbashfully the womanizer side of Anatole Broyard. The scholar also chooses a sexual portrait of the literary critic that, interestingly enough, has nothing intimate about it. The ladies' man persona is weaved through a concatenation of third-person narratives, wink-wink comments, and rumors. Gates tells us that an author and ex-lover of Broyard, Anne Bernays, admitted that "with women, he was just like an alcoholic with booze." A former professor of comparative literature argued that "he was a pussy gangster, really."[64] The *New York Times* managing editor allegedly said, "The trouble with Broyard is that he writes with his cock!"[65] These are only a few of the sexual references that Gates chose to include in his article. The author skillfully stages a sexual subplot to stage the outing of Anatole Broyard, thereby suggesting that a narrative on passing infallibly carries a sexual subtext to be deciphered. More than that, Gates's gossipy reported genre turns out to present Anatole Broyard as an unsubstantiated flat character assembled through disparate public speculations. Gates satirizes, consciously or not, the paranoid compulsion of the passing narrative genre as he relies on the trope of public overexposure, sexualizing, and sensationalizing of the passing as a way to fill the void of racial simulacrum, the secret about nothing. Gates was going to be the first to tell the story, but what precisely was the story?

Bliss Broyard, on the other hand, builds the legitimacy of her voice and authorship on the idea that, unlike Gates's article, her book offers an inside look at her father. Her narrative technique is therefore deprived of gossipy sexual sensationalism. Nonetheless, the daughter leaves the door open to speculations as she admits that her father had a pied-à-terre in New York, where, while her mother was going through a difficult time with alcohol addiction, he may have had extramarital affairs. She also mentions her father's impressive romantic life as a young man, further discussing the hundreds of multiauthored and multilingual love letters sitting at her mother's house. In *One Drop*, this family-invested memoir, Anatole Broyard's sexuality can only be a side story, something that Bliss Broyard's father had, literally speaking, *on the side*, since the extrafamilial sexual activities belong to the pied-à-terre. Anatole Broyard's scandalous sexual life did not set foot in her house and life, and therefore it is an aspect of her father's life that she would deem irrelevant to the story of his passing. By choosing the opposite approach, Gates presents Broyard's public sexual persona as an extension of his racial passing. Anatole Boyard carries meaning not in the acts of sex or passing but in the representation, perception, and telling of them.

Among his people, Anatole Broyard was known as an unfortunate writer manqué in spite of his well-crafted writing skills and intellectual sophistication. After publishing two well-received autobiographical pieces about his family, Anatole was commissioned by *Atlantic Monthly Press* to write a novel on a similar topic. The press waited more than fifteen years for the completion of the novel, after which they asked for their money back. Gates notes, "Some people speculated that the reason Broyard couldn't write his novel was that he was living it—that race loomed larger in his life because it was unacknowledged, that he couldn't put it behind him because he had put it beneath him."[66] Anatole is essentially not a writer but a living protagonist meant to be told about, read, represented, assessed, and handled by literary critics. He once said himself that a personality is no more than a style that one should work to perfection. As Bliss Broyard comments, "He'd always viewed a person's style as the literal embodiment of his personality. As if we were uniquely made instruments, our job in life was to continually tune ourselves, tightening this and loosening that until we hit our most natural, most authentic sound."[67] The compulsive exteriorization of his life is made blatantly visible in Gates's chatty narrative genre. Like many others, Gates believes that Broyard dodged his potential career as a writer to avoid the racial box in which the likes of Richard Wright, James Baldwin, and Ralph Ellison had been confined. For Gates, Broyard "lived a lie because he didn't want to live a larger lie: and Anatole Broyard, Negro writer, was that larger lie."[68] But when Gates quotes Broyard's 1993 memoir ("I wanted to discuss my life with him not as a patient talking to an analyst but as if we were two literary critics discussing a novel. . . . I had a literature rather than a personality, a set of fictions about myself"),[69] another reason for Broyard's failed career comes to mind. As his experience with his therapist shows, even Broyard looked at himself through the scrupulous lens of a literary critic. After all, he was a literary critic, just like Gates, McDowell, and Butler, and as such, he used the unavoidable detour of the literary critic working on racial passing to fashion his own persona: highlighting the sexual persona behind the racial passing, "tightening this and loosening that" until he hit the most "natural" sound for us to read. Gates says that his story about Broyard offers "an image of self-assemblage which is very much in keeping with Broyard's own accounts of himself."[70] There is indeed little doubt that Gates's sensationalizing and sexualizing Broyard's racial passing result from Broyard's own invitation to be read as a sensation. Both Gates and Anatole Broyard tell *around* the subject, by way of the subject's surrounding and fabricated public personality. This circumvention results in a *différance* (as Jacques Derrida explains) of the telling of his real difference. Anatole Broyard's passing is the story ever so deferred, yet to be told, but obstructed by the chatter of his surroundings.

Few are aware that, in his work, Sigmund Freud addressed the question of racial passing, comparing the ambivalence characteristic of the unconscious to racial passing. In the following passage, Freud uses the image of racial passing to pinpoint the location of fantasy, between the preconscious and the unconscious:

> Their mixed and split origin is what decides their fate. We may compare them with individuals of mixed race who taken all round resemble white men but who betray their coloured descent by some striking feature or other and on that account are excluded from society and enjoy none of the privileges.[71]

The critic Daniel Boyarin believes that Freud is referring here to himself as a European Jew, since in the late nineteenth century, as Boyarin argues, "Jews most often appeared as mulattos"; they were qualified as off-white, *Ecru Homo*, and were therefore also subject to the politics of "not white / not quite."[72] Freud's "striking feature" is exactly what is at stake in not only the nature of the passing subject but in many supposedly ambivalent figures, like the Jew or the Creole. The passing subject and the *Criollo* never completely fit in a given group, but at the same time they are so much like the rest of the group, so much like the whites or the metropolitans. The indefinable "striking feature" is what makes those ambivalent figures renegades while they naturally stray from the pack as the normative group. Homi Bhabha would say that this striking feature is "a subject of a difference that is almost the same, but not quite."[73] The ambivalent figure is a metonymical presence that does not fully represent the original; the derivative only partially, hence metonymically, accounts for the source, which in turn creates this continual "slippage, its excess, its difference."[74] The unsettling yet thrilling sense of cultural and racial approximation inherent in the act of passing defines the Creole subject. The incompleteness of kinship is what makes the Creole, just like the passing subject, a born renegade. In that respect, Broyard, as a black passing for a white Creole, embodies perfectly this metonymical displacement. Both the Creole and the passing subject are naturally iconoclastic and disloyal to even their own (assumingly fixed) definition. Ultimately, this intrinsic iconoclasm makes the notion of "Creole renegade" intentionally pleonastic, since the Creole seems to *always already* break the mold of fixed conventions.

But of particular interest here is that the "striking feature," the said slippage, carries the libidinal excess of the *Entstellung*, the process of displacement that Bhabha himself associates with desire.[75] The *Entstellung* is the "displacement, distortion, dislocation, repetition"[76] eating up the norm, disfiguring it. Bhabha uses *Entstellung* within the literary context of the English book (the "original") that undergoes a process of displacement and hybridization due to the colonial presence. In the case of "passing," however, as Butler points out in "Gender Is Burning," there is no such thing as an "original book" that would dictate what the norm—the origin—is. Passing is referential and mostly perceptual. Its realness relies on an unwritten book of racial conventions. Butler's "Gender Is Burning" addresses Jennie Livingston's 1990 documentary about the passing performances of the African-American, Latino, and transgender communities in drag balls of Harlem. As the participants try to emulate the hegemonic models of whiteness and heterosexuality, they rely on what Butler names a "morphological ideal" of what the norms are, an ideal conveying "a figure of a body, which is no particular body."[77]

In Livingston's film, when the performer impersonating an Ivy League student casually struts down the catwalk, the audience here sees no slippage, no excess in the performance. Butler would go on to say, "This is a performance that works, that effects realness, to the extent that it cannot be read. For 'reading' means taking someone down, exposing what fails to work at the level of appearance, insulting or deriding someone."[78] Yet, Livingston's camera serves as a reminder of the mimic nature of the Ivy League boy, which implies that the camera, by definition, always "reads" (in Butler's sense) the performer. The channel through which we see the performance—namely, the camera—signals the unrealness of the Ivy League student. Again, "reading," as seen with McDowell, Butler, Larsen, and Gates, often includes sexualizing the passing subject. At one point in Livingston's film, we hear a voice that does not appear on camera wooing Octavia St. Laurent into posing seductively for the camera. Butler has this to say about the voice:

> What is suggested by this sudden intrusion of the camera into the film is something of the camera's desire, the desire that motivates the camera, in which a white lesbian phallically organized by the use of the camera (elevated to the status of disembodied gaze, holding out the promise of erotic recognition) erotizes a back male-to-female transsexual—presumably preoperative—who "works" perceptually as a woman.[79]

Butler equates the camera with a phallic gaze, the erotic tool of the lesbian filmmaker. Yet, her description could just as well apply to the reader, the literary critic committed to bringing out the sexual appeal of the passing subject. Like in "Paris Is Burning," Broyard's racial passing was also supposedly based on an Ivy League performance. His performance was incidentally outed by a racial scrutinizer who erotized the "striking feature" that gave him away. Gates quotes William Gaddis describing Broyard in his novel *The Recognitions*: "a parody on the moment, as his clothes caricatured a past at eastern colleges where he had never been."[80] Then comes the outing (also quoted by Gates): "his 'unconscionable smile,' which intimates 'that the wearer knew all of the dismal secrets of some evil jungle whence he had just come.'"[81] The "striking feature" here is the evil jungle, suggestive of a primitive, instinctual, and sexual extra something in Broyard's eastern college demeanor. Broyard's inner secret is like Vian's Sullivan prowling after white women surreptitiously in the dark. In Larsen's *Passing*, Irene's eroticized reading of Clare resulted in her being coined a closeted lesbian by several critics, including Butler. Irene lavishly (hence suspiciously?) described Clare's "brilliant geranium-red" lips and her "arresting eyes, slow and mesmeric," bearer of an indefinable "exotic" secret. Reading, in Butler's sense of screening racial realness, carries the pleasure of undressing the passing subject, laying that individual down, body-searching the "striking feature" that will give the passing subject away, which will result in a *jouissance*-producing exposure. In racial passing, in this slight disfiguration of whiteness, the reader gets to peek at the in-betweenness of the passing subject while getting the erotic gratification that comes with peeking at "celle la peau qui scintille entre deux pièces" (the skin flashing between two articles of clothing).[82] By putting side by side Broyard's Ivy League's semblance and the crudeness of his sexual prowess, Gates is able to create the effect of the gap between the shirt and the pants, the promise of a peek at his "jungle" extra something, a eureka moment that would otherwise be incommunicable. Literally speaking, sexuality puts some flesh on racial passing, adding body to an invisible secret.

There is a potential reason why racial passing should so often carry sexual undertones. It has to do again with the question of Creoleness—more specifically white Creoleness. In 1966, the Dominican-born writer Jean Rhys published *Wide Sargasso Sea*, a story that resuscitated Bertha Mason, the Jamaican character from Charlotte Brontë's English Victorian novel *Jane Eyre*. In Brontë's original version of events, Bertha is the secret wife of the British Edward Rochester, a mentally disturbed white Creole who has been kept out of sight in the attic of her husband's manor. In Rhys's rewriting, most of the action takes place in the Caribbean; the author focuses on the marital woes of the European Rochester and his Creole wife Antoinette. By unleashing the crazy white Creole and bringing Antoinette back to her predominantly black native environment, Rhys has opened a Pandora's box. The author tries to suggest that Brontë's Bertha was locked in the attic not because of her supposedly dangerous mental illness but because of her being Creole. Once back on the island, the Creole wife shows—literally speaking—the "dark" side of her Creoleness, turning out to be culturally, physically, and racially too close to the black community for Rochester's white comfort. Even the locals start looking at Antoinette and her now destitute family as "white niggers," as they say.

In her race-oriented revision, Rhys introduces the significant, though implicit, concept of racial promiscuity. Promiscuity, from the Latin *miscere*, meaning "to mix," designates an indiscriminate mixture of things and people. By the second half of the nineteenth century, the word took on a slightly different meaning, having built up a sexual connotation that signifies an indiscriminate exercise in multiple sexual relations. The semantic adjustment underscores a mental convention in the current English language of associating the idea of mixture (indiscrimination) with sexuality, and even more so with sexual deviance. In *Wide Sargasso Sea*, the connotative extrapolation—from indiscrimination to sexual deviance—is very salient in the figure of the white Creole. As Antoinette's race becomes more indeterminate, her image turns out to appear more promiscuous in Rochester's eyes as a result of her approximation with blacks. This approximation is both physical and figurative. Because Antoinette lives *close* to the blacks, her identity is now *close* to being black: literally speaking, her race *approximates* that of the blacks. The subtle allusion to racial indiscrimination resulting in indeterminacy—what the critic Lee Erwin refers to as "taint"—is the impetus of the novel, bringing race and sexuality together. Rhys draws on a rich etiological imaginary based on the phobic idea that race can be contracted through proximity—hence the isolation of the wife in the attic. But the author also implies that racial proximity, and thus racial approximation, are symptomatic of sexual deviance. As Erwin points out, "Rochester's racial imagination is metonymic, expressing itself as a perception of contamination from contiguity, one racial term slipping or 'leaking' into another through sheer proximity, obsessively perceived as sexual."[83] Once doubt enters his mind, Rochester looks at his now racially indeterminate wife as a sexually deviant person, whose deviance implicitly relates to the miscegenation responsible for producing "white niggers."

Since the moment he set foot on the island, after the honeymoon, Rochester felt that a dark secret from Antoinette's past consumed their marriage. The husband set out to find the nature of the secret: "It was a beautiful place—wild, untouched, above all untouched, with an alien, disturbing, secret loveliness. And it kept a secret. . . . 'What I see is nothing—I want what it *hides*—that is not nothing.'"[84] At a critical moment in the book, Rochester gets an important clue as to his wife's mysterious past. Just like Irene in *Passing*, Rochester finally experiences the "ah ha moment" as he finds a crack in Antoinette's representation of whiteness:

> Long, sad, dark alien eyes. Creole of pure English descent she may be, but they are not English or European either. And when did I begin to notice all this about my wife Antoinette? After we left Spanish Town I suppose. Or did I notice it before and refuse to admit what I saw?[85]

Once Rochester decides that his wife, whom he saw as white before their marriage, was not completely white in the European sense of the term, the presumed racial indeterminacy of Antoinette soon enough introduces a hidden sexual past. Daniel, a mixed-race character in the story, reveals to Rochester that he and Antoinette share the same (white) father, making Antoinette his half-sister. The young man proceeds, "You are not the first one to kiss her pretty face. Pretty face, soft skin, pretty colour—not yellow like me. But my sister just the same. . . ."[86] The plot is organized in such a way that racial promiscuity, this indiscriminate mixture of races, is meant to portend sexual promiscuity.

Rhys extrapolates on an already existing connotation in Brontë's *Jane Eyre*: that of the Gothic figure carrying a haunting secret too unthinkable to be openly revealed. What happened on the island, what led Rochester to hide his Creole wife in the mansion's attic after he moved to Europe?[87] As mentioned earlier, in post-Reconstruction New Orleans, the Anglophones accused the white Creoles of having "a touch of the tar brush," meaning that the white Creoles were suspected of being the products of miscegenation. In Larsen's *Passing*, one also sees the power of racial approximation when Clare is publicly outed as black the moment she is caught by her white husband mingling with black people. The semantic unreliability of the word *Creole*—as Murdoch puts it, "this undefinability and strategic slippage of the Creole"[88]—reflects the slippery and ever so elusive racial identification of the Creole. But more importantly, as Pratima Prasad points out, Creole indeterminacy, as visible in nineteenth-century narratives, is fundamentally rooted in the notion of sexual promiscuity:

> "Creole" works as a convenient shorthand for many of the ambiguities and threshold identities that were the product of miscegenation and interracial contact: bodies that were racially unreadable; uncertain lineages; boundary-crossing filiations such as interracial frères and soeurs de lait, et cetera.[89]

First comes sexual promiscuity, then racial indeterminacy. As such, the Creole figure provides a unique paradigm with which to understand the covert sexual connotation underneath the genre of the passing narrative. Passing narratives do not narrate but *reveal*; they do not introduce but *out* their subjects from a language presumably sexually repressed and closeted. This literary genre is unique in its way of subtly bringing together race and sexuality under the common umbrella of promiscuity. Just like the Creole, the passing subject carries the scarlet letter of sexual promiscuity, and it is up to the reader, whether it be a husband, friend, or literary critic, to bring out the presumed truth of the sexual encounter.

Caribbean-born Bert Williams (1874–1922), one of the greatest black entertainers of all time, was famous in North America for his "coon" impersonation accessorized with makeup that exaggerated the darkness of his skin. In his biography of Williams, *Dancing in the Dark*, Caryl Phillips suggests that, had he stayed in the Bahamas, Williams would have never become such an icon:

> [Williams] has heard that anything is possible in the big country to the north. His father has told him this, and he understands that this is the reason why they are leaving their beaches, and abandoning their island. His father is giving them both a chance to improve themselves in the land of opportunity to the north, but freedom comes with a price.[90]

Williams's creativity indeed blossomed in the big country to the north, but his artistic accomplishment came at a price. Many black peers saw in the celebrated comedian a tragic sellout. Somehow, Bert Williams's life is similar and yet opposite to Anatole Broyard's. As a child, Broyard also went to "the land of opportunity to the north," moving from Creole New Orleans to New York. But while Williams exaggerated his blackness in order to distance himself from his color, laughing alongside the whites at the clownlike black, Broyard erased his blackness in order to live and work alongside the whites and possibly also laugh along with them. One may wonder what is more condemnable: challenging the rule of hypodescent—granted for what seem like opportunistic reasons—or, for a black like Gates, to put the passing subject back in his black place on the cover of the (white) *New Yorker*? Given the semantic history of the word *Creole* in the French Caribbean and New Orleans, it seems that race, like Creoleness and racial passing, is mostly determined by the variable context of reception. The real story to be told, therefore, lies in the eyes of the beholder. Gates "outing" Broyard ultimately makes us question the legitimacy of the so-called cultural obligation of blackness. Why this compulsion, this rushing need, in Gates to call on Broyard and bring him back to his black "home" in a striking gesture of devernacularization? Is the Creole Broyard indeed a tragic sellout?

2

# Maryse Condé's *Histoire de la femme cannibale*

## Coming Out in the French Antilles

> Je n'ai jamais eu le sens de la collectivité, . . . de l'origine commune qui
> font que les auteurs antillais, guadeloupéens, martiniquais ont tendance
> à parler d'un "nous" collectif.
>
> (I've never felt a sense of collectivity, . . . of the common origin that
> makes Antillean, Guadeloupean, Martinican authors tend
> to speak in terms of a collective "us.")
>
> MARYSE CONDÉ (INTERVIEW), "J'AI TOUJOURS ÉTÉ UNE
> PERSONNE UN PEU À PART"

Following the footsteps of Aimé Césaire's *Une tempête*, an adaptation of William Shakespeare's *The Tempest*, or Jean Rhys's *Wide Sargasso Sea*, based on Charlotte Brontë's *Jane Eyre*, Maryse Condé contributes to the tradition of Caribbean revisionism in her novel *La migration des coeurs* (*Windward Heights*, 1998), a Creole variation of Emily Brontë's *Wuthering Heights*. The appropriation of European classics by postcolonial writers often comes with expectations, given that postcolonial revisionism is primarily meant to be oppositional in the vein of the "Empire writes back" postcolonial discourse.[1] However, Condé visibly fails to meet those expectations when she opens the book with a kindhearted dedication to Emily Brontë: "A Emily Brontë, qui, je l'espère, agréera cette lecture de son chef-d'oeuvre. Honneur et respect!" (To Emily Brontë, who I hope will approve of this interpretation of her masterpiece. Honor and respect!). Instead of writing back to the center *with a vengeance*, a role that Salman Rushdie envisioned for postcolonial writers in his 1982 *Times of London* article, Condé rewrites the Western canon with "honor and respect." The critic Chris Bongie sees Condé's failed horizon of militant expectations as a "commercially canny"[2] move on the part of a "cross-over" writer who, he posits, carries the particularity of catering to both an academic audience and mainstream readers because she writes mainstream pleasing literature under the guise of the highbrow "postcolonial" genre. Condé wrote *La migration des coeurs* at a time when so many critics, Bongie pursues, would go "into spasms of high seriousness every time a name like Caliban, Ariel, or Bertha Mason got mentioned."[3] The market climate in which *La migration des coeurs* was published unarguably makes the book prone to be viewed as a manifestation of what Graham Huggan calls the "postcolonial exotic," referring to the global commodification of the postcolonial. Like a number of critics recently, Bongie has been persistent in what he sees as a pressing matter—namely, questioning the politics of production and commodification of the postcolonial in a global market. However, the case of *La migration des coeurs* seems to say more about the critical reception of those sorts of books than about their politics of production.

Postcolonial Studies is a field saturated with conventions, trends, and expectations where rules of popularity do not apply only to the mainstream market but also to the academic readership. The spasms-inducing names Caliban and Bertha are, granted, highly commodified, but they are, even more so, highly codified. They come with critical expectations of a very specific nature (high-seriousness, militancy, revisionism, etc.). It seems that the real "comprador intelligentsia"[4]—the culture brokers of the postcolonial—are not, as Kwame Anthony Appiah states, the handful of writers who produce postcolonial literature in the global market but rather the handful of critics who set the postcolonial trend with their expectations and assume that the authors will comply with them. By not conforming, Condé may, as Bongie argues, disinvest her revisional book of an oppositional discourse—the type of discourse found in Césaire or Rushdie—but the book carries an oppositional voice of a different kind, one least expected in a postcolonial context. As Carine Mardorossian rightfully suggests, *La migration des coeurs* "defies the tenets of postcolonial revisionism so unashamedly that it makes readers question their own assumptions rather than the colonialist representations it is rewriting."[5] In precisely that, *La migration des coeurs* comes across as an oppositional discourse, not so much in terms of "postcolonial militant" discourse as in an "individual against the trend" discourse of resistance. Because she resists, while seemingly adopting, the postcolonial trend, Condé is strictly speaking a postcolonial renegade or a "postcolonial antipostcolonial." Though she is technically a *jus soli* (right of the soil) postcolonial, the Guadeloupean-born author refuses to partake in so-called Postcolonial Studies.

By playing a role of hide-and-seek, constantly distorting the truth, or rather what one expects the truth to be, Condé has been coined *une nomade inconvenante* (an inconvenient nomad).[6] Nomadism always holds the potential of being inconvenient because by definition nomadism is meant to err and deviate from the assumed "proper" location. But in Condé's case, what makes her truly an inconvenient author is her errant narrative deviating from the presumed course of interpretation. Her narrative, in Freudian terminology, is one of *Enstellung*, the German for the distortion of the truth by disfiguration. Condé's writing is like Caliban himself, a token of the postcolonial that was originally disfigured (in Shakespeare's *The Tempest*) and whose distortion is a simulacrum. The disfiguration hides the fact that there is no real truth behind the guise of distorted truth. Condé's revisional gimmick recalls that, to begin with, the postcolonial is a chimera whose void the critics fill with their own expectations.

Condé projects an image of her life that bears a resemblance to her text. Her life is unsettling like the inconvenient nomad that she is. Condé is somehow the wandering Jew of Caribbean literature. The writer deems nationalities an obsolete characterization and calls for a "redéfinition de la littérature antillaise" (redefinition of Antillean literature).[7] By her own admission, Maryse Condé's relationship with her countrymen has always been challenging. She has nonetheless made two attempts to move back home. The first attempt was in the 1980s, when she felt financially secure enough after the success of *Ségou* to start a new life in Guadeloupe. As she says, "Le pays que je retrouvais ne ressemblait nullement à celui qu'avait gardé ma mémoire" (the country I found in no way resembled what I remembered).[8] Estranged from her country and feeling inadequate and unwelcome, Condé ultimately left again. Upon receiving an invitation from the University of California, Berkeley, she moved to the United States. After twenty years in American academia, Condé retired as a professor emerita from Columbia University in New York City. She then once again entertained moving back to Guadeloupe, which would turn out to be another failure. She describes her experience in a recent interview:

> For example, two years ago, I left Guadeloupe. I could have left without saying anything, letting people think that I was leaving for health-related issues. When the television asked me, I could not resist telling what I thought of Guadeloupe. I explained that it is still a colony with no room for creativity, a place where, during my twenty-two years there, I didn't do

anything interesting. When I think of what I have accomplished at Columbia and at other American universities, I think it is sad. Guadeloupe is my country. I made the mistake of saying what I thought. My protagonists are like me. It is a way to share how I am but also to criticize myself for what I am.[9]

She has paid a high price for publicly opening up about her departure; as she said, "Some people sent me e-mails saying that they will never read a book by Maryse Condé ever again. I had to face a raging storm."[10]

The author's on again/off again relationship with Guadeloupe reads like a Fanonian allegory of the *débarqué*. The *débarqué* refers to a person who has freshly landed back home and, unlike the prodigal son, is not welcome back after his or her time abroad. In his 2008 English translation of Frantz Fanon's *Peau noire, masques blancs*, Richard Philcox (who is coincidentally Maryse Condé's husband) has translated the word *débarqué* as "new returnee," not just "returnee." Likewise, in a 1967 translation, Charles Lam Markmann translated *débarqué* as "the newcomer" and "the newly returnee Negro." The idea is that the *débarqué* has not yet rejoined the pack, so the subject will always come across as "newly" returned, regardless of the time elapsed since the landing. The *débarqué* is notoriously not up-to-date with the changes that have occurred while he or she was away. In *Peau noire, masques blancs*, Fanon says the following about this unique figure:

> Le noir qui pendant quelques temps a vécu en France revient radicalement transformé. Pour nous exprimer génétiquement, nous dirons que son phénotype subit une mue définitive, absolue.[11]

> (The black man who has lived in France for a length of time returns radically changed. To express it in genetic terms, his phenotype undergoes a definitive, an absolute mutation.)[12]

The phenotype is a genetic mutation shaped by the social environment and, for Fanon, observable through specific behavior; it only exists through the social gaze that can detect the alterations. Fanon skillfully describes the new returnee in a syntactic framework that purposely highlights the observable-by-witness changes in the subject's behavior. The Antillean who returns home after a stay in the *métropole* is so changed that he is like a demigod, says Fanon. Instead of a wide sweep of the arm, the new returnee now bows slightly to greet people, and instead of the usual deep voice, the voice of the *débarqué* is a gentle inner stirring as of rustling breezes. Only the one who always belonged, who never left and never betrayed, can describe the *débarqué*, given that that the scrutinizer needs the privileged perspective of the settled group.

In his novel *Bleu-blanc-rouge* (*Blue White Red*, 2013), the French Congolese writer Alain Mabanckou replicates Fanon's *débarqué*. In his illustration of a black Congolese who returns home after a trip to France, the first-person narrator, who is the designated sedentary observer, describes the genetic mutation of the new returnee as follows:

> Je me rappelle ses multiples retours au pays alors que je n'avais pas encore mis les pieds en France. Ce pays de blancs avait changé son existence. Il y avait une mutation, une métamorphose indéniable. . . . La France l'avait transfiguré. Elle avait cisaillé ses habitudes, lui prescrivant une autre manière de vivre. Nous le constatâmes avec convoitise.

> (I remember his multiple returns home at the time when I had yet to set foot in France. This country of white people had changed his existence. There was a mutation, an undeniable metamorphosis. . . . France had transfigured him. It had redefined his habits, giving him a new way of living. We noticed it with envy.)[13]

Mabanckou's novel is an unequivocal adaptation of Fanon's *débarqué*: same tone, same humor, same lightness in the *débarqué*'s body mass.[14] As Mabanckou describes the expectations of the sedentary observer and the pressures that those expectations bring to bear upon the new returnee, the author lays emphasis on the admiration that the sedentary observer has for the one who has returned.[15] The Congolese-turned-Parisian is idolized, emulated, and respected, which is the reason why Mabanckou's *débarqué* is relentlessly pressured to live up to his people's high expectations. But while phenotypic mutation is a token of success in the Congolese's *débarqué*, the same mutation is the reason for the new returnee's demise in the Antillean version. Once the Antillean-turned-Parisian goes back home, he or she must shed the extra phenotypical characteristics gained in Metropolitan France before fitting back into the group. The new returnee is forced into genetic involution. Fanon tells us the story of a son who returns home and fakes cultural amnesia (he had spent only a few months in France and upon his return claims not to remember the name of a common tool). His father dropped the heavy tool on his feet, and "l'amnésie disparaît" (the amnesia vanishes).[16] The slightest misstep betraying the in-authenticity of his *Parisianism* will bring his downfall, "c'est qu'on l'attend";[17] the italicized *on l'attend* here does not refer to the literal meaning of "looking forward to seeing the new returnee" but rather "*on l'attend au tournunt*," which literally means "waiting around the corner to catch the *débarqué*," like bullies lurking behind their prey. There is only one alternative, Fanon writes: get rid of the *Parisianism* or die at the pillory. But as we know from Condé's experience, there is yet another alternative: leave the country again.

When Condé first returned to Guadeloupe after spending years in West Africa, she was invited to a local separatist radio station. At the end of the show, many called: "Qui était cette Maryse Condé qui au micro d'un organe indépendantiste ne s'exprimait pas en Créole?" (Who was this Maryse Condé who on the microphone of a separatist station would not speak Creole?)[18] Even though her lack of ease with the Creole language was not due to her stay in metropolitan France but was rather the product of her bourgeois upbringing in Pointe-à-Pitre, Condé's speech wore the scarlet letter of the *débarqué*. The writer sounded like Fanon's amnesiac in need of a heavy tool falling on her feet. Ironically enough, this kind of native amnesia often calls for another form of amnesia—what we could refer to as Calypso amnesia. Memory lapse becomes the sine qua non condition of cultural reinsertion in the Antilles. As Condé says about the Creolists:

> Il est vrai que l'on n'entend guère que la voix d'écrivains en résidence au pays. Il est savoureux de constater que tous ont été des "négropolitains" ou des "nègzagonaux" pendant une période plus ou moins longue de leur vie. Néanmoins, ils l'oublient commodément et défendent une définition de l'Antillais, de l'être créole digne du temps où Lady Nugent visitait la Jamaïque (autour de 1839). Paradoxalement, pour se convaincre de "l'authenticité" de l'image de leur pays natal contenue dans leurs écrits, ils s'enorgueillissent de faire recette dans les milieux littéraires de l'Hexagone, toujours à la recherche de nouveaux exotisme.

> (It is true that we only hear the voice of writers in residence in the Antilles. It is worth noticing that they were all "negropolitans" [black metropolitan French] or "negzagonals" [black hexagonal French] at one point, short or long, in their lives. Nonetheless, they conveniently forget and put forth a definition of the Antillean, of the Creole subject, straight from the time when Lady Nugent visited Jamaica (circa 1839). Paradoxically, to convince themselves of the "authenticity" of the image of their native country given in their writings, they are proud of their marketing success in metropolitan France, always in search of exoticism.)[19]

Condé thus suggests that authors such as Chamoiseau and Confiant have deleted their metropolitan or foreign experience in order to offer an exclusively in-residence image to their readership. This memory lapse reads like a survival technique against the pillory.[20] The Creolists present themselves as some sort of literary *djobeurs*, a moribund Creole profession that Confiant and Chamoiseau portray in their literature. Like *djobeurs*, Chamoiseau and Confiant hold on to the *local* market of Creole traditions, valiantly resisting the spell of globalization.[21]

Fanon's *débarqué* is called today the *négropolitain* (Negro/black metropolitan French) or the *nègzagonal* (Negro/black hexagonal French). But aside from the terminology, not much has changed. Negropolitans (more commonly used than *negzagonals*) are Antilleans who have spent a long enough time in metropolitan France to undergo what Fanon would call an alteration of the personality. The word *negropolitan* itself suggests a mutant condition of ambiguity, half black and half metropolitan—nothing complete. The word also carries pejorative undertones, since it pinpoints, like Fanon's *débarqué*, the manifestation of a "décalage, un clivage" (discrepancy, cleavage) with "la collectivité qui l'a vu naître" (the birth collectivity),[22] something that approximates the idea of family betrayal. Rather than an addition to an already hybrid Creole culture, this discrepancy is often seen as a sign of cultural alienation and pretense. The Martinican writer Tony Delsham has made a unique contribution to the question of negropolitanism in his novel *Négropolitains et Euro-blacks* (Negropolitans and Euro-Blacks).[23] Like Fanon in *Peau noire, masques blancs*,[24] Delsham deconstructs the phenotypical characteristics of contemporary negropolitans, which, surprisingly, he associates not with Antilleans living in France but with Antilleans-in-residence who "affirmez être autre chose que des Français alors qu'aux Antilles vous avez [ils ont] les mêmes lois politiques, les mêmes lois économiques, les mêmes lois sociales" (claim to be something other than French when in the Antilles [they] have the same political laws, the same economical laws, the same social laws) as in France.[25] The author accuses Antilleans of using the history of slavery as an accessory for cultural authentication, as Antilleans-in-residence capitalize on their history in the same way they wear the "colliers-choux," a popular necklace in the Antilles that imitates, in solid gold, the chains of a slave. Delsham replaces one dichotomy with another for the sake of provocation. The author does not do away with the *negropolitan* stigma but only ships it back to the sender. While Delsham's rhetoric is interesting mostly for the sake of provocation, it brings attention to the nonetheless serious need in Antillean culture to discard the old pillory. Times have changed, and, as Condé says, "Il y a une centaine d'année, il était simple de définir les Guadeloupéens, les Martiniquais ou les Haitiens" (A hundred years ago, it was easy to define Guadeloupeans, Martinicans, or Haitians),[26] but today, not only do those islands host many nationalities but they also breed new generations of future intermittent migrants, just like Condé who is from Montebello (Guadeloupe), New York, and Paris all at once.

Admittedly, one cannot ignore the colonial factors at play in the figure of the negropolitan. The fear of French assimilation concomitant with Antillean cultural erosion should not be downplayed even though amputation and forced amnesia may be inadequate responses to those fears.[27] A new generation of writers is slowly reacting against the obsolete "to be or not to be Antillean" position. For example, Gisèle Pineau (Guadeloupe) and Fabienne Kanor (Martinique), both born and raised in France by Antillean parents, manage to go beyond the dichotomy in order to negotiate a deeper cultural collaboration between metropolitan France and the Antilles. They show that Antillean identity can germinate in continental soil and end its gestation on Antillean grounds. Pineau's *L'exil selon Julia* (*Exile According to Julia*, 1996) and Kanor's *D'eaux douces* (Freshwater) praise cultural atavism and autonomy. The two books offer their own version of the out-of-residence Antilleanism: metropolitan but equally so Antillean. That said, their position remains within the metropole-Antilles spectrum and does not reach out beyond this dichotomy, unlike Condé's pluri-nomadism.

*Débarqué* should work as an umbrella term understood in the broader sense of that which deviates from the presumed course of action, whether it be geographical (home) or professional (the field of Postcolonial Studies). *Débarqué* suggests a deviance and an antinormative position that strays from, paradoxically enough, an inexistent norm. The *débarqué* is like Caliban, the Shakespearean subject who is always already disfigured from a nonexistent original undistorted figure. The *débarqué* is, in that sense, a peculiar kind of renegade because he or she strays from what is, supposedly, always already an uprooted and deterritorialized Creole culture. Thus, the not-so-prodigal son is ostracized for having left what has become an essentially territorialized diasporic culture.

## From *Débarqué* to *Macoumé*

As the anthropologist David A. B. Murray points out in his article about Martinique, class is "a matter of economic wealth equaling higher status: education, *time spent abroad* [my italics], language, age, and race must be factored into any analysis of status in the Caribbean."[28] Though all of those factors are matters of common knowledge and may not apply to the Antilles alone, "time spent abroad" is a measuring tool the cultural importance of which has been overlooked in the Antilles. This critical omission is partly due, as discussed earlier, to the social pressure put on the new returnee to amputate his or her time spent abroad. In other words, the "time spent abroad" entity is incomplete without the entity "where they are no longer" that Patricia Noxolo and Marika Preziuso mention in their study on Maryse Condé:

> In fiction, this geography of disorientation addresses not only where people or things are in relation to other people or things but also *where they are no longer* [my italics], where they are coming from or going to, as well as where they could have been or might have been.[29]

"Where they are no longer" identifies more explicitly the negative impact of the departure on the ones left behind, the lingering effect of what once was and no longer is, and maybe to a larger extent, the fear of the home community to lose the status quo and let the threat of change creep in.

Following on Fanon's ample use of psychoanalytical terminology, it could be said that the idea of return in Fanon's new returnee (*débarqué*) symbolically stands for the resurfacing symptom. Because for Sigmund Freud, trauma does not manifest itself in the real event (primal scene) but in its reoccurrence, meaning in its re-presentation (mnemonic symbol); it is through a secondary event—a reminder of the primal event—that the subject experiences the traumatic nature of the first event. In other words, trauma does not exist in the immediate present but in its return, or rather, as Laplanche puts it, in "a circumstance contingent to the traumatic event, which unlike that event, has remained in memory as a symptom or 'symbol' of the first scene."[30] In the Antillean culture, the *returnee* embodies, as the name suggests, the *return* of the repressed. In *Peau noire, masques blancs*, the concept of returning back home psychoanalytically suggests the exposure of a deviance and thus the inhospitality of the sedentary group toward the new returnee. On the surface, Fanon suggests that cultural alteration is the main "deviance" of the returnee, but between the lines, or rather in a footnote, we find out there is more to Fanon's *débarqué* than a mere question of cultural mutation. "Time spent abroad" and "where they are no longer" potentially suggest also sexual deviance:

Mentionnons rapidement qu'il ne nous a pas été donné de constater la présence manifeste de pédérastie en Martinique.... Rappelons toutefois l'existence de ce qu'on appelle là-bas "des hommes habillés en dames" ou "Ma Commère." Ils ont la plupart du temps une veste et une jupe. Mais nous restons persuadés qu'ils ont une vie sexuelle normale.... Par contre en Europe nous avons trouvé quelques camarades qui sont devenus pédérastes, toujours passifs.[31]

(Let me observe at once that I had no opportunity to establish the overt presence of homosexuality in Martinique.... We should not overlook, however, the existence of what are called there "men dressed like women" or "godmothers." Generally they wear shirts and skirts. But I am convinced that they lead normal sex lives.... In Europe, on the other hand, I have known several Martinicans who became homosexuals, always passive.)[32]

Fanon's assertion dates back to the 1950s. Few in current Martinique would seriously posit the absence of homosexuality in Martinique, let alone its manifest presence only in patriarchal societies like France. Of more relevance today is Fanon associating time spent overseas with so-called sexual deviance, *abnormal* behavioral characteristics. In *Peau noire, masques blancs*, Fanon draws an implicit parallel between the *débarqué* and the homosexual, who share the common experience of developing, once overseas, characteristics that are foreign (and thus undesirable) to Antilleans. This is not to say that Fanon, who was somehow a disappointed old *débarqué* himself, identified with the Antillean-turned-homosexuals living in France. He did not necessarily even identify with Antilleans in France. Fanon's situation was unique in that, like Maryse Condé, he made several inconclusive attempts to go back home and ended up living his life away from Martinique.[33] But Fanon seems to have felt equally inadequate in the company of Antilleans in France. The biographer Alice Cherki quotes Fanon telling his fellow Antilleans in Paris, "The less we see of each other, the better we behave."[34] What is striking in Fanon's indirect association of the *débarqué* with the Antillean-turned-homosexual is that both figures have undergone cultural alterations while being in metropolitan France, yet only one brings those alterations back home. As the word precisely implies, the *débarqué* is defined by his or her return home, while the homosexual is precisely defined by what exists and flourishes abroad: the word *homosexuel* is made in France and stays in France.

As Murray says, "Homosexuality is a dirty, and in some cases taboo, word in Martinican public life."[35] Instead, Antilleans often use the word *macoumé*, the modern version and contraction of *ma commère* (French for "my god-mother" or "my gossiper"). But *macoumé* is not a semantic substitute for homosexual; it is only a shy and bashful cover-up for the French word, just like— as Fanon's footnote indicates—the *macoumé, ma commère*, is "dressed up." *Macoumé* is not denotative but connotative, used either as an insult, a joke, or an accusation. When Thomas C. Spear says in "Carnivalesque jouissance" that "homosexuality is not evoked save in an exceptional manner among the West Indian novelists in order to make a joke, for example, when a character is treated as a "faggot" (*macoumé*),"[36] the author hereby implies that homosexuality does not exist in the Martinican semantic life, but the joking about *it* does. *Macoumé* refers to the second-degree joking about homosexuality, while the French word *homosexuel* is the real thing.

In his research from the late 1990s, David A. B. Murray came across Martinicans who, like Fanon, argued that homosexuality did not exist in Martinique. Those Martinicans claimed to know of homosexuality by reading about its existence in other societies, "especially throughout Europe, but as they knew no one in Martinique who was that way, it was therefore obviously a foreign problem."[37] Similarly, Jarrod Hayes questions why, in *Traversée de la mangrove* (*Crossing the Mangrove*, 1995), Maryse Condé uses the Creole word *macoumé* instead of the French word for homosexuality. For Hayes, Condé's semantic choice suggests that "the homosexuality she describes is so Caribbean that only a Creole word would do."[38] By "Caribbean," Hayes means "gossip." The word *macoumé* is unique in that the word refers to both, simultaneously, the *ideas* of homosexuality and gossip. *Commère* as gossiper makes complete sense here, since the idea of something—the alleged existence of something-is nothing more than gossip. It needs therefore to be stressed that *macoumé* stands for what is said, in a nontruthful joking or insulting manner, about the other and not what the other is. Homosexuality is foreign to Antilleans, but speculating and joking about it are not.

Unlike the *débarqué*, the Antillean-turned-homosexual is, semantically speaking, not meant to return to the Antilles. When Fanon writes that the Antillean homosexual is a European condition, he himself adopts the perspective of an observer located in Europe, using the distal deictic "là-bas" (there). No one returns home to address the topic, neither the homosexual nor the observer. If homosexuality is daringly addressed, it most often depicts female homosexuality. Condé recently mentioned, "Looking back on it, I remember now that there were women called Zanmi, they were lesbians, they lived together, dressed alike, and went out together. Nobody told us who they really were."[39] It is interesting to note that Condé looks at Guadeloupean lesbianism in terms of a discrete community of women who retrospectively happen to have been gay. The said lesbianism is conveniently out of reach. More recently, another Guadeloupean, Ernest Pépin, wrote a novel about lesbian love. In *Cantique des tourterelles* (*Song of the Turtledoves*), Pépin describes the love of two women in a double-voiced narrative: the woman conducting the lesbian affair shares half of the first-person narrative, while the betrayed husband shares the other. Pépin's novel is groundbreaking for two reasons: first, because the author uses the voice of a female character, a rare occurrence in an Antillean novel written by a man, and second, because Pépin describes lesbian love, a taboo topic in the Antilles. That said, the novel remains, to some extent, framed in terms of male heterosexuality. The husband is presented as the guard of a harem, a gatekeeper who fantasizes about lesbians as he witnesses the perfect heterosexual fantasy of "forêt de femmes, il recevait nos offrandes de seins nus, de paréos transparents, de dessous ciselés, de hanches en balançoires, de cuisses dénudées" (forest of women, [who] received the offerings from naked breasts, see-through wrapping skirts, embroidered undergarments, swinging hips, uncovered thighs).[40] When the text happens to bend toward queerness, the author soon enough straightens it up, as if to say that there are no words in the Creole culture allowing for a full exposure of homosexuality. Because homosexuality cannot be made fully visible, the Creole culture remains a culture of *macoumés*, this word being the only reference to homosexuality that fits the proximal deictic "ici," right here.

## *Histoire de la femme cannibale*

Nowhere is the nexus between *débarqué* and *macoumé* in the Antilles more manifest than in Condé's *Histoire de la femme cannibal*, a novel that revisits the question of the one no longer here through the theme of homosexuality. Maryse Condé is the only Antillean writer who has used homosexual characters in her books with such frequency. In *Traversée de la mangrove*, in addition to the two Haitians, Désinor and Carlos, who discover homosexual rapture by chance, Condé's main character (Francisco Sanchez) is, as mentioned earlier, simultaneously the source of gossip (*commère*) and the alleged homosexual (*macoumé*). In *La migration des coeurs*, Cathy finds sexual pleasure in her maid's attentive care, while her brother, Aymeric, feels sexual attraction for a young male relative who looks like his deceased beloved. With time, Condé has become more daring with the subject of homosexuality, more generous with the quantity of homosexuals sharing her stories. In *Célanire cou-coupé* (*Who Slashed Célanire's Throat?* 2004), many characters are either closeted or open homosexuals: Hakim rejects women because of his sexual orientation, and Bokar engages in an affair with Hakim at the same time Célanire is having an affair with Amarante. In *La belle Créole* (*The Beautiful Creole*), Luc fondles Dieudonné, which reminds the latter of the guilty pleasure he took, as a child, with a *macoumé* dressed like a dragonfly. Finally, in *Histoire de la femme cannibale* (*The Story of the Cannibal Woman*, 2007), homosexuality is no longer a side plot but the critical element that leads the story to its eventual climax. Rosélie, a Guadeloupean woman, is married to Stephen, a white English professor who is also a closeted homosexual carrying on an affair with a male student. Stephen is tragically assassinated in the streets of Le Cap, in South Africa. Rosélie has no knowledge of her husband's sexual orientation. At the end of the story, she discovers the truth when the police inform her that her husband's murderer was also his young male lover. In *Histoire de la femme cannibale*, the question of homosexuality comes close to home, not so much in a geographical but more in a personal sense. The novel introduces the story of a white British husband (like Richard Philcox, Condé's real-life husband) and a black Guadeloupean artist (like herself) faced with the social challenges of biracialism in South Africa. In this novel, Condé brings homosexuality inside her house, inside her life, and, even more so, inside her man. Prior to this book, Condé's homosexuals have always been either foreigners (Sanchez, Désinor, Carlos, Hakin, Bokar) or characters living in a foreign land (an imaginary island in *La belle Créole*, South Africa in *Histoire de la femme cannibale*, Ivory Coast in *Célanire cou-coupé*). Granted, there are two noticeable exceptions to the tendency of locating homosexuality abroad. It is in Guadeloupe that, in *La migration des coeurs*, Aymeric and Cathy show homosexual tendencies. But even then, Condé chooses to locate Guadeloupean homosexuality in the white Creole world, Aymeric and Cathy being white Creoles. In the Antilles, white Creoles, known as *békés*, have traditionally rejected miscegenation with either French or black Creoles in favor of exclusive white Creole inbreeding, which makes them stand apart from mainstream Guadeloupe.[41] The second exception occurs at the end of *Célanire cou-coupé*, when Célanire returns to Guadeloupe in search of her biological father and discovers a large sapphic community that has spread throughout the island:

Des Zanmi! C'était du jamais vu dans cette commune rurale! Elles dor-
maient la nuit et faisaient la sieste le jour sous la même moustiquaire.
Elles se baignaient ensemble dans le même baquet, se récurant le dos
avec des baisers. Toute la journée, c'était une litanie de noms doux et
d'impudentes caresses.

(Zanmis! It was never seen before in this rural community! They slept
at night and napped during the day under the same mosquito net. They
bathed together in the same bucket, brushing each other's backs with
kisses. The whole day, it was a litany of sweet words and impudent
caresses.)[42]

But as mentioned earlier, Condé carries the tendency to speak about the *Zanmi* as a retrospective construction of things past, which purposely avoids the
present reality of Antillean lesbianism. Célanire discovered this community
as an adult after she returned to Guadeloupe, just as Condé became aware of
the sexual orientation of this community much later as a well-traveled adult.

When asked in an interview why she always associates homosexuality with
foreignness, the author replied that she was raised in a culture that was convinced of the absence of Antillean homosexuality. Because of her upbringing,
she is now afraid to bring homosexuality home:

It comes from a fear of bringing homosexuality where it is, to acknowledge that it can also happen in Guadeloupean places. It is a fear to admit,
to confess, shyness even though I know it is there. I do not dare, I do not
really have the courage to say it, to go all the way.[43]

It may be surprising to hear a Guadeloupean woman such as Maryse Condé,
the cultural offspring of the *neg marron la Mulâtresse Solitude*, the author of the
no less defiant Tituba, the revolutionary woman strong enough to stand alone
against such dominating male figures as Chamoiseau and Confiant, claiming
fear, shyness, and timidity toward her native island. But there is a special reason why Condé would lose her usual composure when faced with the question
of homosexuality. The author has recently addressed the question:

In my personal life, I can say it now, it is not a secret, my son, the only
son I had, who is dead now, was gay. One day, he was maybe sixteen, he
revealed to me: "Mom, I think that I am a homosexual." It is a blow for
a mother. Everybody around me rejected, denied homosexuality, and
there it was, the closest to home, right in my personal life.[44]

The son is now out, the story is in the open. Condé has (albeit rarely) mentioned her daughters in interviews, articles, and biographical pieces, but never her son. She did break her silence once before, in 1999, in a piece from Thomas Spear's edited volume *La culture française vue d'ici et d'ailleurs* (*The French Culture Seen from Here and from Elsewhere*). Condé begins the story with the following words:

> Je suis la mère de Denis Boucolon à qui cet ouvrage est dédié. Je n'ai pas souvent reconnu ce fait. En tout cas, je ne l'ai jamais écrit . . .

> (I am the mother of Denis Boucolon to whom this work is dedicated. I have not often acknowledged that fact. At least, I have never written it before . . . )[45]

Ten years after the initial confession, Condé admits that her son lives in the recurrent and uneasy presence of homosexuality in her books: "I learned to believe that homosexuality does not exist, or if so, it is the other. And I see my son, my own son, in this confinement. I had a hard time adjusting and this is why my books are a bit ambiguous."[46] Condé says she has struggled with the discrepancy between her (Fanonian) upbringing in regards to homosexuality and the sudden appearance of this disavowed existence in her life, her man, and her genes. That said, Condé did not choose to biographically reenact the coming out of her son when she decided to fearlessly address homosexuality in *Histoire de la femme cannibale*. Instead, she began the novel with the following inscription, "Pour Richard," presumably alluding to Richard Philcox, her real-life husband. The story focuses on the closeted homosexuality of Stephen, a protagonist who daringly borrows some of Richard's features (like Richard, Stephen is white, British, and erudite and shares his life with a black Guadeloupean creative woman in a foreign land). The novel is built on a flashback. The couple has been living in Le Cap, South Africa. In the first pages, Stephen is already dead. After his death, Rosélie, his Guadeloupean life partner, is left alone in Le Cap. The story then works its way back to the specifics of Rosélie and Stephen's life together and ultimately to Stephen's death. The narrative is presented through the perspective of Rosélie, who is blindly incognizant of Stephen's big open secret. As the story progresses, Rosélie begins hearing conflicting reports about Stephen. She is told on several occasions that Stephen was not the good loving partner that she had thought. At first, the widow shuns rumors, but soon enough she begins exploring the circumstances of Stephen's death. Suspicions grow. After talking to a school official about Stephen's close relationship with one of his male students, Rosélie is relieved to see that her suspicions are not confirmed—at least not quite yet: "curieusement rassurée sans toutefois s'avouer ce qu'elle avait redouté" (curiously relieved without however admitting that she had doubted).[47] Soon after, the wall protecting her disavowal mechanism starts crumbling. Finally, she admits:

> Au fond de moi-même, je savais. Depuis le début. Accepter? Je ne sais pas si j'acceptais. Je niais la vérité pour n'avoir pas à décider.
> Voilà! C'était dit.

> (Deep down, I knew. From the start. To accept? I don't know if I accepted. I was denying the truth so that I would not have to decide.
> Here it is! I've said it.)[48]

"Voilà! C'était dit" is a double-edged sword in the context of its production: the words refer admittedly to Rosélie's confession, but it also builds on Condé's long-time *macoumés*-populated writing. It's finally done: *Here it is! I've said it.* Condé has let the homosexual out, with both a public and printed coming out. The *macoumé*, as an alleged but never confirmed homosexual in the Antillean culture, has become an open homosexual. The homosexual is out; there is no way back—just as there is no way back for Condé as a Guadeloupean native who repeatedly failed her *Aliyah*. In *Histoire de la femme cannibale*, when Rosélie is asked whether she ever considers going back to Guadeloupe, she replies:

> Elle disait "rentrer." Rentrer dans l'île comme dans le ventre de sa mère. Le malheur est qu'une fois expulsée on ne peut plus y rentrer. Retourner s'y blottir. Personne n'a jamais vu un nouveau-né qui se refait foetus. Le cordon ombilical est coupé. Le placenta enterré. On doit marcher crochu quand même jusqu'au bout de l'existence.

> (She was saying "going back." Going back to the island as one goes back into a mother's womb. The sad thing is that once expulsed, one cannot go back in. Snuggle back inside. Nobody has ever seen a newborn turn into a fetus again. The umbilical cord is cut. The placenta is in the ground. One has to keep walking bent forward to the end of existence.)[49]

The homosexual is like the Guadeloupean-out-of-residence, a motherless vagrant bent forward to the end of existence. Rosélie has finally made up her mind: she will stay in Le Cap. She has decided to stay close to her stateless homosexual, both being out of place in their own ways—not able, and to some extent not willing, to go back *home*. Stephen and Rosélie are like David, the American homosexual living in Paris in James Baldwin's novel *Giovanni's Room*. Originally published in the 1950s, in Paris, David was free to openly love a man, although in the United States, he was still in the closet and engaged to an American woman. At one point during his love affair with Giovanni, David questions his out-of-residence bliss:

> Yes, it was true, I recalled, turning away from the river down the long street home. I wanted children. I wanted to be inside again, with the light and safety, with my manhood unquestioned, watching my woman put my children to bed.[50]

The idea of being inside again carries a fetal connotation not lost on Baldwin, who implicitly associates the domestic bliss of heterosexuality with the warmth of a reproductive womb. Yet, as Condé said earlier, once the umbilical cord is severed, there is nothing to pull the subject back in. And indeed, David soon comes to that realization when his home becomes a mirage that can only be reached from a distance: "You mean I have a home to go to as long as I don't go there?"[51] Like Baldwin, but within her own Caribbean culture, Condé is able to show in *Histoire de la femme cannibale* that *out* is a condition shared by both the Antillean-out-of-residence (Rosélie) and the homosexual living in a foreign land (Stephen). The irreversibility of the status of being "out" is due to the impossibility of bringing unhomely phenotypical characteristics home—unhomely in the strict sense of not belonging home (Bhabha). Coinciding in a meaningful way, Condé has grown to be more public about her alleged "inconvenient" nomadism as she has been increasingly explicit about her personal interest in the subject of homosexuality. The two questions come together in the homonym "out," addressing both the "where they are no longer" entity and the reality of homosexuality.

## Cannibal/Caliban as Semantic Displacement

As said before, Bongie identifies *La migration des coeurs*, the Creole adaptation of Brontë's *Wuthering Heights*, as the novel by Condé that best shows her work of "inauthentic" postcolonial revisionism given the book's mainstream appeal and its lack of serious commitment. Condé's book *Histoire de la femme cannibale* also dabbles in the tradition of postcolonial revisionism. In addition to the book's protagonist—Ariel (also the name of a sprite at the service of Prospero in Shakespeare's *The Tempest*)—the word *cannibal* in *Histoire de la femme cannibale* evokes the anagramic Caliban, a key name (also originally from *The Tempest*) in the tradition of postcolonial revisionism. Contrary to *La migration des coeurs*, *Histoire de la femme cannibale* is not marketed as a Creole rewriting of a classic because it does not call into question its loyalty to the postcolonial genre. What the book does, however, is question the concept of displacement and, more particularly so, semantic displacement, which is the main component of the revisional practice. With *Histoire de la femme cannibale*, instead of offering a scripted book following the conventions of post-colonial revisionism, Condé proposes a more personal reflection on a black Caribbean-born postcolonial woman writer caught in an academic world of conventions and expectations.

During his 1492 trip to the Americas, Christopher Columbus encountered unknown indigenous tribes in the Caribbean, which made the explorer look at the world and its inhabitants in a new way. As Michael Dash points out in his book *The Other America*, Columbus's diary is a unique New World piece of literature, since it is the first of its kind to document the Caribbean alterity seen and tentatively translated through the prism of the European schemata. Columbus's diary is a neological practice exhibiting, as Dash says (quoting Roberto González Echevarría), "how to write in a European language about realities never seen in Europe before."[52] The word *cannibal* sums up the experience of the colonial encounter in the Americas. It is alleged that local Indians told Columbus that a tribe called the Carib were well known to be hostile warmongers and, more importantly, anthropophagic. Because of the challenges of translation (from the Taino Indian language to Spanish), it seems that Columbus heard "cannibal" instead of "Carib."[53] Columbus then applied the neologism to this mysterious tribe whose presumed anthropophagism was never proven. Thus, the word *cannibal* was born out of a misunderstanding—or, more accurately, out of colonial untranslatability. As George Lamming observes:

> Columbus's journal speaks about meeting a Caribbean aboriginal on arrival and conversing with him. Yet, as far as I know, Columbus spoke not a word of any aboriginal Caribbean language, and the aboriginal spoke neither Italian nor Spanish; it is peculiar that they could understand each other; what Columbus really did was to create what he ordered, because he represented power"[54]

Though today *cannibal* unequivocally means "anthropophagite," the trace of its illegitimate birth lingers. The fact that Columbus's neologism is based on a distortion of reality initiated by, literally speaking, hearsay, or what Dawn Fulton calls "second-hand reports,"[55] did not fall on deaf ears. Condé situates her story, suitably titled *Histoire de la femme cannibale*, in a world of freely spoken words carrying unverifiable presumptions. *Cannibal* in the strictest sense refers to the distorted representation of the Caribbean. By extension, the term denotes the alleged yet never proven existence of a sensational story about the Caribbean figure, which turns out to be, essentially, Condé, the misunderstood so-called postcolonial writer. But in her book, Condé capitalizes on the connotative richness of the cannibal concept through the story of a woman presumed to be a cannibal. The presumed cannibal, Fiéla, is depicted exclusively through media coverage, gossip, hearsay, and Rosélie's speculations. Fiéla is on trial for murder in Le Cap, and Condé describes the sensationalistic attention surrounding the trial. Condé's story about Fiéla is inspired by the real story of a cannibalistic murder in Paris of a Dutch college student by a Japanese classmate in the early 1980s. The Paris killer cut his victim's body into pieces, stored the pieces in the freezer, and later cooked and ate the flesh with peas. Because he was deemed insane, the young murderer was sent back to Japan with no charges brought against him. The story received ample media coverage in France and has now become part of the media-initiated collective memory of the French. Condé cannibalizes the old headline story and incorporates it into her own sensational story of a closeted husband. Unlike her Japanese counterpart, Fiéla is only accused (by her son-in-law) of having committed a cannibalistic act with her dead husband's remains. The case is mainly based on speculation, something that Condé greatly highlights in the story. Condé's *Histoire de la femme cannibale* is a story about the word: the word that is spoken, shared, and distorted in its act of sharing. Condé's use of semantic displacement is essentially *catachrestic*, meaning applying the wrong word to a given context. As Ross Chambers explains:

> Catachresis is the name given to a kind of lexical error or making do, a form of bricolage whereby in the absence of a "proper" term another term is inappropriately, but necessarily (and hence in a sense legitimately or at least pardonably) *détourné*, turned away from its dedicated function, and pressed into alternative functions.[56]

The misuse can be fortuitous (a slip) or intentional (rhetorical figure). The use of "arm" for the "arm of a chair" is a catachresis forced by semantic poverty, while saying "don't talk *black* to me" instead of "don't talk *back* to me" is the result of a slip. In both cases, the misuse is not random but based on a partial truth that diverts the original meaning of a word in a process of metonymical displacement. As in all catachreses, the slip from "Carib" to "cannibal" in Columbus's mishearing episode is based on a partial (phonetic) truth, since the two words sound similar. Condé's catachrestic rhetoric plays on the accepted assumption that distortion always branches out of some kind of truth. The author plants autobiographical elements in the story (Stephen and Rosélie taking after her husband and herself), while making it clear that the final product, the book itself, is a distorted version of the truth. Just like *La migration des coeurs*, a book accused of borrowing the "authenticity" of the postcolonial tradition for the sake of an "inauthentic" cause, *Histoire de la femme cannibale* is the epitome of the crossover book, mixing truths and false facts. Both books are openly, and strategically, misleading. The novel ends with Rosélie rushing to her studio to work on a painting that she will name *Femme cannibale*:

> Cette fois, elle était en possession de son titre. Elle l'avait trouvé avant même que de commencer son ouvrage. Il avait surgi du plus profond d'elle-même au bout d'une marée incontrôlable: *Femme cannibale*.

> (This time, she was in possession of the title. She had found it even before starting to work on the piece. It had come from deep inside of her, from the bottom of an uncontrollable flood: *Femme cannibale*.)[57]

Fiéla—from *fiel*, the French for "bile"—refers to extreme anger threatening to squirt out of a spiteful body. Is Fiéla the alter ego of Rosélie, or is Rosélie the alter ego of Condé? Does cannibalism refer to Fiéla's alleged act—Rosélie's painting—or to Condé's novel? Mireille Rosello said of Condé's novel, "There are so many allusions and references to other films, texts, and people in the novel . . . as well as easily recognizable colleagues and students, that it is tempting to suggest that Condé's novel "cannibalizes" her contemporaries, and more particularly the academic world."[58] As such, the book is even more a crossover than *La migration des coeurs*, seeing as it brings together the alleged "mainstream" gossip genre and the high-seriousness of academia by revealing gossip that takes place precisely in academia. Suffice it to say that one way for Condé to cannibalize the academic world is to flesh out its assumed high-seriousness in order to reveal its mundane and human all too human gossipy nature.

If cannibalism means feeding on the substance of others, incorporating their lives into one's own body, it can indeed be argued that Condé takes a bite out of other people—in particular, a mouthful out of her husband. Condé tells an interviewer that her husband did not like the book "pour des raisons personnelles, intimes" (for personal, intimate reasons).[59] In this specific interview, Condé tiptoes around her cannibalistic performance, never directly addressing it. Instead, she says:

> J'ai eu envie de parler d'une chose dont personne ne parle jamais: le couple mixte; la femme noire dans un couple mixte. . . . Et c'est intéressant, c'est le seul de mes romans, je crois, que mon mari déteste. Il le trouve trop intime. Pourtant, il y a beaucoup de fiction, énormément de fiction dans *Histoire de la femme cannibale* qui change complètement ce que nous avons vécu bêtement tous les deux mais quand même la base le dérange beaucoup. Et je me suis aperçu en interrogeant les amis que c'est un roman qui les a un peu déstabilisés. C'est un roman on dirait qui a gêné beaucoup de gens.

> (I wanted to talk about something that nobody ever talks about: the mixed couple; the black woman in a mixed couple. . . . And it's interesting, it is the only one of my novels, I believe, that my husband hates. He finds it too intimate. Yet, there is a lot of fiction, a huge amount of fiction in *Histoire de la femme cannibale* that changes completely what the two of us simply lived, nonetheless the basis greatly bothers him. I have noticed, when asking around, that this novel somehow startled friends. It seems that it is a novel that put a lot of people at unease.)[60]

Condé uses the interview to set a horizon of expectations for readers now anticipating an uncomfortably personal story in the novel. She surrounds her novel with an aura of broken secrets even though, in the same interview, she insists that her novel is intimate (sharing her true feelings) though not autobiographical (sharing her true life). In another interview that took place a year before the publication of *Histoire de la femme cannibale*, Condé hints at her tendency to expose other people's private stories in her writing, which results in these individuals feeling intruded upon. But as she says, "J'y suis habitué maintenant. Ce n'est pas nouveau" (I'm used to it by now. It's not new).[61]

Not only does Condé seek to tell a story about a broken secret, but she also makes sure that, outside the diegetic space, the book is marketed and sold as such. Condé uses the interview as an "epitext" authenticating the claim of a broken secret in the book. In addition, *Histoire de la femme cannibale* is complemented with the inscription to Richard, a central paratext that confirms Condé's simulacrum of exposed truth.[62] Just as the media speculates about Fiéla's alleged cannibalistic act, Condé invites readers to speculate as well about her own cannibalistic act against Richard. The end result is that readers take pieces of truthful elements inserted in Condé's novel and try to come up with a truthful conclusion in a setting that, as yet, only allows for speculation and no reliable conclusions. The critic Mireille Rosello describes the experience of reading *Histoire de la femme cannibale* as follows:

> Condé accumulates obvious, perhaps even ostentatious references, allusions, and pointers. If this is what the French call "un roman à clés," are the keys in question going to help us open some of the scary closets of a ferocious Bluebeard's castle? Or is my thinking about Bluebeard and the bloodstain on a key a sign that I have already fallen into an interpretative trap?[63]

Condé proceeds to a series of metonymical displacements, forcing readers to constantly shift and readjust their leap of faith: Who can be trusted? Where is the cannibal? What or who is really outed? Condé is a temptress of critical extrapolation, admitting in one interview that she purposely created in that novel a misleading mix of voices to disconcert her readership: "I wanted to create a work in which you really don't know where all these voices you hear are coming from. Is it Maryse Condé? Is it Rosélie? Is it the narrator who's expressing an opinion?"[64] *Histoire de la femme cannibale* is a masterpiece of plurivocal embedded patterns, a book about gossip that at the same time intends to produce gossip. Rosélie's friend, Dido, avidly reads gossip magazines, Fiéla is the tragic victim of a headliner sensational story, and Rosélie is the talk of the town. Condé is fully conscious that her island, Guadeloupe, is "a country of hearsay, gossip, crossing glances."[65] But what she really wanted to get back at, in *Histoire de la femme cannibale*, is academia:

> I think that when I wrote *La femme cannibale*, I was going to or I had just left Colombia. I felt that there was a world I had never talked about and it was a bit of a shame. I willingly wanted to talk about the university but not in a positive way. Look closely, there are only people who are quite mean and envious. The university as I experienced it is a place of power struggles. One wanted to get things and the university was a means by which to get them. At least twice or three times I thought that some colleagues were my friends, and I realized that it was not the case. As I was the Francophone specialist in the department, the Francophone writer, they too wanted to be in good standing with someone who was not me, me the woman with a given number of problems, etc. In fact, it is a story of farewell to the university before it is too late.[66]

*Histoire de la femme cannibale* is somehow an attack on the mentality of small worlds within larges one, both the island and academia. Condé uses the Caribbean genre of storytelling and gossipy circulation of information to give her own account of the academic world as Condé experienced it. In the interview dedicated to *Histoire de la femme cannibale*, Condé describes her literary intentions in the following terms:

> When you read yourself, you realize to your astonishment that you wanted to shock people, to hurt them. In general, that's what writing is—a kind of revenge against those around you. You can say things as they are. It's at once an intimate act and a social act. One writes for oneself, but it becomes an act directed toward others.[67]

Condé gets back at people by using the same ammunition that they used against her: she creates a gossipy narrative structure where she throws her look-alike real surroundings (students, colleagues, husband) into the lion's cage of gossip. But eventually, in a parabolic way, what Condé really gets back at is Caliban.

One of Condé's obvious pointers in the novel is the presence of a protagonist named Ariel, which is also the name of the *mulâtre* in Aimé Césaire's *Une tempête*. In Césaire's play, Ariel shares the stage with Caliban. In Shakespeare's original version, Caliban is a hideous monster, while in Césaire's version, like in many other colonial-inspired texts that reused the Shakespearean figure of Caliban,[68] Caliban is a rebel figure symbolizing the defiant colonized.[69] Condé joins the chain of cannibalistic appropriations of the original Caliban. Yet, as aforementioned, it can easily be argued that there is no such thing as an "original" Caliban, since Caliban is the anagrammatic distortion of the word *cannibal* (and more precisely the Spanish word *canibal*), which is itself a distortion of the word *Carib*. The *mise en abîme* boils down to an endless, or rather beginning-less, series of semantic alterations. When Freud depicts the work of displacement and distortion in the work-dream, he uses the word *Entstellung*, which means both "distortion of the truth" and "disfiguring." Caliban, Shakespeare's enigmatic monster, is just that: a disfigured anagrammatic distortion. But Caliban is also a semantic alteration of an unknown original, a revision of a nonexistent original word and of a nonexistent original truth. The fact that Caliban is an intertextual catalyst for appropriation, revision, and distortion incidentally explains why Caliban is a monster in Shakespeare's play. There is no revision without distortion, and as such, Caliban is *always already* a disfigured token, a Shakespearean monster flaunting the distortion of a nonexistent primal figure. To paraphrase Jacques Derrida, Caliban, as a readable text, is a copy of a text with no original prints, since the so-called original is *always already* a copy:

> [Caliban is] a text nowhere present, consisting of archives which are *always already* transcriptions. Originary prints. Everything begins with reproduction. Always already: repositories of a meaning which was never present, whose signified presence is always reconstituted by deferment *nachträglich*, belatedly, *supplementarily*: for *nachträglich* also means supplementary.[70]

*Histoire de la femme cannibale*, like Caliban, is a reproduction with no original truth, with no originary print of the author's life. Condé plays with the idea of truth as a premise for her semantic displacement, but as it is for Caliban, the purported truth is already a distortion of a nonexisting, though assumed, original. As Rosello says in "Post-Cannibalism in *Histoire de la femme cannibale*," cannibalism epitomizes the never-achieved truth because it functions like a mirage: the truth receding as one approaches it. Cannibalism is that which one talks about but never witnesses, just as Columbus never saw the so-called cannibals who supposedly had one eye in the middle of their foreheads. As a matter of fact, mirage-like sensational truth is intrinsic to the discourse on cannibalism. Tobias Schneebaum's 1969 memoir on cannibalism, *Keep the River on Your Right*, is a good example of it. The author of the memoir is an American artist turned anthropologist who received a Fulbright Fellowship in 1955 to go to Peru. The original purpose of the fellowship was to visit the ruins of Machu Picchu, but once in Peru, Schneebaum discovered that "out there in the forest were other peoples more primitive, other jungles wilder, other worlds that existed and that needed my eyes to look at them."[71] In the memoir, Schneebaum confesses, "I am a cannibal. That four-word sentence doesn't leave my head."[72] Schneebaum, indeed, ate human meat with the Akaramas, the alleged anthropophagite tribe in Peru, yet the cannibalistic act occurred while he was living in seclusion with his fellow tribe members. No Western outsider—that is, the targeted audience of his memoir—can attest to the authenticity of his sensational claim. After a whole year living with this Peruvian tribe, Schneebaum came back from the forest in his most simple apparel, his naked body covered with paint, with a story of homoerotic cannibalism from "out there" to share.[73] But here is the point: cannibalism is always "out there," somewhere impenetrable, full of sensational presumptions and opaque to the outside gaze.

Like Schneebaum's, Condé's "out there" is unverifiable; it lies in the deep forest of her intimacy. The closer one gets to the truth of the novel, the more the semblance of truth seems to recede. *Histoire de la femme cannibale* materializes Condé's phenomenal idea that, in a Derridean sense, there is no primary truth, only copies of a nonexistent original in her storytelling. Again, just like Freud, who argues that the meaning is to be found not in the dream but in the dream-work, which includes a work of condensation, displacement, and distortion, Condé essentially creates meaning through secondhand telling, thus producing the intended effect of discursive distortion. Condé has a tendency to skip the original version of events, directly jumping to what is said, hence already altered, about a primal event. The most idiosyncratic feature of Condé's writing lies in the way she introduces new characters, always using the outside gaze of the village people as a referential point. In *La vie scélérate* (*Tree of Life*, 1992), for example, most of her main events are introduced through the perception of a collective, exterior eye. This eye belongs to the gossipy villagers, whom Condé repeatedly and almost obsessively refers to as "les gens":

*Les gens* [my italics] jasèrent beaucoup quand le père Seewal donna sa fille à un Guadeloupéen.
(*People* gossiped a lot when the paternal Seewal gave his daughter to a Guadeloupean.)[74]

Au bout de quelques mois, *les gens* [my italics] s'aperçurent que son ventre s'arrondissait et ils comprirent qu'il y aurait bientôt un troisième occupant dans la case.
(After a few months, *people* noticed that her belly became rounded and they understood that there would be soon a third person living in the house.)[75]

C'est vers cette année-là, l'année 1906, que *les gens* [my italics] de la plantation Boyer-de-l'Etang virent revenir Aldans dans les bras un enfant palot . . .
(That year, year 1906, *people* from the Plantation Boyer-de-l'Etang saw Aldans come back with a pale child in his arms . . . )[76]

*Les gens* [my italics] racontent que lorsque Albert Louis revint de son séjour de dix ans à l'étranger, il confia tant de dollars américains à la banque que le directeur blanc lui-même sortit de son bureau pour contempler ce fleuve vert.

(*People* say that, when Albert Louis came back from his ten-year trip abroad, he deposited so many American dollars in the bank that the white manager himself left his office to look at the green flow.)[77]

Un tranquille matin de septembre, *les gens* [my italics] de La Pointe purent voir . . . une caravane de porteurs, les jambes arquées, le dos voûté sous le poids d'énormes caisses.
(On a calm September morning, *people* from La Pointe saw . . . a trailer being carried, bent legs, arched backs under the weight of those enormous cases.)[78]

A quatre heures de l'après-midi, *les gens* [my italics] de Petit-Canal, ceux qui étaient sur le devant de leurs portes, virent passer un homme noir à califourchon sur son cheval noir.
(At four in the afternoon, *people* from Petit-Canal, those standing at their doors, saw a black man riding astride on his horse.)[79]

In most of her novels, Condé uses a similar rhetorical approach to introduce characters and key events. The author frequently uses the perspective of villagers who, having never moved from their birthplace, are available to witness strangers coming into town and natives returning home. In *La migration des coeurs*, the author presents Razié, the foreigner who comes into town, also from the anonymous perspective of "les gens." In *Histoire de la femme cannibale*, Condé substitutes the generic term "les gens" for a more precise village voice introduced as "les voisins" or "les habitants." The end result is identical: all the new characters, whether they are returnees or strangers/foreigners, pass under the village's scrutinizing eye before entering the domestic space:

Déjà quelques années plus tôt, quand elle était descendue avec son blanc du camion de déménagement Fast Move, *les voisins* [my italics] s'étaient offusqués. Des renseignements, ils avaient déduit que ce nouveau venu, Stephen Stewart, n'était pas un natif-natal.
(Already a few years earlier, when she came out of the moving truck Fast Move with her white man, *neighbors* had gotten offended. From the information, they had deduced that the newcomer, Stephen Stewart, was not a real native.)[80]

Un matin, Rosélie, . . . était descendue d'une 4 × 4 de Navitour. . . . *Les habitants* [my italics] de l'immeuble étaient restés estomaqués.

(One morning, Rosélie, . . . got off a 4 × 4 from Navitour. . . . *The residents from the building were flabbergasted.*)[81]

In all the examples above, Condé is able to make it sound as if she were being superseded by the village people—as if *les gens* had to be the ones to tell the story.

In *The Dialogic Imagination*, Bakhtin looks at how in polyphonic phenomena miscellaneous speeches coexist within one language or within one voice. For Bakhtin, Dostoevsky was one of the rare writers able to produce true heteroglossia because he had the ventriloquistic ability to reproduce within one voice (his authorial voice), the multivoicedness of all his characters.[82] But Condé subverts Bakhtin's ideal image of heteroglossia by giving the impression that her authorial voice is in fact taken over by the dominating pluralistic presence of *les gens*. The characters rebel against the almighty author. Dostoevsky is depicted as the master of his writing, the one able to sit back and listen to his perfectly designed heteroglossic creation. Condé's heteroglossia, on the other hand, is intrusive, gossipy, and overbearing, so much so that it cannibalizes the voice of its creator.

Condé's compulsive intrusion of *les gens* in her writing is a unique genre of Caribbean discourse, a much less perfect, more human, and potentially more truthful representation of the Creole voice, compared to Glissant's ideal of Caribbean solidarity and community. Condé has persistently looked at the Caribbean writer as someone who has probably more to say about his or her Creole condition while abroad than at home. For her, what was once an isolated position has become a trend. As she once observed, "second- and third-generation-exile Caribbean writers . . . brought up outside of the country of their parents"[83] hold today a strong voice in Caribbean literature, like Edwidge Danticat (Haiti), Caryl Phillips (St. Kitts), or Neil Bissoondath (Trinidad). That said, there is something intrinsically different between Condé, born and raised in Guadeloupe and who has chosen to live and write about the Creole condition far from home, and second- and third-generation-exile Caribbean writers who were born into displacement. For these writers, displacement is an intrinsic component of their identities, while Condé uses displacement as a borrowed strategy, allowing her to make it out of her native land. But paradoxically enough, displacement is what brings her home, closer to her villagers. Condé offers a literature of *débarqués*, the only one that knows what *les gens* in the Caribbean sense really means, the only one capable of capturing the Creole gaze, the Creole representing, as paradoxical as it may sound, true sedentariness.

## Out and On the "Down Low"

In *Traversée de la mangrove*, Condé emulates the Creole tradition of storytelling, which relies on a heteroglossic spiral movement rather than a teleological form of telling. Condé's use of the mangrove image novel, the multibranched horizontal rhizome, is presumably a reference to the non-Western, and thus nonlinear, Creole narrative structure. To complete the Creole furnishings, Condé locates the story in Guadeloupe. This is the only novel by Condé that takes place entirely on her native island.[84] But Condé's Caribbean story would not be complete without a foreign presence around which the entire village can come together. The (allegedly) Colombian Francis Sancher, who happens to be also the alleged *macoumé* in the story, is the deceased and silent protagonist around whom the village gathers during his wake in order to create a dialogical Creole story about his identity. Sancher does not exist outside of the village's voice; he is made out of mere heteroglossic speculation. This very speculation is the reason why he is a *macoumé*. Again, *macoumé* is what is said about the subject, no matter what the "true" identity of the subject is. *Les gens* are responsible for producing the *macoumé* as a signifier with no signified. Conclusively, the *macoumé* is self-referential in that the word refers to nothing other than itself, there being no original truth behind it.

More than ten years after *Traversée de la mangrove*, the *macoumé* suspicions are finally confirmed with the truthfulness of homosexuality. In *Histoire de la femme cannibal*, Condé creates a male character that is truly a homosexual and not merely suspected of being one (*macoumé*). Condé's choice could be read as an endeavor on her part to finally give substance to the *macoumé*'s absence of the signified, to finally offer a character produced outside of *les gens'* speculative gaze. Condé's literary production was, until then, invested with the omnipresence of remote (foreign) homosexuality, which is a safe way to talk *around* (geographically too) the topic. It almost looks as though Condé had been testing how far her semantics of speculative circularity could take her. Her literary production up to *Histoire de la femme cannibale* was like foreplay: Condé moved around the erogenous zone but never touched it. Then comes *Histoire de la femme cannibale*, the novel where the author chooses to lay out all her cards. The big coming out is finally here. We are introduced to the face behind the *macoumé*. The feeling of completion is, however, short-lived, since it very soon comes to mind that the supposed homosexual is dead before we even get to meet him. In the very first pages of the novel, it is announced that Stephen has been murdered. Since Condé has killed him before the story even begins, Stephen has the ghostly presence of a postmortem character. Condé is the alter Fiéla, the woman who kills her husband, cuts him up, and throws the pieces down to us readers and ravenous crows. Stephen's deadly immateriality makes him an unreliable source and, most of all, an unreachable firsthand source, just like Sancher, the other homosexual mirage. Stephen is incidentally a *macoumé* whose only materiality is in the spoken word: the coming out.

The concept of "coming out" is used, in *Histoire de la femme cannibale*, as a rhetoric of *Aliyah*, the tentative of return. It addresses the underlying association in the Antilles of geographical (*débarqué*) with homosexual displacement. When addressing Condé's outsider status in Caribbean literature, it is essential to keep in mind that Condé comes from a black diasporic culture in the Americas, a culture convinced that homosexuality does not exist on its own turf, which therefore treats homosexuality as the epitome of cultural outsideness. As said earlier, the disavowal of homosexuality has been mainly articulated through the immaterial and speculative figure of the *macoumé* in the Antilles. The *macoumé* is an assumption of homosexuality self-assured of its unfoundedness. The ancestral disavowal is the reason why Condé cannot bring homosexuality back home. The Guadeloupean author is struggling with the stigma of phenotypical characteristics that one acquires abroad and seeks, to no avail, to bring home. Coming out, revealing the covert presence of Creole homosexuality, allows Condé to break open the walls of sedentariness in the French Antilles responsible for rejecting what has become foreign, altered, and deviant while abroad. Some may argue that homosexuality in *Histoire de la femme cannibale* is nowhere near close to home because the author chose to locate the coming out in South Africa and in a character that is incongruously British, not to mention white. Yet, within the larger context of disavowed black homosexuality in the Americas, Stephen can still be considered as an intimate rhetorical choice given that in her fictional characterization of Stephen Condé implicitly deconstructs the questionable equation of sexual deception with blackness.

Homosexuality, as a strong source of repression in black cultures, has paved the way for a specifically black sexual identity in the Americas, called the *Down Low*. Being on the Down Low in America refers to the condition of being black and secretly gay while cheating on your heterosexual partner. In the 1990s, the Down Low expression was a sleek R&B term referring to heterosexual infidelity.[85] Around the year 2000, the expression underwent a semantic alteration, resurfacing in the mainstream language as a designation of black gay infidelity toward a heterosexual (usually) black woman. More recently, the expression has become sleeker, sexier, and even more underground. It has made black homosexuality sound like hip-hop: hip, hypermasculine, and an essentially black product for the white audience to enjoy. The Down Low culture has received much media hype since the 2003 *New York Times* article "Double Lives on the Down Low," by Benoit Denizet-Lewis. In this article, the author brings to public consciousness this subculture, which was then on the rise, explaining that "today, while there are black men who are openly gay, it seems that the majority of those having sex with men still lead secret lives, products of a black culture that deems masculinity and fatherhood as a black man's primary responsibility—and homosexuality as a white man's perversion." The news of the Down Low culture broke out due to the allegedly alarming side effect of this underground life: a disproportionate number of black—as opposed to white—heterosexual women were diagnosed HIV positive. The Down Low practice was blamed for this statistical trend. Denizet-Lewis explains:

> DL culture has grown, in recent years, out of the shadows and developed its own contemporary institutions, for those who know where to look: Web sites, Internet chat rooms, private parties, and special nights at clubs. Over the same period, Down Low culture has come to the attention of alarmed public health officials, some of whom regard men on the DL as an infectious bridge spreading HIV to unsuspecting wives and girlfriends. In 2001, almost two-thirds of women in the United States who found out they had AIDS were black.

The direct connection between the Down Low culture and the high number of HIV-positive black women has been disputed.[86] Whether it is an accurate statistical conclusion is subject to debate, but what is undisputable is that the black woman has been made (indirectly) responsible for the public coming out of the black gay man. It is her HIV status that has been the alleged trigger for waving the red flag on the secretive and underground existence of a dangerously undercover black homosexuality in America.

*Histoire de la femme cannibale* was published the same year as Denizet-Lewis's *New York Times* article, both texts addressing in their own ways the black woman as a silent victim of closeted homosexuality. Two years later, in 2005, Keith Boykin, an openly gay African-American broadcaster, editor of the *Village Voice* and CNBC contributor, came to the defense of the Down Low culture in his *New York Times* bestseller book *Beyond the Down Low: Sex, Lies, and Denial in Black America*. In it, the author strives to define the evasive concept of the Down Low and eventually concludes, "You don't have to be black, you don't have to be male, you don't have to be HIV positive, and you don't even have to be in a relationship to be on the down low."[87] It remains the case that the Down Low is like R&B: you don't have to be black to sing R&B, but R&B is nonetheless a black form of artistic expression. Likewise the singer Eminem has proven that one does not need to be black in order to be a credible rap music artist, even though a white rap artist will inevitably come across as a creative anomaly. Eminem is catachrestic in the sense that he appropriates an expression that is not meant to fit him. Stephen is equally catachrestic. Given the year of production, *Histoire de la femme cannibale* calls to be read in the context of the controversy surrounding the media exposure of the Down Low culture. Just like in the real meta-story produced by the media around the Down Low, Rosélie is also presented as a black woman victim of the dangerous Down Low deception. Rosélie is the black woman responsible for the homosexual's sudden public exposure. But of course, the main difference between the *New York Times* article and Condé's novel is that Stephen is inappropriately white. As mentioned earlier, one of the functions of the catachresis is to fill in for semantic poverty, semantic misuse being an alternative to silence. Given that black homosexuality does not exist in Condé's semantic home, Stephen is a catachrestic strategy that brings the question of homosexuality indirectly home. Stephen is a sort of semantic stand-in, one that may have to suffice. In a safe platform far from home, with Stephen in South Africa, Condé can freely address her role in the question of homosexuality, her role as a black woman carrier of the secret, the one responsible for breaking the silence of "homosexuality," highlighting her efforts to bring the word home through a detour. By bringing the word home, she attempts to bring her "deviant self"—in the etymological sense of "off road" (from the Latin *deviare*)—home.

As we know, the Antiguan and naturalized American writer Jamaica Kincaid followed a similar itinerary in her 1997 controversial memoir, *My Brother*. Jamaica Kincaid is very similar to Maryse Condé in that both writers come from a small Caribbean island that they left at a relatively young adult age; both write about their respective islands from the outsider perspective of someone culturally altered by their time spent abroad; and both choose to construct one of their stories around the cannibalistic act of outing someone close to home. In her book, Kincaid makes the homosexuality of Devon, her brother, public. Her outing is quite intrusive, since her brother had until then, and even beyond death, been successful at painstakingly hiding his homosexuality from the people of his small island. The narrative recounts in Kincaid's first-person narrative voice, Devon dying of AIDS, her assisting him with the necessary material and medical privileges brought or shipped from America, and the eventual discovery of her brother's homosexuality after his death. Her brother had always been a notorious womanizer, even when knowingly HIV positive, even when dying. Devon was clearly doing what the media would call living "on the Down Low." Kincaid was told about her brother's closeted sexuality in Chicago while giving a reading for her latest book. An Antiguan woman who attended the reading introduced herself to Kincaid as the person who had offered a safe shelter for gays, including Devon, at her home, because "homosexual men had no place to go in Antigua."[88] Devon is outed to his sister by this woman, but Kincaid will out him to the world.

Kincaid participates in the aforementioned concept of the black woman being somehow responsible for the outing of the black man on the Down Low. That being said, Kincaid's proxy confession does not bring us much closer to a tangible coming out, since Devon is dead at the time he is outed. Just like Stephen, Devon is the silent *macoumé* who is alleged to be a homosexual. Both Condé and Kincaid are black women *débarquées* trying unsuccessfully to go home while bringing homosexuality home along with them. They both use the detour of their remoteness from home to reach the semantically unreachable. This detour ends up biting its own tail as it circumvents the very question of homosexuality. The homosexual is infallibly turned into a *macoumé*, a product of hearsay, a Caribbean turned cannibal, a Caliban. In *My Brother*, Kincaid uses homosexuality, the phenotypical characteristic of time spent abroad, to break into the impenetrable space of her native island, but she never makes it inside. The Down Low figure may be black (Kincaid's Devon) or catachrestically white (Condé's Stephen), but it is never a confirmed homosexual. Devon and Stephen are mere reflections of their authors' failures to break the cycle of "once out of the pack, never back." Their attempted outings attest to the self-referentiality of their *débarqué* status doomed to never again reach home.

Condé, through the omnipresent theme of homosexuality (*macoumé*) in her writing, shows the price of leaving, the price of—in all its polysemy—being *out*. Because getting out or coming out goes against the grain of the Creole fabric, Maryse Condé as a spokeswoman for both the *débarqué* and the homosexual, can be said to be an unapologetic Creole Renegade. Arguing that what makes Condé's Caribbean writing "authentic" is her incidentally uprootedness, Noxolo and Preziuso wrote, "Condé insists that it is precisely this nomadic existence, the fact that she has not remained 'rooted' in Guadeloupe, that fosters her creativity in relation to writing from a Caribbean perspective."[89] We could conversely argue that, even more than her uprootedness, the so-called authenticity of Condé's literature lies in its failed attempts to go home.

# Edwidge Danticat and Dany Laferrière

## Parasitic and Remittance Diaspora

> Bowing my head in shame at being called a parasitic dyaspora.
>
> EDWIDGE DANTICAT, *CREATE DANGEROUSLY*

Peter Hallward, the author of a book on the former Haitian president Jean-Bertrand Aristide, writes in his preface, "This is not a book motivated by any personal association with Haiti. . . . A philosopher and a literary critic by training, I have visited Haiti only twice, and make no claim to the sort of insider or anthropological knowledge that authorizes much published work on the country."[1] In response to Hallward's disclaimer, the critic Jana Evans Braziel insists in *Duvalier's Ghosts* that "a direct knowledge of Haiti . . . does matter"[2] if one seeks to be a credible source. This allows Braziel to legitimize her own credibility by then closing her "acknowledgments" with an expression of gratitude for the person who risked his life in order to bring her closer to the action in Haiti: "[He] took me into Cité Soleil when I pressed him to do so and even when he felt that it was against his better judgment."[3] Braziel's "acknowledgments," as a paratextual guarantee of so-called direct exposure to the subject, carries the effect of, if not fully identifying, at least partially associating the author with the survivors, the "ghosts of Cité Soleil." "The Ghosts of Cité Soleil" refers to a song by Wyclef Jean, featured in Asger Leth's 2006 documentary of the same title that recounts the dangers of daily life in Cité Soleil, a neighborhood on the outskirts of Port-au-Prince deemed to be extremely dangerous. The lyrics depict Wyclef's wife and mother begging the singer not to go to Cité Soleil, but to no avail. Upon Wyclef's return, they call him "the ghost of Cité Soleil" because he survived an experience with presumably no way out. Yet, as Braziel argues in her preface, "Those with the privilege to come and go, those who have the means to find a way out, are not the ghosts of Cité Soleil."[4] For her, the real ghosts live in Cité Soleil and as such face the daily danger of being kidnapped, raped, or killed there: "they are the ones for whom there is no way out."[5] But the "real" ghosts do not come out to tell their story. The go-betweens, on the other hand, like Braziel and Wyclef, are the ones who, as transnational brokers, bring and even sell the story to the overseas party.

Every contribution to the history, politics, or culture of Haiti produced outside of the country seems to come with some sort of disclaimer, given that the contribution is always already guilty of its not-direct-enough exposure to the country. In an Adorno-resonance of "no poetry after Auschwitz," the immediacy of the Haitian experience does not tolerate an outside, an after. The fact of getting out, even only to report the story, grants a privilege to the survivor whose credibility is refuted by the mere fact of reporting from the other side—what the Haitians call *lot bod dlo*, "the other side of the water." Though "the guilt of absence,"[6] as Nick Nesbitt calls it, consumes the Haitian diasporic writer, it undeniably also fuels his or her writing. For immigrants, absence is often nourishing, immigration being the backbone of an economy of production, exchange, and two-way circulation between the adopted land and the home country. Economically challenged countries, in particular, rely on a Western Union type of immigration. Western Union is an international money transfer service, and its frequent use by Caribbean migrants shows, as Kezia Page pointedly argues, the "material cultural evidence of the active interchange between Caribbean migrant and diaspora communities and their communities at home."[7] The argument is equally valid for an economy of creative production. The migrant goes to the other side of the water to produce a story on Haiti that could not have been produced in the homeland. One side relies on the other in order to boost diasporic creativity. The Haitian Creole expression itself, *lot bod dlo*, which insists on a border-to-border perspective, calls to mind the uncut umbilical cord between the homeland and the adopted land, with the water between them the amniotic fluid nourishing both sides. Absence, in the Haitian context of *lot bod dlo*, is not a barren rupture but rather the profitable (to a few) outsourcing of the memory, history, and even culture of Haiti.

Reflecting on Haitian scholarship, Braziel ponders, "What if years on the street do lend an intellectual and political credibility that a 'well-paid' and 'sheltered' academic life does not?"[8] But all things considered, we could further argue that, to some extent, it is precisely the scholarship on Haiti that *supports* the "well-paid" life of the "sheltered" academic. Because the report on Haiti generates a type of safety (money, shelter) that is lacking in Haiti, one could wonder whether the profitable nature of the report holds the risk of undermining the credibility (and good faith) of the report itself. In the case of the Haitian diasporic writer, the guilt is twofold: the guilt of absence comes along with the guilt of profit, a profit made possible by the absence. And yet, how could one write otherwise, since, as Nesbitt convincingly argues, the direct witness can be "impeded by the burden of immediacy,"[9] immediacy depriving the witness of the (physical, emotional) means of getting the story out. The dilemma is how to get the story out if the tellers of the story become illegitimate ghosts, and potentially unreliable sellouts, as soon as they tell the story.

The critic Martin Munro has drawn attention to the relation between the growing number of internationally known and successful Haitian / Haitian Diasporic writers and Haiti's ever more desperate social situation, concluding that "perhaps great writing feeds off and is inspired by misery and despair."[10] It is difficult to miss the (probably involuntary) irony in Munro's words, particularly in the leech metaphor ("feed off") that Edwidge Danticat has incidentally heard many times before. "You are a parasite and you exploit your culture for money and what passes for fame"[11] is, as it were, the most common criticism that Haitian diasporic writer Edwidge Danticat says she has received from the Haitian community. Danticat lived in Haiti under the Jean-Claude Duvalier regime until the age of twelve, when she left Haiti for New York. In America, she became a *dyaspora*, as Haitians call their countrymen living abroad. Danticat, a literary prodigy, published her first work at fourteen and released her first novel, *Breath, Eyes, Memory* (which would later become a lucrative Oprah Winfrey Book Club selection) at the age of twenty-five. Probably the most "en vogue" writer from the Haitian diaspora today, Danticat carries the particularity of writing in English, holding a master's degree in fine arts in creative writing from Brown University. In 1999, she won the American Book Award for her fictional account of the 1937 persecution of Haitians in the Dominican Republic. Her recent testimonial book on her beloved uncle's tragic death in the Miami immigration detention center (Krome), *Brother, I'm Dying*, was a finalist for the National Book Award. In 2009, she was awarded the MacArthur Foundation "Genius Award," a fellowship worth $500,000. Danticat's career is a mix of superior academic achievement and commercial and critical success, which invites some to say that her American success story clashes somehow with the topic of her choice: Haitian suffering. To some degree, Danticat is indeed a "parasite" in that she is a diasporic organism that lives off the history of the land to which she no longer belongs. The author seems to be sucking it all in for cultural survival. But for an immigrant writer, cultural parasitism is not necessarily negative, unless, of course, there is not just human but also capital gain involved in writing about Haitian suffering.

In his recent book *Lénigme du retour* (*The Return*, 2011), Dany Laferrière, another well-known Haitian diasporic writer, alluded to the questionable position of the outsider making money while working in (and by extension working on) Haiti. In this book, Laferrière is sitting in the expensive Hotel Montana in Port-au-Prince, having a drink with a German engineer working in Haiti. The two have a discussion about Haitian misery. The engineer tells Laferrière that his father once told him that "on était tous des salauds à vivre dans cet hôtel luxueux et bien protégé tout en se faisant croire qu'on menait une vie dangereuse et difficile" (we were all jerks, living in luxury hotels, all safe, while giving the impression of leading a dangerous and difficult life).[12] Laferrière and Danticat's American land of exile is somewhat like Hotel Montana: a luxurious and well-protected space offering the beneficial illusion to those working for/on Haiti that they are working *dangerously*. Case in point, in 2010, Danticat published a collection of essays for the Toni Morrison Lectures Series titled *Create Dangerously: The Immigrant Artist at Work* that reads like an attempt at (self)-justifying the role of the Haitian immigrant writer:

> Perhaps this is why the immigrant artist needs to feel that he or she is creating dangerously even though she is not scribbling on prison walls or counting the days until a fateful date with an executioner. Or a hurricane. Or an earthquake.[13]

Danticat's attempt at rehabilitation in this collection of essays is filled with palpable guilt and self-doubt, emotions that run through her entire body of work. Danticat is the epitome of the survivor's guilt that tortures the Haitian immigrant.

As said before, Danticat has been endorsed by Oprah Winfrey, which, as both Chris Bongie and Nick Nesbitt argue, makes Danticat's books guilty of their—"middle brow" (Bongie)—popularity. Winfrey's imprimatur could impact the seriousness of Danticat's contribution, all the more so because this popularity came as an indirect result of her leaving Haiti. However, Nesbitt comes to the defense of Danticat by arguing that the author is able to overcome the debilitating effect of her absence by contributing creatively instead of physically to Haiti. This deferral, or what Nesbitt calls "distanciation," is potentially more beneficial than immediate presence because immediacy—

Nesbitt claims—can be paralyzing (muting), while reflection produces its own kind of act-ivism. Nesbitt concludes that Danticat compensates her passivity by her "*act* [my emphasis] of aesthetic creation."[14]

Bongie, in return, offers an interesting twist on Nesbitt's defense of Danticat. Bongie sees the role of Nesbitt as too similar to that of Winfrey; in some way, he suggests that Nesbitt "bought into" Winfrey's marketing strategy. Both Nesbitt and Bongie agree that Winfrey's imprimatur makes Danticat's books guilty of their *commercial* success. But, as Bongie argues, while confirming the commodified nature of the book, the role of the endorsement is, paradoxically enough, to guarantee the seriousness of the contribution. Winfrey's endorsement calls for a leap of faith; it asks readers to forget its marketing nature in order to see only its message: the value of the book as a must-read. Bongie argues that it is exactly what Nesbitt, as a literary critic, has done. While Nesbitt first takes notice of the commodified nature of Danticat's books (Nesbitt wrote that her books are guilty of their Winfrey's Book Club popularity), the critic then overlooks this dimension in order to focus only on their "intrinsic values."[15] Bongie contends that, like Winfrey's endorsement, Nesbitt asks us to disavow the blatant politics of production, circulation, and consumption of the book in order to look only at what the book promises to do as an act of aesthetic production:

> By the end of [Nesbitt's] paragraph, in other words, we have come a very long way away from the "properly sociological investigation of [francophone literature's] production and reception" that its opening seemed to promise, and that Nesbitt himself identifies, in a footnote, as a pressing task facing those who study this literature.[16]

One of the main preoccupations of Bongie's book *Friends and Enemies* is to bring attention to the marketing of Caribbean literature. Bongie's mission is to start "considering the 'aesthetic value [of a francophone book]' in relation to the increasingly commodified ways in which that value is produced and consumed today. . . ."[17] The disavowal for which Winfrey's endorsement calls requires overlooking the politics of global capitalism in the marketed book. This leap of faith, as Nesbitt showed, makes the act-ivism in the "act of the aesthetic production" possible. What Bongie asks for, on the other hand, would necessitate a synecdochical transfer where the paratext (Winfrey's stamp of approval on the book cover) would take precedence over the text and where the book as a product of consumption—to paraphrase Marshall McLuhan's "the medium is the message"—would be the message.

Laferrière's writing strategy is, in fact, based on this synecdochical transfer. Compared to Danticat, Laferrière stands at the other end of the marketing spectrum. The writer has built his literary persona on the very question of writing as monetary gain based on a basic, all-American, every-man-for-himself attitude. Laferrière claims to have done his best to get the Haitian dictator out of his life, but he also admits in a deliberately unscrupulous tone that "que pour ce faire il m'a fallu jeter parfois l'enfant avec l'eau du bain" (to do so, I sometimes had to throw the baby out with the bathwater).[18] When he first left for exile at age twenty-three, Laferrière made a living doing odd jobs in Montréal, until the 1985 publication of his provocative and commercially successful novel *Comment faire l'amour avec un nègre sans se fatiguer* (*How to Make Love to a Negro without Getting Tired*, 1987). Laferrière's book tells the story of a look-alike Laferrière writing his autobiographical book in Montreal while fully enjoying the pleasure of interracial sexuality. In addition to the marketability of the topic and of the book title, *Comment faire l'amour* comes across as a black immigrant's "how-to" guide (as the title suggests) for gaining fame and money in America. The Laferrière protagonist alleges to have started writing out of opportunism; as he says, if a black man cannot dance or sing, he might as well claim to be a writer. In *Cette grenade dans la main du jeune nègre est-elle une arme ou un fruit?* (*Why Must a Black Writer Write about Sex?*, 1994), Laferrière presents the act of writing as an escape from proletarianism: "en tapant huit heures par jour sur une vieille machine à écrire déglinguée. C'était ça ou l'usine. Ça a été ça et l'usine. Et petit à petit, ça a été seulement ça" (typing eight hours a day on my old, raggedy typewriter. It was either that or the factory. It was that and the factory. Little by little, it became only that).[19] Writing means money, which for Laferrière is the only meaningful currency in America: "En Amérique, c'est l'argent qui rassure. L'argent, c'est vivant" (In America, money reassures. Money is alive).[20]

Laferrière comes across as the epitome of the proletarian immigrant. From the Latin *proles*, meaning "offspring"—suggesting that the proletarian's only wealth is his offspring—but also close to the Latin *alere* meaning "nourishing," what defines the *proletarius* is his basic role to feed (the offspring). By extension, the foremost goal of the proletarian immigrant is to use the adopted land not as a source of personal, cultural, or intellectual enrichment but rather as a land that will provide basic necessities for his people in return for labor. Belinda Edmondson has made a very interesting semantic distinction between the Caribbean "exile" and "immigrant." For her, while the "primary motives" of the "immigrant" in the adopted land are, as she says, "to make money,"[21] the "exile" carries a "glamoured image of the educated—if tortured—exile, thinking and writing in a 'cultured' cosmopolitan center."[22] The "immigrant," she pursues, is a menial worker relying on "physical, not intellectual, labor."[23] Edmondson's distinction is mainly based on a question of generational gap. The older Trinidadian-British V. S. Naipaul, who moved to England to study at Oxford, and to a lesser degree the Martinican Aimé Césaire, who studied at the prestigious Ecole Normale Supérieure in Paris (though he moved back to Martinique after his education), exemplify the old generation of privileged and educated exile writers. In contrast, Laferrière's first job in North America was in a Canadian factory, while Jamaica Kincaid first came to America to work as an au pair. In her book *Reclaiming Difference*, while elaborating on "the critical shift of exile to migrant literature"[24] that Edmondson initially addressed, Carine M. Mardorossian emphasizes the importance of the location and gender-based nature of the shift. Mardorossian points out that the first generation of "predominantly male Caribbean writers 'in exile'" relocated to Europe, whereas "the second generation of predominantly female 'immigrant' writers"[25] migrated to America. The feminization of migration concomitant with a labor-oriented migrant force hints at, once again, a "nourishing" metaphor. The female immigrant is a *nourrice* in the sense of both a nanny and a wet-nurse (feeding). Being sent to America as an au pair in order to provide for her family back home, Kincaid is the embodiment of the Caribbean *nourrice* (nanny / wet-nurse) immigrant. The proletarian immigrant is highly feminized in her nourishing role.

Cultural currency gives way to hard money, the European metropole is traded for America, and male exile is exchanged for female immigration. Laferrière, as a man, falls one characteristic short of fitting Edmondson and Mardorossian's profile of the modern-day Caribbean immigrant. But more than a question of gender, Laferrière does not qualify as a *nursing [nourrice] immigrant* because, as a diasporic subject, the writer strongly rejects a putative role of overseas provider. Unapologetically, Laferrière offers no sense of amniotic *lot bod lo* in his writing, no mention of a Western Union type of immigration, financial or otherwise. Laferrière's strategy, to put emphasis on the self-serving nature of the immigrant's book, is, however, not necessarily less political than Danticat's aesthetic act. Both Laferrière's and Bongie's focus on the financial value and the marketing of the Haitian diasporic book over its aesthetic and political purpose is based on a chiasmic switch. The politics of marketing takes precedence over the marketing of politics. In both cases, the immigrant writer addresses the difficult question of how to sell a book on Haiti.

## "I am not a Journalist": *Engagée* versus *Dégagée* Literature

Laferrière has published more than fifteen books, ten of them encompassing what the author refers to as his "autobiographie américaine." In the scope of his entire American autobiography, the author intended to speak only about himself, thus carefully avoiding the topic of Haitian misery. In *Je suis fatigué* (*I Am Tired*), Laferrière points out that he purposely did not use the word *Haiti* in his first book, adding "Je ne me sentais pas digne" (I didn't feel worthy it).[26] Instead of writing about those left behind, as Danticat did, Laferrière chose to write about frivolous matters, which could have been his own bashful way of coping with his survivor's guilt. In 1985, the year of the publication of *Comment faire l'amour*, the Barbadian George Lamming asserted in a public lecture, "But wherever you are, outside of the Caribbean, it should give you not only comfort, but a sense of cultural obligation, to feel that you are an important part of the Caribbean as external frontier."[27] For some, cultural obligation may be a comfort, but for others it is cumbersome—especially for immigrant writers who are often perceived as the ambassadors of their native culture. In an interview, Danticat laments the fact that the Haitian community imposes on minority writers a duty of national representation: "It is a burden that most writers who are from smaller groups face. There is a tendency to see our work as sociology or anthropology, an 'insight' into a complex culture. Readers have to remember that we're writing fiction, telling stories."[28] The idea that writing individually is "a freedom," as Danticat claims, not "allowed" to "minority groups,"[29] and even less so to Haitian immigrant writers, has undeniably influenced Danticat's writing. Laferrière and Danticat are different types of Haitian immigrant writers offering two perspectives on the cultural obligation of the diasporic subject: one avoids addressing Haitian misery at all costs, and one makes Haitian misery her main concern. In both cases, the line between cultural obligation and opportunism gets dangerously thin for the immigrant writer at work. Could Haitian immigrant writing be seen as an inverted case of remittance in which the immigrant feeds off Haiti rather than feeding Haiti? Or is diasporic writing, as Danticat suggests in *Create Dangerously*, an act of remittance, a way of giving back to the community through a journalistic duty of memory? Danticat explains, "My purpose, then, as an immigrant and a writer, is to be an echo chamber, gathering and then replaying voices from both the distant and local devastation."[30]

Danticat, who left Haiti for Brooklyn at age twelve, is referred to as a *dyaspora*, which encompasses the tenth department, "the floating homeland, the ideological one, which joined all Haitians living outside of Haiti, in the *diaspora*."[31] *Dyaspora*, unlike the more generic spelling *diaspora*, is a Haitian Creole concept. Like many words in the Creole language, *dyaspora* is an empirical concept that defies definition: one has to live it to understand it. Danticat, as a writer, struggles with her ambition to put the meaning of *dyaspora* into words. Lacking adequate semantics, Danticat chooses to define it through a series of personal life vignettes, which once assembled will create a collage of intimate shame, embarrassment, and guilt, the sum of her *dyaspora* experience. Danticat writes:

> I meant in that essay to list my own personal experiences as an immigrant and a writer, of being called *dyaspora* when expressing an opposing political point of view in discussions with friends and family members living in Haiti, who knew that they could easily silence me by saying, "What do you know? You're living outside. You're *dyaspora*." I meant to recall some lighter experiences of being startled in the Haitian capital or in the provinces when a stranger who wanted to catch my attention would call out, "Dyaspora!" as though it were a title like *Miss, Ms., Mademoiselle*, or *Madame*. I meant to recall conversations or debates in restaurants, at parties, or at public gatherings where members of the *dyaspora* would be classified—justifiably or not—as arrogant, insensitive, overbearing, and pretentious people who were eager to reap the benefits of good jobs and political positions in times of stability in a country that they'd fled and stayed away from during difficult times. Shamefacedly, I'd bow my head and accept these judgments when they were expressed, feeling guilty about my own physical distance from a country that I had left at the age of twelve during a dictatorship that had forced thousands to choose between exile and death.[32]

The first draft of the previous description dates back to the year 2000. Ten years later, when the writer edited the draft with the intention of including it in her collection of essays, Danticat wrote, "Now I am back in the old essay, back to bowing my head in shame at being called a parasitic *diaspora*."[33] When Michael Dash states, "The burden of guilt is one of the defining features of the 'tired ghosts' of the Haitian diaspora, guilt at having survived while others were massacred,"[34] he is referring in particular to Danticat, the known tortured writer. Danticat uses empathy when depicting the 1937 persecution of Haitians in the Dominican Republic in *The Farming of Bones*, when writing about a prostitute mother or a despairing father's suicide in economically deprived Haiti in *Krik? Krak!*, when describing the humiliating death of her beloved uncle in the Miami Krome Detention Center for illegal immigrants in *Brother, I'm Dying*, and when writing about the 1964 public execution of activists Marcel Numa and Louis Drouin and the 2000 assassination of journalist and radio personality Jean Dominique in *Create Dangerously*. The editor and poet Rodney Saint-Eloi once wrote that Haiti means death or exile, *Sak pa kontan anbake*,[35] love it or leave it. Saint-Eloi's slogan suggests that there is still a choice for Haitians, albeit a bitterly ironic one: one can leave or one can keep living in Haiti and keep dying for it. Some of those who chose life over death, like Danticat, became willful *dyaspora* survivors. As a consequence, Danticat's literature comes across as a constant negotiation and justification of her choice to live, often giving tribute to the ones who stayed.

Jan J. Dominique, the daughter of the assassinated Haitian radio personality and activist journalist Jean Dominique, writes in her memoir about her exile, "The French say *nègre*, the English, more poetic, call it the 'ghost writer,' 'ce fantôme qui s'efface derrière une voix qui pleure, derrière un corps qui souffre, pour que la lumière doucement le réchauffe. Je veux devenir ce fantôme'" (the ghost who disappears behind a crying voice, behind a body in pain, so that the light softly warms it up. I want to become that ghost).[36] J. J. Dominique's words are evocative of Danticat's "tired ghosts" of the Haitian diaspora" (Dash), as the survivor's guilt translates into a ghostwriter's testimonial literary genre. In the same manner as Aimé Césaire, who wrote, "Ma bouche sera la bouche des malheurs qui n'ont pas de bouche, ma voix, la liberté de celles qui s'affaissent au cachot du désespoir" (My mouth will be the mouth of the sorrows that have no mouth, my voice, the freedom of those sinking in the dungeon of despair),[37] Danticat is the ghostwriter who is committed to speaking for the martyr's silenced voice. J. J. Dominique stopped writing on the day of her father Jean Dominique's assassination to only start again once a *dyaspora*, whereas Danticat picked up her pen to write about *dyaspora* the very day of Jean Dominique's death: "I meant, in the essay that I began writing the morning that Jean died, to struggle to explain the multilayered meaning of the Creole word *diaspora*."[38] One assassination, two converging stories of writing and *dyaspora*.

Jonathan Demme chose to name his documentary *The Agronomist* in memory of what Jean Dominique once told him: "You will be surprised but I am not a journalist. I am an agronomist."[39] By introducing Jean Dominique as an agronomist instead of a journalist, Demme drew attention to the particularity of being a journalist in Haiti, a *de facto* profession born out of contingencies. Before he was forced into exile, Laferrière was also a journalist in Haiti, working for *Le petit samedi soir* newspaper and for Radio Haiti in Port-au-Prince. The young man was responsible for the cultural section of the newspaper, while his colleague and friend, Gasner Raymond, was in charge of politics. Gasner, the political *engagé*, was savagely assassinated by the *tontons macoutes*, the Duvalier special police force. To avoid Gasner's fate, Laferrière immediately left Haiti for Montreal, a painful departure at the age of twenty-three, which the author narrates in *Le cri des oiseaux fous* (*The Cry of Crazy Birds*). The particularity of Laferrière's position is that, as a journalist, he refused to be politically engaged; he was only interested in culture, a position that was a cultural anomaly in Haiti. Laferrière says, "Chez nous, il n'y a qu'une seule section dans tous les journaux: la politique. . . . Le journalisme ne peut être qu'une lutte infatigable contre la dictature" (In our country, there is only one section in the newspapers: politics. . . . Journalism can only be a tireless fight against dictatorship),[40] which leads the young Laferrière to further conclude, "Ça me frustre énormément de ne pas pouvoir emprunter le si joyeux chemin de la frivolité, simplement parce que je suis né dans un pays du tiers-monde gangrené par la dictature" (It frustrates me enormously not being able to take the oh so joyous road of frivolity, only because I was born in a Third World country ravaged by dictatorship).[41] Once in Montreal (and then Miami), Laferrière freely chose the delight of frivolity. Danticat herself calls Laferrière a funny writer, a good diversion from Haitian misery. After the 2010 earthquake in Haiti that threw her into despair, Danticat says that she needed to laugh for release: "I too needed to laugh, so I began reading my friend Dany Laferrière again. Dany is one of the funniest people I know, and his sense of humor often infuses his work."[42] But once she opened Laferrière's most recent book, *L'énigme du retour*, Danticat realized that this one was not funny. *L'énigme du retour* is the book of the prodigal son looking Haitian misery straight in the eye, without feigned frivolity or funny diversion. What happened to funny Dany?

From 2000 to 2008, Laferrière took a hiatus from writing, during which time he worked on the big-screen adaptations of several of his novels, including *Le goût des jeunes filles* (*Dining with the Dictator*, 1994) and *Vers le sud* (*Heading South*, 2009). In the year 2000, to give closure to his monumental

"American Autobiography," Laferrière released two books whose purpose was to announce the end of his writing career: *J'écris comme je vis* (*I Write As I Live*) and *Je suis fatigué*. *Je suis fatigué* hints at the possibility that Laferrière may not have said his last word, given that the book introduces itself as the last word that cannot stop talking: "un livre pour dire que tu ne fais plus de livres" (a book to say that you will no longer write books).[43] Sure enough, Laferrière began writing again a few years later, but the writer came back this time as a different person, surprisingly less frivolous. In 2008, Laferrière published *Je suis un écrivain japonais* (*I Am a Japanese Writer*, 2010), a postmodern narrative selling itself as a book with nothing to say ("Quand on a le titre, le plus gros de l'ouvrage est fait. Mais il faut quand même écrire le livre" [When one has the title, the biggest part of the work is done. But one has yet to write the book]).[44] *Je suis un écrivain japonais* picks up where *Je suis fatigué* left off, with a Laferrière persona at a loss for words but in need of one more lucrative publication ("Vendu! On signe le contrat: 10,000 pour cinq petits mots" [Sold! We sign the contract: 10,000 for five little words]).[45] *Je suis un écrivain japonais* carries an intended air of déjà vu. Laferrière chooses to reenter the stage with a taste of his old strategy as if he wanted to remind readers of his old persona before introducing the new one. In this novel, Laferrière combines self-centeredness, wit, and absurd nothingness à la Samuel Beckett.

But a year later the author did a ninety-degree turn with the publication of *L'énigme du retour*, a serious chronicle of modern Haiti. A year after that, the release of *Tout bouge autour de moi* (*Everything Moves around Me*) confirms his new direction. Laferrière shows, once again, an earnest concern with Haitian misery. While *L'énigme du retour* is, to paraphrase Laferrière, the book *manqué* of a well-fed writer, the book that will never be the great Haitian novel about the experience of hunger ("le grand roman haïtien dont le sujet ne peut être que la faim" [the great Haitian novel of which topic can only be hunger]),[46] *Tout bouge autour de moi* chronicles Haiti's latest natural tragedy, the January 12, 2010, earthquake, which, as a witness, Laferrière shares with the world. With Laferrière's two most recent books, readers discover a writer willing to embrace the role of the journalist, the ghostwriter for the ones who are fallen, starving, and crushed. Laferrière's literary itinerary, with its hiatus, hesitations, and final surrender, retraces an immigrant writer's journey as he sways between his basic need for subsistence and his journalistic inclination. His itinerary could lead to the conclusion that he must resume his journalistic duty when, as a novelist, he has nothing left to say. In his recent publications, Laferrière abandons his initial focus on the marketing value of the book; the content is now the message. However, for most of his career, Laferrière had adopted a blatant antifetishistic approach, in which the book was presented literally as a product of consumption. Fetishism is based on a disavowal such as Octave Mannoni's formula "I know but nevertheless." I know that an author makes profit off a book, but I choose to see the aesthetic over the marketing value of the book. The fetishistic act chooses to overlook, as Bongie laments, the "commodified ways in which [the aesthetic value of a book] is produced and consumed."[47] Once the book has been stripped of its fetishistic protection, however, reverting to the value of the content of the book over its marketing value is almost impossible. Now ignoring the marketing strategy of Laferrière's book about the 2012 Haiti earthquake and believing in its *act* of aesthetic and journalistic production require another leap of faith.

In *Create Dangerously*, Danticat hints at the pivotal role of journalism in Haitian culture, a role that tends to look at all *engagé* Haitian writers as journalists by default. The author recounts a trip back to visit her seventy-five-year-old aunt living far out in the Haitian mountains of Beauséjour in a location only accessible by foot. Aunt Ilyana has not seen Danticat for years. The old woman seems to remember that Edwidge was a journalist, which Danticat confirms. Following the journalist discussion, Danticat describes her emotions and those of her aunt:

> I hear a hint of pride in her voice, pride that this person, who she has momentarily forgotten is myself, has spent some time with her. A *jounalis*, or journalist, is the most common kind of writer in Haiti. A mix of usefulness—you are offering a service to others by providing information—and notoriety makes it an occasionally respectable profession. . . . Though *I am not a journalist* [my italics], I know that this is her way of calling me a writer. I am overjoyed, thrilled. . . . I am the niece and the *journalis*, a family writer in the eyes of my aging aunt, who has never read a word or a sentence, who has never met and will never meet another writer.[48]

After the chapter in which the above passage is included, Danticat titles the next chapter "I am not a journalist," a reference to what the agronomist Jean Dominique told Jonathan Demme, the director of the documentary *The Agronomist*. The chiasmus highlighted by Danticat speaks for itself: the writer Danticat, though not a journalist, is mistaken for a journalist, and Dominique, though an agronomist, is a journalist after all. One is and the other is not, yet both end up being *journalis*. Dominique, Danticat, and Laferrière are acciden-tal journalists made to report as tragedy unfolds.

It is precisely to deflate the pressure of the "journalist culture" imposed on Haitian-born writers that Laferrière has chosen to chronicle the mundane, the frivolous, and the entertaining in his early books. Frivolity is a key theme both in his novels addressing the life of Haitian exiles[49] and those taking place in Haiti.[50] Laferrière's literary strategy appears to be a reaction to Haiti's enduring stigma of exceptionalism, something that the scholar Michel-Rolph Trouillot strongly condemns: "We need to drop the fiction that Haiti is unique—Trouil-lot [quoted by Michael Dash] argues—if by unique one means that it escapes analysis and comparison. Haiti is not that weird. It is the fiction of Haitian exceptionalism that is weird."[51] The tendency to see Haiti as a historical ex-ception arches back to the 1804 Haitian Revolution, admittedly a truly unique historical event. As the critic Nick Nesbitt said, "The Haitian Revolution led by Toussaint Louverture and his lieutenant Dessalines and Henri Christophe has become an international symbol of anticolonial contestation, well known as the world's only successful overthrow of a slave-holding society by the en-slaved themselves."[52] From then on, Haiti has been caught in its superlative historiography, the uniqueness of its inception calling for ever more unique-ness. As Laferrière points out, first Haiti became the first black independent Republic in the world; in the later 1980s, it became the poorest country; and finally, postearthquake, it was labeled "maudit" (cursed),[53] which brings us to the image of an unsalvageable nation beyond superlatives.

Haiti's historiographic agenda of exceptionalism is surely not easy to re-linquish. Paul Ricoeur explains in *Histoire et vérité* (*History and Truth*, 1965) that in order to sort out and make sense of past events, the work of the histo-rian precisely proceeds through interpretive schemas, since going from the "past" to "history" requires a work of sequencing:

L'objectivité de l'histoire consiste précisément dans . . . cette ambition d'élaborer des enchaînements de faits . . . car il n'y a pas d'explication sans constitution de "séries" de phénomènes: série économique, série politique, série culturelle, etc.

(The objectivity of history precisely consists in . . . this ambition to elabo-rate the chain of events . . . because there is no explanation without the constitution of "series" of phenomena: economical series, political se-ries, cultural series, etc.)[54]

In the case of Haiti, we see a historiographic compulsion to sequence the past of this nation in terms of exceptionalism. Superlativism becomes that which brings the disparate events of the past into a coherent generic narrative. As Michel-Rolph Trouillot says regarding Haitian historiography, at stake in history, and in Haitian historiography in particular, is the "archival power . . . to define what is and what is not a serious object of research, therefore, of mention."[55] In other words, Haiti's selective narrative of "exceptionalism" leaves little room for ordinariness. This widely perceived lack of Haitian mundaneness explains why the *journalis* holds a pivotal role in Haitian culture and why writers like Laferrière, once in exile, are faced with the difficult choice of either writing dangerously like a *journalis* or writing individually like a novelist.

## Against Exceptionalism

To some extent, *Le cri des oiseaux fous*, Laferrière's autobiographically inspired account of his last day in Haiti before his secret departure for Canada, could be viewed as Laferrière's own version of Danticat's *Create Dangerously*—not because it carries an apologetic tone like Danticat's book but rather because it explains why the author left Haiti. In *Le cri des oiseaux fous*, Laferrière explains why he chose life, hence exile, over his death. The book also addresses national responsibility, a question that Laferrière frames within the larger issue of his choice to live. In this book, Laferrière brings no communal dimension to the tragedy; on the contrary, the author makes special efforts to present the consequence of the journalist's death (Gasner) and his subsequent exile, as a personal plight, a profoundly individual, almost existentially absurd situation reminiscent of Mersault's fate (Albert Camus). After the violent assassination of Gasner, Laferrière's mother, fearing for her son's life, forces him to leave the country the following day. The entire novel takes place the night preceding the departure, as Laferrière wanders in the streets of Port-au-Prince, looking for his friends to whom he will indirectly communicate his farewells while painfully pretending that he will see them the following day to resume their daily battle for survival. As the young Laferrière witnesses the impact of Gasner's death on his friends and as he observes his friends' fearless quest for immediate retaliation and justice, Laferrière comments, "Il y a des types comme ça. Moi, je suis plutôt lâche" (There are guys like that. I, on the other hand, am rather a coward).[56] The public image of Gasner takes on a heroic quality as the night progresses and the news of his death spreads. Laferrière simply writes, "Gasner est en train de le [un héros] devenir dans la conscience populaire, alors que je ne fais que penser à moi. Je suis un individualiste né" (Gasner is becoming [a hero] in people's consciousness, whereas I only think of myself. I am a born individualist).[57] Like Mersault, Laferrière does not attempt to turn his personal tragedy into a cathartic moment for the reader. His choice to leave Haiti, which is in itself symbolic of Haitian suffering and the traumatic severance with the mother(land), is presented as no more than a personal choice of someone who does not want to end up like Gasner, the Haitian hero.

Michael Dash has skillfully argued that Haitian Diasporic literature did away with Haitian exceptionalism by deterritorializing Haiti and presenting a more global, multifaceted vision of its people and culture. Dash credits Danticat and Laferrière for broadening the Haitian literary horizon. According to Dash, the deterritorialized writings of Danticat and Laferrière opened up the old *terroir* literary canon of works such as Jacques Roumain's *Gouverneurs de la rosée*, "a narrative directed itself uniquely at those people, places, memories, and cultural forms that were seen to be uncontaminated by modernity and consequently imbued with a Haitian specificity."[58] But with deterritorialization comes the fear of erosion, and particularly so in small countries that have experienced big tragedies. As Edouard Glissant says about Martinicans' exposure to the world, "Nous n'en finissons pas de disparaître, victimes d'un frottement du monde. . . . Il reste à crier le pays dans son histoire vraie: hommes et sables, ravines, cyclones et tremblements, végétations taries, bêtes arrachées, enfants béants" (We never stop disappearing, victims as we are of world friction. . . . We have yet to cry the country in its true history: men and sands, ravines, cyclones and earthquakes, dry vegetation, torn animals, gaping children).[59] To avoid erosion, historical protectionism becomes a civic duty and the cultural obligation of the deterritorialized—the so-called tenth department. As seen earlier, Jan J. Dominique and Danticat think of *dyaspora* as carrying a duty of memory, something that already suggests a mission against historical erosion. "In Danticat's case," Dash writes, "there is increasing evidence of an oeuvre that moves beyond fiction to give the placeless subject a voice as witness to the unspoken and unspeakable horrors of recent Haitian history."[60]

Yet, Laferrière chooses to offer a different take on protectionism, one that is more provocative because it is *dégagé* rather than *engagé*. For him, Haitian protectionism means protecting oneself, coming first. Laferrière's main claim: "Le droit de penser à moi. Ah! j'y tiens à ce droit" (The right to think of myself.

Ah! I hold on to that right),[61] and Laferrière's main accomplishment "Un Haïtien a réussi à ne penser qu'à lui-même (pas dans le sens physique du terme,
mais plutôt métaphysique). C'est l'une des opérations les plus épuisantes de
ma vie" (A Haitian succeeded in thinking only about himself [not in the physical sense of the term, but rather metaphysically]. This is the most exhausting
endeavor of my life).[62] In *Le cri des oiseaux fous*, Laferrière sets the scene of
his departure around the theme of *Antigone*, Sophocles' Greek tragedy to be
performed in Creole the night of his departure. *Antigone* is a tragedy about
civil disobedience: "l'histoire de cette ardente femme qui a affirmé en face du
pouvoir politique et de tous les pouvoirs que seul l'amour l'intéressait, que
l'amour était au-dessus du devoir d'Etat" (the story of this fervent woman who
asserted in front of the political power and all the other powers that she was
only interested in love, that love was above the duty of the State).[63] Danticat's
*Create Dangerously*, on the other hand, sets the scene of her preoccupations
around Albert Camus' *Caligula*, a tragedy that seems to best reflect Haiti at
the time when Marcel Numa and Louis Drouin, the two young revolutionaries, were publicly executed by the forces of the Duvalier regime. "In his play
*Caligula*, Albert Camus, from whom I borrow part of the title of this essay,
has Caligula, the third Roman emperor, declare that it doesn't matter whether
one is exiled or executed, but it is much more important that Caligula has
the power to choose."[64] The main difference between Danticat and Laferrière
plays out in their chosen tragedies. Both may use tragedy as a background for
their writing, yet Laferrière identifies with the play that promotes civil disobedience for the sake of individual passions, while *Caligula* projects a more
general, nation-based reflection on political consciousness.

While some of Laferrière's narratives take place in Haiti,[65] he makes a point
of using Haitian history only to set the scene, just as *any* writer (meaning
any writer who does not supposedly come from a history of exceptionalism)
would do. For example, in the first short story from *La chair du maître* (The
flesh of the master) precisely titled "To Set the Scene" (Pour planter le décor),
the author makes a point of referring to Baby Doc's dictatorship only as a way
to situate the importance of sexuality in Haiti in the 1970s, the time when the
story takes place. The same is true for *Le goût des jeunes filles*, whose historical background is based on the 1970s sexual decadence of Jean-Claude (Baby
Doc) Duvalier. Laferrière does not use the Duvalier setting to get back at the
dictator's violent regime in a direct *engagée* literature; instead, Duvalier is only
there to show that private pleasures and physical ecstasy are good remedies for
repression. As he says:

Mon livre le plus politique est *Le goût des jeunes filles* parce que la question se pose sur un plan privé comme sur un plan public. Le sexe dans
un contexte de dictature.

(My most political book is *Le goût des jeunes filles* because the question is
addressed at a private as much as at a public level. Sexuality in a context
of dictatorship.)[66]

In *L'odeur du café* (*An Aroma of Coffee*, 1991), a sentimental and nostalgic book
about Laferrière's childhood in Petit-Goâve with his dear grandmother, Da,
the context of the Duvalier regime is relevant to the extent that it explains the
premise of the story. After his dissident father left for exile in New York when
Laferrière was five, Laferrière's mother thought it safer to keep her son in a
discreet rural place, far from the public exposure of Port-au-Prince, which
is why, as one can see in *L'odeur du café*, the young Laferrière lives with his
grandmother and not his mother.[67] *L'odeur du café* does not address the suffering of being raised under the Duvalier regime; instead, the impetus of the
novel lies in the homage made to a beloved grandmother.

Laferrière gives a new meaning to Haitian exceptionalism and the *journalis* culture. Through his chronicle, based on the pleasure of everyday life, the
author is able to show that one's cultural origins, and the history that comes
with them, does not necessarily take precedence over the individual. Haitians
are just as prone to be ravished by the sight of a dragonfly covered with ants[68]
and just as inclined to write about the beauty of inconsequential fragments of
life[69] as any other writer endowed with a so-called unexceptional collective
history.

In his first book, Laferrière chose to exclude Haiti, but with time, the immigrant writer has learned to include his native island in his writing. Laferrière presents a country where a Creole Proust can also enjoy doing nothing, merely sitting on the front porch of the family house next to his beloved
grandmother, both grandson and grandmother looking at the horizon while
daydreaming. The irony of Laferrière's literary strategy lies, paradoxically
enough, in the subversive nature of ordinariness. Comparing Haitians to other
peoples, Laferrière asks himself, "Are we that different from others?" Aware
of the blasphemous nature of his question, Laferrière then adds, "Chaque fois
que j'essaie de poser le problème sous cet angle, on m'accuse d'être un vendu
qui refuse d'accepter la spécificité authentique de la culture haïtienne" (Every
time I try to raise the question from that angle, I'm accused of being a sellout

who refuses to accept the authentic specificity of the Haitian culture).[70] Accused of being a sellout for claiming cultural unexceptionalness, for being an ordinary novelist, Laferrière is confronted with the lack of *acti*vism in his act of aesthetic production.

In *The Location of Culture*, Homi Bhabha promotes a theory of hybridity and argues, "In the fin de siècle, we find ourselves in the moment of transit where space and time cross to produce complex figures of difference and identity."[71] In this 1994 study, Bhabha foresees postcolonial studies moving toward an interstitial nexus, "beyond narratives of originary and initial subjectivities," and right into "those moments or processes that are produced in the articulation of cultural differences."[72] Laferrière's own take on transit theory tends to turn Bhabha's question of hybridity upside down. Laferrière moves beyond dichotomous definitions of identity, as Bhabha advocates, to simply almost unambitiously reach ordinariness. In other words, Laferrière does deconstruct the idea of "originary and initial subjectivities,"[73] but for the single sake of a poetics of cultural common ground. In a Fanonian twist, Laferrière rejects the fixating Western gaze that imposes on Haiti an overdetermination that ultimately turned Haiti into a "cursed" country.[74] Laferrière's demythification of Haiti, his calculated lightness regarding Haiti's series of tragic fates, does not necessarily amount to apoliticalness. The writer creates a politics of *dégagement* (unaffectedness) and a literature of *désengagement* (disengagement) as an act of resistance against the Haitian culture of journalism-itis.

Because Laferrière has built his entire persona on *désengagement*, using Haitian misery only as contextual background, his books *L'énigme du retour* and, even more so, *Tout bouge autour de moi* are very much of a surprise, since both feed on Haitian tragic fate. The first addresses with compassion social and economic problems and, more specifically, the painful question of hunger in Haiti, while the second deals with a devastating natural disaster. Either Laferrière has decided to meet Danticat on her turf of *engagement*, rolling up his sleeves to embody the role of the "echo chamber, gathering and then replaying voices from both the distant and local devastation"[75] or Laferrière's new literary strategy is simply a marketing move by a writer who has nothing more to say about himself and moves on to the next topic: Haitian tragedy. Or again, as *Je suis un écrivain japonais* seems to suggest, it could be that it might not matter what Laferrière wants and who he is; the writer will come to embody whatever readers project onto him. For example, if you are Japanese, he might as well be Japanese for you ("Qui peut m'empêcher d'être un écrivain japonais? Personne" [Who can stop me from being a Japanese writer? Nobody]).[76] If readers want to see a sense of *engagement* in his most recent books, they can also freely do so. As a floating signifier fixated by public opinion alone, Laferrière is a cynical response to the *journalis* culture, a culture that assigns an act (as in *acti*vism) in any Haitian aesthetic production.

## Diasporic Testimonial Writing

Ross Chambers observes that the inhospitable nature of the traumatic truth justifies why some testimonial narratives do not benefit from a "compensatory partnership of witness and audience."[77] Indeed, the audience will not always respond collaboratively to the challenging literacy of testimonials such as Holocaust or AIDS testimonial narratives. The main challenge that Chambers sees in testimonial writing is the impertinence of the story: first, the impertinence of survival, "The witness must have *survived*, or more accurately, *be surviving*,"[78] and second, the impertinence of the unspeakable story meant to be told—the witness being faced with "the trope of 'words fail me' or 'I can't express.'"[79] In the case of diasporic testimonial writing, another layer of impertinence comes into play, which is the questionable legitimacy and authority of the diasporic testimonial narrative. Even if immigrant writers happen to be present in the native land at the critical moment of a tragedy, claiming or taking the right to report the story back to the surrogate home can be subject to controversy. Should the testimonial that has been written from the safety of the adopted home be perceived as opportunistic in the eyes of those left behind to pick up the pieces? Or is it simply the duty, as Danticat and J. J. Dominique see it, of the diasporic writer to leave the native home behind in order to tell the story of the victims who remain there? In *Create Dangerously*, Danticat uses a passage from Laferrière's *L'énigme du retour* to justify her identity as a diasporic writer: "What is certain," writes the novelist narrator [Laferrière], "is that I wouldn't have written like this if I had stayed there / maybe I would not have written at all / living outside of our countries, do we write to console ourselves?"[80] In other words, leaving provides the opportunity to report (*reportare*) or, etymologically speaking, to carry *back*.

*My Brother*, by the Antiguan-American writer Jamaica Kincaid, offers a good illustration of the dual parasitism and remittance inherent in the diasporic testimonial genre. *My Brother* could be defined as a proxy testimonial, since Kincaid tells not of her dying but of someone else's dying. In it, Kincaid recounts the experience of losing her brother to AIDS. The writing of the story was initiated after the brother's death, a condition that obviously prevented the brother from ever telling his story. *My Brother* is all the more a proxy kind of testimonial given that Kincaid does not live in Antigua and thus writes the story in a location other than the site of the event. The misplacement, or physical inadequacy, of the testimonial production is the main feature of the proxy genre of telling. Literally speaking, the sister tells the tragedy *in lieu* of the brother, in the *place* of the brother, when in fact the place of death is Antigua and not America, where Kincaid lives and writes. Kincaid's appropriation of her brother's story can be seen as a form of metonymical usurpation: speaking *instead* of the brother is an unscrupulous substitute for speaking *in the space of* her brother. There is a kind of irreverence in the displacement of the event, as Kincaid voraciously takes both the elocutionary place and the physical place of the victim. Indeed, even if Kincaid made several trips to Antigua to support her brother through his ordeal of dying of AIDS, it cannot be said that she belongs to the place of the dying brother. As she admits, when she heard of her brother dying (via the phone), Kincaid "was in [her] house in Vermont, absorbed with the well-being of [her] children, absorbed with the well-being of [her] husband, absorbed with the well-being of [her]self."[81] And after the death of the brother, she says:

> Not really more than a week after he was buried in the warm and yellow clay of the graveyard in Antigua, I resumed the life that his death had interrupted, the life with my own family, and the life of having written a book and persuading people simply to go out and buy it.[82]

Kincaid depicts the consequences of her brother's death on her life with startling emotional transparency. The author's crude honesty leaves us no choice but to question the legitimacy of her *place* as a diasporic witness writer. Is it Kincaid's place to tell the story instead of the people left behind? This type of questioning will inevitably jeopardize, to paraphrase Chambers, the audience's supposed "collaborativeness in the reception of witnessing narratives."[83]

Mireille Rosello, in *Postcolonial Hospitality*, looks at the rhetoric of French politicians regarding immigration; the critic questions the motivation behind the use of "host" and "guest" when speaking about France and its immigrant population (*terre d'accueil*). After all, as Rosello rightly points out, an initially welcome guest can turn out to be a "bad Guest who overstays his or her welcome, pockets the silver, or ransacks the fridge."[84] For that reason, according to Rosello, the image of the immigrant as a guest is insidiously ambiguous and not necessarily a positive one. In a similar rhetoric of *terre d'accueil*, the returnee can also be seen as a form of immigrant, a nonnative visitor. The prodigal child holds a comparable duplicity, being both a welcome and potentially overbearing guest. When he or she returns for a visit, the diasporic subject is, in most cases, no more than a guest of the native people, with all the limitations that the ambiguous connotation of the word entails. Laferrière learned the hard way of his "guest" status while on a visit to Haiti. In *L'énigme du retour*, the author recounts an awkward incident where he attempted to buy a newspaper in the street for which the vendor demanded an unusually large amount of money. Laferrière let the vendor know that he was a local and that, as such, he expected to pay the local price. The vendor, however, insisted that Laferrière was not one of them: "Pour moi vous êtes un étranger, comme n'importe quel étranger" (For me you are a foreigner, like any other foreigner).[85] It is assumed that, as a *dyaspora*, Laferrière should pay the price of a guest as well as be a guest. As a guest in his own country, the diasporic visitor must also be on his best behavior. Everybody already knew that Laferrière had checked into a room in a nearby hotel (as a guest) during his visit instead of staying with his mother—a definite faux-pas for a *dyaspora*?

Within the context of diasporic testimonial writing, the above image of the *dyaspora* helping himself to food from the refrigerator raises the question of authorship as ownership, a question that haunts *My Brother*. Kincaid's testimonial is concerned with sexuality and physical decay, two intimate issues often not willingly exposed to the public eye. Kincaid's brother, Devon, is no exception. Toward the end of the book, Kincaid admits that her brother "would not have wanted to hear how he looked when he died, he would not have wanted to know how everyone behaved, what they said and what they did"[86]—all the more reason to believe that he would probably not have wanted the rest of the world to hear the specifics of his dying. Kincaid candidly concedes that her brother would not have approved of being exposed as a person with AIDS. Like anyone else in Antigua, Devon did not want to open up to the public for fear of retaliation. Talking about a gay Antiguan man who had paid the price of becoming an anathema for openly sharing the news of his dying of AIDS, Kincaid says, "It is perhaps because of the reaction to his publicly identifying himself as a person with AIDS that no one in Antigua will do this again."[87] Likewise, when she finds out about her brother's closeted homosexuality a few weeks after his death, Kincaid mentions the valid reasons why her brother would not have wanted to publicly share his homosexuality: his "fear of being laughed at, his fear of meeting with the scorn of the people he knew best were overwhelming and he could not live with all of it openly."[88] Kincaid repeatedly reminds the reader that her brother did not want his intimate story to come out. Ironically enough, Kincaid stresses Devon's unwillingness to *come out* in a narrative that precisely does just that: out him. As Chambers says again to tell the story, "The witness must have *survived*, or more accurately, *be surviving*."[89] Kincaid has indeed the asset of survival on her side, the opportunistic impertinence of life, a life that she resumed in Vermont as a writer telling about the not-to-be-shared suffering of her people back home.

It remains to be asked whether Kincaid's proxy testimonial calls for a stealing-the-goods-from-the-fridge metaphor. Kincaid indubitably profits from her impudent chance of being alive, of being in the position to tell the story instead of the dead brother who is stripped of words. Unlike Danticat's aforementioned survivor's guilt, Kincaid exhibits the convenience of survival, which she daringly flaunts in the materiality of her written testimonial. In the following passage, the author even presents the opportunism of life as the exclusive purview of the testimonial writer:

> When I heard about my brother's illness and his dying, I knew instinctively, that to understand it, or to make an attempt at understanding his dying, and not to die with him, I would write about it.[90]

The testimonial itself, the telling of the other's death, is not only the proof but also the reason for the teller's survival. Like a crow, the sister feeds off the brother's cadaver in order to stay alive. Sucking in his story and then spitting it out to the world are her means of survival as a diasporic writer. But with poised reflection, what first sounds self-serving and parasitic can also be interpreted as a sharing and generous act of witnessing. In her article on *My Brother*, Kezia Page draws a parallel between Kincaid's material contribution to the effort to fight her brother's disease and the book that came out of the experience. The author sees *My Brother* as a remittance text on two levels:

> One, it tells the story of the author maintaining her family, specifically her sick brother, with cash and kind from abroad. Two, *My Brother* is written outside of the geographical location of the Caribbean, outside of Antigua, then sent home to Antigua. Undoubtedly, this involves a remembering and representation of home from "foreign" eyes. Kincaid's decision to call on memories and revisit Antigua is indeed a form (however warped) of preserving home from the outside. Even though this act of nonfiction may be construed as much more self-centered than a monetary remittance, it does play its part in a cultural economy.[91]

Page's take on Kincaid's testimonial is very forgiving because it situates *My Brother* in a logic of a cultural economy in which, regardless of the real intent of the diasporic writer, the mere act of writing about home means giving back to the community. In Page's logic, national memory is the stable currency of diasporic testimonial writing; it is the mental preservation of home, no matter what kind of light the testimonial will shed on home.

Page's logic is a double-edged sword, for while it validates the purpose of telling about home, it also justifies why the community at home feels that the diasporic writer owes them. When Danticat released *Breath, Eyes, Memory*, a fictional story that mentioned a presumed Haitian tradition of a mother finger-testing her daughter's virginity, the Haitian community vilipended Danticat for false and wrongful representation of their country. Danticat felt compelled to defend herself. She wrote an afterword in the next edition of *Breath, Eyes, Memory* in which she explained, in the form of an open letter to the victim of the testing, that she had not expected that her character's singular story would be made to represent every Haitian woman. In a 2003 interview, Danticat further discussed her motivation for writing the afterword:

> I was so naive that I never anticipated that people wouldn't be able to make the distinction between one family's story and an entire group's story. I wanted to write the afterword not as an apology or a defense, but as a clarification.[92]

Interestingly enough, what caused so much opposition to Danticat is also what justifies her role as a diasporic writer. As mentioned earlier, when Danticat says that it is maybe her "purpose, then, as an immigrant and a writer—to be an echo chamber, gathering and then replaying voices from both the distant and the local devastation,"[93] she meant this was a positive and fulfilling function of the immigrant writer. The diasporic writer gives back through reporting (*reportare*, "carrying back"), through speaking *in lieu of* and *in the place of* the people of Haiti. But the diasporic function, as enunciated by Danticat, also carries a dark side. The diasporic voice, in that sense, reports, records, and speaks for the one and indivisible Haitian community. Danticat's voice, as an echo chamber of her people's suffering, is intrinsically linked to the collective, each word serving her community, for better and for worse.

If indeed the diasporic writer is the voice of the community, and as such, each testimonial is *always already* a remittance text giving back to the community through preservation of memory, what first sounds self-serving is never totally so. The goods are never unduly ingested by the guest but only taken and used to bake a dish that will somehow eventually serve the host. As Page notes, what makes one person Caribbean is not merely his or her Caribbean residence but also, or instead, the memory of the native Caribbean land that one is able to share: "Kincaid's work is called Caribbean literature not only because she is from Antigua, but also because Kincaid's texts are all set in her memory of home and in many ways reflect her own experience as a Caribbean native and migrant."[94] But the fact that those memories are taken out of the native land and catered to a readership outside of the native land, sometimes against the will of the native, is something on which Page does not dwell. Even though the critic pertinently lays out the cultural remittance value of diasporic writing, her angle washes out the "dirty" side of the testimonial work. And yet, it is a side that the diasporic writer is not afraid to acknowledge and share with the reader. By insisting on how private Devon meant to remain, Kincaid purposely presented her writing as intrusive and inhospitable. It is clear that the writer did not seek a collaborative partnership between writer and audience; *My Brother* provocatively flaunts its impertinence, making it difficult for the reader to embrace it. Likewise, Danticat willingly admits that her task can be at times opportunistic and quite self-serving. For example, her love for her family and community did not stop her from outing her cousin as an AIDS victim, despite her aunt's plea for discretion. In *Brother, I'm Dying*, Danticat speaks about her cousin, Marius, who died of AIDS in Miami five years after he illegally immigrated to the United States. In *Create Dangerously*, a few years after the publication of *Brother, I'm Dying*, Danticat reveals that her aunt had earlier pleaded with her never to reveal in her books that her beloved son had died of AIDS, a cause of death that the aunt herself still refused to acknowledge: "I know this is what you do now. This thing with the writing. I know it's your work, but please don't write what you think you know about Marius."[95] Reporting the most private pain is, however, Danticat's means of living. Reporting is her subsistence as a *dyaspora* who needs to cling to anything that ties her back to the severed native home, but reporting also means telling on home, another form of subsistence for an immigrant writer who lives off her writing. Danticat never had a moment of hesitation about the decision to expose her cousin,[96] even at the very moment when her aunt was pleading with her: "I bowed my head in shame, wishing I could apologize for that, but the immigrant artist, like all other artists, is a leech and I needed to latch on. . . . I wanted to ask for forgiveness for the essay that in my mind I was already writing."[97]

Duplicity is part of diasporic writing. Writers, like Kincaid or Danticat, admit to struggling with it. This duplicity creates a mixing of genres that is oxymoronic by nature. Diasporic testimonial writing is self-serving and parasitic on the one hand but meant to be shared and distributed on the other. Chambers said the following about testimonials:

> The audience responds with anxiety to a text that poses a difficult taxonomic, and hence also interpretative, problem: it appears to espouse a familiar genre but to be making unfamiliar and possibly inappropriate use of the genre; it feels like an error or an infraction, yet the error is apparently deliberate and designed to be expressive of a truth.[98]

In the case of diasporic testimonials, the taxonomic problem does not inhere so much in the coexistence of the familiar and the unfamiliar, which Chambers approximates with Sigmund Freud's *unheimlich*, but rather in the ambivalence between friend and foe, welcoming and repelling. Following on Freud, Ross Chambers calls "untimely" the ambivalence of the "time out-of-joint,"[99] while Homi Bhabha uses the word "unhomely" to express the in-between space, a blurring of frontiers between the domestic and the private space. Following in the tradition of the Freudian *déclinaison* of *unheimlich*, the ambivalence at play in diasporic testimonial can be said to be "unwelcome-ly." The neological "unwelcome-ly," from *will* (desire) and *cuma* (guest), designates the unwillingness to be a pleasing host in spite of having expressed a desire to invite the reader in as a guest.

While Kincaid's testimonial writing embodies the taxonomic ambivalence of genres (friendly/unfriendly) with defiance, Danticat expresses it with apologies and shame, and Laferrière presents it with his usual air of unaffectedness and casualness. Laferrière was in Port-au-Prince when the earthquake shook Haiti on January 12, 2010. Soon after the earthquake, Laferrière was able to drive with a fellow writer to his mother's house to check on the damages and potential casualties. With great relief, Laferrière was to learn that everybody was safe. During his short visit, he was able to talk with his nephew. While looking at fissures on the wall, he told the nephew:

-Je vais écrire, fais-je
-Ah, oui . . .
-Je vais écrire sur ça.
Je n'arrive pas encore à le nommer.

-(I am going to write, I say
-Oh, yeah . . .
-I'm going to write about all this
I can't put a name on it yet.)[100]

To which the nephew bluntly replied, "J'aimerais que vous n'écriviez pas là-dessus" (I'd rather you didn't write about this).[101] The nephew claimed that the 2012 earthquake belongs to his generation. Dictatorship is Laferrière's turf, while telling about the earthquake should be left to the nephew. Laferrière's reaction is no different from Danticat's when faced with a similar family request: "Je ne peux pas te faire une pareille promesse, aucun livre ne prend la place d'un autre" (I can't make you that promise, no book can take the place of another).[102]

## Timeliness and the Exclusivity of Reporting

Drawing a paradigmatic relationship between personal and collective tragedy is a delicate maneuver, just like comparing Danticat's and Kincaid's testimonials on family members affected by AIDS with Laferrière's chronicle of the 2010 Haitian earthquake. In both cases, however, the personal soon overtakes the collective. Whether it is a private body infected by a deadly virus or a whole nation coping with the aftermath of a natural disaster, the telling of those tragedies initiates a breach of family trust. It all boils down to the diasporic writer's unwillingness to remain silent in spite of a brother's, an aunt's, or a nephew's plea. To what extent is diasporic status, the safe distance physically separating the telling from the told, responsible for this defiant breach of trust? The diasporic writer is in many ways, indeed, a ghostwriter: missing but haunting in action in the homeland. In his study of the testimonial genre, Chambers argues that "the constants (an experience of a certain kind, the witnessing of the experience, the anticipated and real reception of the witnessing)"[103] bring the singularities of each atrocity, whether it be personal or national, together under a common umbrella for discussion. In the context of diasporic witness narratives, the same is true: whether it be Kincaid's testimonial on dying of AIDS in Antigua, Danticat's revealing the story of her cousin who died of AIDS, or Laferrière's chronicle of the 2010 Haitian earthquake, the constant in those three singular events is the impertinence of the witnessing voice. The witnessing voice is noticeably absent in the homeland after the tragedy has struck.

Laferrière's *Tout bouge autour de moi*, however, is still different from Danticat's and Kincaid's testimonials in that Laferrière's text is defined by a unique immediacy of witnessing that blurs the frontiers between the diasporic and the firsthand testimonial genre. Danticat and Kincaid offer instances of diasporic testimonials in which the witness does not attend the tragedy, or at least not the premise of it. Danticat's and Kincaid's returns to their respective islands were initiated after or as a consequence of dying or death. This kind of testimonial is defined by the distance separating the immigrant writer's voice from that of the victim. Especially with Danticat, the poetic of geographical discrepancy or misfire is an important part of her writing. Danticat always seems out of place; she is never where things seem to be happening for her people. In *Brother, I am Dying*, Danticat could not reach her uncle at the crucial moment of his death when he needed her the most to survive the ordeal of mistreatment at Krome (the detention center for illegal immigrants in Miami). During the 2010 Haitian earthquake, Danticat once again missed her chance to be present. She was scheduled to attend the Etonnant Voyageurs International Book Festival in Port-au-Prince in January 2010, which is when the earthquake hit Haiti. Because of health concerns about her one-year-old daughter, however, the writer had canceled the trip. Danticat describes the challenge of vicarious suffering and the guilt of absence. After the earthquake, Danticat was on the phone with family members, crying and apologizing, telling them, "I'm sorry I can't be there with you."[104] Laferrière, however, attended the Etonnant Voyageurs festival and was in Hotel Karibe, the designated hotel of the festival, enjoying an early dinner with Rodney Saint-Eloi, the editor of the Montreal publishing house Mémoire d'encrier, when the magnitude 7.5 earthquake shook the island. Many writers and scholars were in Hotel Karibe that day because of the festival. Luckily, the hotel did not collapse, unlike another luxury hotel, Hotel Montana. On January 12, 2010, Laferrière became a surviving witness of the biggest natural disaster to ever hit his native land.

There is no doubt that the timeliness, though fortuitous, of Laferrière's presence in Haiti at the time of the earthquake makes his testimonial voice more pertinent. In *Tout bouge autour de moi*, the author stresses the critical role of timeliness in the experience of the 2010 Haitian earthquake. In a chapter appropriately titled "J'étais là" (I was there), the author targets the politicians, intellectuals, and demagogues who "ne rateront aucune occasion pour glisser un 'j'étais là'" (won't miss a chance to sneak in an "I was there")[105] as a way to flaunt the exclusiveness of their firsthand witnessing. The substantiation of "j'étais là" ("*a* 'j'étais là'") is Laferrière's way of pointing the finger at the commodification of this natural disaster. The pride that some have taken in having been there that day, the human vanity of trying to build envy of being present at a tragedy around the earthquake carries indeed an air of self-promotion, as if one could gloat over the skills of serendipity. In this chapter, Laferrière discusses also the geopolitics of the "j'étais là" phenomenon, arguing that the earthquake changed the national landscape of Haitian identity. He explains:

> Un type qui a toujours vécu à l'étranger et qui se trouvait à Port-au-Prince par hasard ne sera pas affublé de l'horrible qualificatif de "diaspora," il est à l'instant anobli. Il devient un "j'étais là." Tandis que quelqu'un qui a toujours vécu en Haïti et qui était absent du pays ce jour-là perd un peu de son lustre national.
>
> (A guy who always lived abroad and who happened to be in Port-au-Prince won't have to suffer from the horrible designation of "diaspora," he will at once be ennobled. He becomes an "I was there." While someone who has always lived in Haiti and was out of the country that day will lose a bit of his national lustre.)[106]

Laferrière's comments bring to mind the difference between the 2010 earthquake in Haiti and the 9/11 attacks on the Twin Towers in New York City. As Danticat points out, September 11, 2001, brought people from different cultures and nationalities together under the same sentiment of being "all Americans."[107] The 2010 earthquake in Haiti, on the other hand, as described by Laferrière, had the consequence of exacerbating the identification of physical presence with national identity. In other words, having been in Haiti on January 12, 2010, at 4:53 p.m. is what makes the witness a "true" Haitian. Next to the real experience, brandishing an "I ♥ Haiti" in the streets of an American city does not amount to much. The appropriateness of location in the act of witnessing seems to have never mattered so much as in the instance of the 2010 Haitian earthquake. The earthquake literally shook the Haitian ground, removing the right to the land out of reach of the dyaspora. Michael Dash's question "Are Haitian writers of the diaspora truly Haitian or just the creations of a global postcoloniality or migrant literature in North America?,"[108] though asked in 2008, ironically became obsolete in the geopolitical climate that immediately followed the earthquake. As Laferrière demonstrates, Haitian-ness has become, at least temporarily, a mere question of physical and punctual pertinence, two qualities that Laferrière was arbitrarily granted the day of the earthquake. In *Illness as Metaphor*, Susan Sontag argues that "real events often seem to have no more reality for people than images,"[109] which may explain the aforementioned sentiment that September 11 belongs to all and made us all American. While experiencing the 9/11 attacks through a television set gave everybody a sense of proximity with the tragedy ("j'étais là"), the Haitian earthquake remains a visual-less event exclusive to those who lived through it. Those who were not firsthand witnesses only saw the aftermath of the quake on television, not the event itself. In that sense, the Haitian earthquake can be said to be not "real" due to its lack of confirmation through immediate images. Jean Baudrillard argues that September 11 is before all an image to which is added, as a bonus, the reality of the event.[110] The Haitian earthquake, in contrast, is an event without the bonus of the image. Through reporting and testifying, the physical witness is the only one who can turn the abstraction of the earthquake into a real visual representation.

Laferrière, as an exclusive "j'étais là" subject, is part of the group of witnesses that can account for the Lacanian objet petit a event—namely, the ineffable earthquake. Because of the Etonnants Voyageurs festival, Laferrière's group happens to be mostly writers, and most of them were from abroad. The bitter irony of the timeliness of the book festival accounts today for the series of firsthand testimonials published since January 2010. Along with *Tout bouge autour de moi*, Rodney Saint-Eloi's *Haiti Kenbe la!* (*Haiti Never Give Up!*), Lionel-Edouard Martin's *Le tremblement* (*The earthquake*), and Michel Le Bris's *Haiti parmi les vivants* (*Haiti, Among the Living*) add to the list of firsthand testimonials.[111] Laferrière, Saint-Eloi, Martin, and Le Bris were all participants at the book festival and all guests at the Karibe Hotel at the time of the earthquake.[112] In their respective books, they offer distinct testimonials on the same event that they experienced in the same location. This is a unique situation in the production of testimonial writing. The result is an intertextual echo chamber of singular yet common voices.

Interestingly enough, there is one common and omnipresent token that brings those testimonials together: Thomas C. Spear, professor of French at Lehman College, CUNY. Spear was at the festival to record the activities, and he was also staying at the Karibe Hotel. In this nexus of testimonials, Spear is presented as a trope, a rhetorical tool, a literary device—something that, interestingly enough, Spear the scholar is wont to use, expose, and deconstruct in his own work. In *Tout bouge autour de moi*, Laferrière uses the image of the funny professor as a device to counterbalance the gravity of the moment. To do so, Laferrière uses three main figures: himself waiting for the lobster he has just ordered, Rodney Saint-Eloi waiting for his fish dinner at Laferrière's table, and Spear drinking a beer nearby. Here is how Laferrière stages the scene:

> Spear a perdu trois précieuses secondes parce qu'il voulait terminer sa bière. On ne réagit pas tous de la même manière. De toute façon, personne ne peut prévoir où la mort l'attend. On s'est tous les trois retrouvés à plat ventre, au centre de la cour.

> (Spear lost three precious seconds because he wanted to finish his beer. We do not all react the same way. Anyway, nobody can tell where death awaits you. We all three ended up lying flat on our stomachs in the middle of the courtyard.)[113]

In Laferrière's staging, Spear serves as a distraction from the unfathomable real event. The event is never really mentioned, the description focusing instead on Spear's amusingly out-of-character reaction to the event. In the tradition of the Shakespearean buffoon, Spear carries the truth of the event even though he is presented as a mere diversion from the real. Spear is the solecism of the reporting: seemingly inadequate and a failure in its syntactic appearance but profoundly telling in effect. Spear fills in the blanks of the unrepresented tragedy, filling in the silence between the first signs of the seismic event and the moment when the guests are on the floor. The emphasis Laferrière puts on the inconsequential detail of Spear finishing up his beer is a manifestation of the author's lack of words to convey the real event. Because Laferrière cannot do justice to the event, he uses Spear to disguise the silence. Ironically enough, Spear somehow fulfills his role as a scholar and literary critic, bringing his contribution to the author's silence as he meaningfully connects the dots.

In Lionel-Edouard Martin's version of events, Spear holds a comparable role. The following moment takes place after the earthquake, when all the hotel guests gather outside, waiting for the next step. Martin has just met Spear, who kindly offers him a cigarette. A group that includes Martin and Spear is conversing on the tennis court of the Karibe Hotel, where all the hotel guests took refuge after the earthquake. Spear says the following (reported here by the author in free indirect speech):

> Là, ni petits-fours ni champagne, et Spear ne cessait de le déplorer: on devrait, dans de telles situations—"on," la direction de l'hôtel—donner du "rhum" aux survivants que nous sommes, faisant sonner "rhum" et "som-

mes" comme pour marquer la rime, car on ne savait à quel assaut, dans les heures qui suivraient, nous aurions à monter. Comme à la guerre, voyez-vous, celle de 14–18, où le rhum des colonies était une arme, comme le fusil, la baïonnette . . .

(Here, neither petits fours nor champagne, and Spear kept lamenting over it: one should, in such situations—"one" being the hotel manager—give "rum" to all of us survivors, stressing "rum" [rhum] and "are" [sommes] so as to emphasize the rhyme, since who knows which assault we will have to overcome in the following hours. Like at war, World War I, where rum from the colonies was an arm, like a gun, a bayonet . . . )[114]

Unlike with Laferrière, in Martin's account of events, Spear is not a diversion during the event; he is a diversion *after* the event. Nonetheless, as in Laferrière's book, Spear is the jester, the diversion and distraction from the ever-postponed telling of the event. Spear is like the well-needed rum that unwinds the body and the brain after a trying experience.

The third version, Saint-Eloi's version, is somehow different from the two previous ones. This writer's intentions seem more ambitious and thus more constrained than those of Laferrière and Martin. Saint-Eloi seeks to reach transparency and exactitude in the description of the exact moment of the earthquake, which makes the tone of his testimonial less anecdotal and less concerned with the participants at the festival. Saint-Eloi's testimonial is exactly that: a testimonial that does not use rhetorical tools, figures of speech, and literary devices to report the event. Because of it, Spear only plays a very practical and serious role in his narrative; the French professor is mentioned as the one who helps Saint-Eloi get his suitcases after the earthquake, a dangerous task: "Je repère les valises. Je les sors par la terrasse et les glisse à Tomas [Spear]. Ensuite, je ressaute la balustrade. Chaque second compte" (I locate the suitcases. I carry them out through the terrace and hand them to Thomas [Spear]. Then, I jump over the baluster again. Each second counts).[115]

It can still be argued that, even in Saint-Eloi's narrative, Spear is the middleman. Spear is again presented as the one who gets the writer out of a difficult situation, alleviating the weight of his responsibility, down to the weight of a suitcase.[116]

The literary critic, as usual, has the last word. Spear did not remain speechless after the publication of Laferrière's and Martin's testimonials. Here is what he had to say:

At one point in my teaching career, Kurosawa's classic 1950 film *Rashô-mon* was used as a tool in the campus's introductory humanities seminar to develop critical perspectives from different points of view. Four perspectives of an event—a crime in the film—lead to four different stories. Reading Lionel-Edouard Martin's *Le tremblement* and Dany Laferrière's *Tout bouge autour de moi*, the first books published about the event, I thought of the divergent perspectives of *Rashômon* as I discovered a character, played by myself, in these earthquake narratives of January 12, 2010, alternatively preoccupied with distributing cigarettes and dreaming of rum, or risking his (my) life for a beer. While I might want to correct some detail—for example, that I do not smoke Marlboros—something of the insignificant truth inevitably transpires from these two voices; the tennis court of the Karibe Hotel in Port-au-Prince becomes a curious echo chamber of the life and death stories of a disaster of epic proportions. But there are millions of perspectives of what was seen and felt, as with those of September 11, 2001.[117]

When Spear says "echo chamber," the expression does not only refer to the multiple stories surrounding the event, but it also touches on the intertextual nature of the reporting. Spear adds his own echo to this intertextual chamber by giving his feedback on Laferrière's and Martin's characterizations of himself. In this passage, it is assumed that Spear sees that his clownlike and Diogenic characterization clashes with the life and death stories of "epic proportions." Yet, Spear does not condone this somehow faulty characterization but instead reproduces it. After the initial pretense of rectifying the injustice done to the true story of the earthquake (and mostly his role in it), Spear ends up correcting only the brand of cigarettes. Like Laferrière, Spear diverts the so-called true story of the earthquake with a Spear gimmick. By focusing on the inconsequential, laughable, and mundane detail of his cigarette brand, Spear repeats Laferrière's synecdochical tactic: replacing the magnitude of the event with the minuteness of the mundane. In so doing, Spear confirms that the story can never be fully told, not even by an eyewitness who happens to be an academic. This synecdochical shift is not unlike the one in Charlotte Delbo's *Auschwitz et après: aucun de nous ne reviendra* (*Auschwitz and After: None of Us Will Return*, 1997), which condenses the horror of the Holocaust into an image of a single tulip on the windowsill of a Nazi working at the concentration camp. The tulip stands for everything that cannot be conveyed through words, everything left to the imagination.

The synecdoche is, in some cases, a noble expression of discretion, as it reveals a bashful intention of minimizing the measures of epic proportions in order to make the tragedy fit into a human frame of understanding. In the cases aforementioned, it also calls upon the selfless act of seeking, for purposes of relief, laughter in the midst of the tragic. But the synecdochical practice can also create a taxonomical challenge (to paraphrase Ross Chambers), given that it offers ambiguous genres caught between selflessness and individualism. These writers are special in more than one sense. The mention of the lobster, the fish, and the beer at the luxurious Karibe Hotel; the staff running around to assist the guests sleeping on the tennis court after the earthquake; and the jokes about the absence of petits fours and other delicacies all leave an aftertaste of incongruity and discordance next to the known death toll and the extent of the apocalyptic destruction. If the jarring gap between individual lightness and epic gravity is read in sole terms of rhetoric and literary devices, the ambivalence is appropriate. It becomes less so, however, if the testimonial is expected to function as a *journalis*-like "echo chamber" of human tragedy. In that latter context, the unbearable lightness of telling would make smarty Spear or funny Dany the epitome of incongruousness.

Coming back to the "j'étais là" phenomenon, the particular strength of *Tout bouge autour de moi* lies in the concept of timeliness as, paradoxically enough, an out-of-place situation. The pertinence of the attendance is, so to speak, hijacked by the location of the attendance. The book festival scheduled at the Karibe Hotel on the day of the earthquake has created a special kind of testimonial genre, very much self-referential and relatively cliquey. Le Bris (*Etonnants voyageurs*), Spear (CUNY), Saint-Eloi (*Mémoire d'encrier*), Laferrière, and Martin are staged in an exclusive enclave, while the real action is described as taking place outside the hotel:

> L'hôtel est situé un peu à l'écart de la route principale. Cette centaine de mètres suffit pour nous couper des autres. Nous quittons cette vie d'hôtel pour tomber dans la chaudière de Port-au-Prince et son étouffante réalité.
>
> (The hotel is located slightly off the main road. Those 100 meters are enough to isolate us from the others. We leave the hotel life to go into the furnace of Port-au-Prince with its suffocating reality.)[118]

The bitter timeliness of the festival brought writers and university scholars within the confines of a luxury hotel, recreating what Laferrière had described a year earlier in *L'énigme du retour* concerning Hotel Montana (quoted earlier), a somewhat safe place that still gives the feeling of living dangerously. Unlike Karibe Hotel, Hotel Montana was heavily hit by the earthquake, which shows that there is no guaranteed safe place during an earthquake. Yet, the guests of Karibe Hotel were fortunate enough to have been spared in that specific hotel described by Laferrière as a "vie d'hôtel," protected from the Port-au-Prince reality. Their survival at Hotel Karibe has granted a particular cachet of exclusiveness to the testimonials produced on the 2010 earthquake. Aside from the guest list of the Karibe Hotel, other well-known characters appear in those testimonials, among them the Haitian writers Lyonel Trouillot and Franketienne, and the American scholar Joëlle Vitiello (Macalaster College). The "timeliness" of the festival had the privilege of bringing writers and scholars together on the scene, which instantly turned the event into literary material, making not only Spear but all of the other Haitian literature–related characters key figures in the telling of the tragedy. As Haitian literature–related characters, they all know one another and reappear in distinct testimonials, which gives the impression of a literary world set apart from the rest of the earthquake-impacted island.

Concerning Laferrière, his timeliness is out of place not only due to the question of exclusiveness that pervades his testimonial narrative in *Tout bouge autour de moi*, but it is also instigated by the opportunity, a semantic parent of "opportunism," that the timeliness of his presence in Haiti has granted him. As previously discussed, Laferrière has never dwelt on the misery of his native land in his writing. Rejecting the stigma of tragic exceptionalism, the writer has favored a literary world where normalcy and individualism prevail over sociopolitical concerns and activism. Up to *L'énigme du retour*, Laferrière has held on to a complex fictional Dany, a fictional alter ego who, though he has made a name for himself in the literary world, does not have much to give back to the Haitian community. Laferrière refuses to sentimentalize his *dyaspora* returnee condition; he has no problem admitting in his books that he usually stays at a hotel when he visits his mother in Haiti. The writer nonetheless acknowledges the guilt inherent in his condition of being a returnee: "Je me sens mal à regarder ma ville du balcon d'un hotel" (I feel bad looking at my city from the balcony of a hotel).[119] The narrative in *L'énigme du retour* is built on a duality between the pressures of conforming to the model *dyaspora* involved in remittance and Laferrière's distant (physically and emotionally) position. The aunt asks Laferrière to rescue Dany, Laferrière's nephew of the same name. "From what?" asks Laferrière. In *L'énigme du retour*, Laferrière never confirms his intention to help the nephew but only comments on the fact that the aunt should not be talking for her son who is old enough to decide for himself. Laferrière makes no efforts to present himself as a Good Samaritan *dyaspora*. "Ton père a été, malgré sa disparition, le seul homme de cette maison" (Your father, in spite of his disappearance, was the only man in the house),[120] pursues the aunt. Laferrière simply comments, "Une façon de me reprocher mon absence des derniers jours, sinon des dernières décennies" (Her way to blame me for my absence of the last few days, if not the last few decades).[121]

Laferrière's literary impersonation has matured over the years, but in *L'énigme du retour*, the reader finds the same sense of provocation as in *Comment faire l'amour* (controversy has paid off for him). The older fictional Dany character shows the same aesthetics of dandyism and casualness as before, yet with an added and significant touch of pathos. Laferrière is different from Danticat, who feels the need to express her guilt at being a powerless *dyaspora*. When asked to help a family member migrate to America, Danticat openly expresses her embarrassment at not being able to meet her family's high expectations of her back home: "My family members in Haiti have always overestimated my ability to do things like this, to get people out of bad situations. . . . I hope I can help. I have sometimes succeeded in helping, but mostly I have failed."[122] Instead, Laferrière chooses the high road of offhandedness by providing no justification, no excuses for his inactivity and immobility. His unaffectedness is, undoubtedly, a literary pretense. Danticat herself, in her short story "Night Talkers" (*The Dew Breaker*), presents a fictional Laferrière (Dany) character who is remarkably human and committed; this Dany must be close to what she knows of the real person. In "Night Talkers," the character is named Dany, like Laferrière; he is nicknamed Old Zo (*Vieux Os*), also like Laferrière; and he is depicted as being very fond of his aunt named Da, which is similar to the young Laferrière's relationship with his grandmother, also named Da. The Dany of Danticat's short story is presented as being humanly, emotionally, and financially expressive. Danticat's characterization of Laferrière would lead us to conclude that Laferrière's literature of unremittance is not based on an unwillingness to give back but rather on an unwillingness to *admit* giving back. This brings us back to our initial observations on Peter Hallward's disclaimer and Jana Evans Braziel's "acknowledgments." Laferrière forces us to question whether the Haitian diasporic book and the academic book on Haiti are themselves caught in a politics of exceptionalism in which any publication on Haiti must come with a guarantee of immediacy, direct knowledge, and contribution to the community. If the academic assures in her book to have *direct* knowledge of Haiti, does her assurance guarantee the credibility of the reporting? If the author admits in the book to give back, does his admittance guarantee that the book itself gives back to the community?

It is January 12, 2010—the day of the earthquake. The world is in turmoil, Haiti has been hit by the most devastating natural disaster in its history, people are trapped under collapsed buildings, many lay dying in the streets, and many more are dead. Just as Haitian disasters call for external rescuers to repair the destruction and protect those who have survived, those disasters also call for external rescuers to salvage the memory of their history and the story of their survivors. In other words, UN Peace Makers, Médecins Sans frontières, and international volunteers do in the field what the gatekeepers of memory aim to do in their books. Laferrière has always claimed to keep two things with him at all times: his passport and his little black notebook. That day was no different. After the earthquake, his notebook was at hand, ready for its owner to jot down some ideas for the next book. There was, however, a dilemma: should he be a man of action, given the immediacy of the situation, or should he remain a man of letters? Laferrière infallibly chose the latter. In *Tout bouge autour de moi*, Laferrière depicts himself as his usual immobile character: "La révolution est possible et je reste assis dans mon coin" (Revolution is possible and I stay put in my corner).[123] The title of his testimonial, *Tout bouge autour de moi* (*Everything Moves around Me*), refers first to the land impacted by the seismic event and second to the people reacting to the seism. In both cases, Laferrière remains the stoic pillar, the unshakable "moi" of the title. Laferrière himself stresses the irony of men of letters unexpectedly finding themselves in an immediate disaster zone: "Nous discutons de cette situation inédite tandis qu'autour de nous les gens courent dans toutes les directions comme si l'on se trouvait dans une zone de guerre" (We are reflecting on this unprecedented situation while people around us run in all directions like in a war zone).[124]

Laferrière does not stay put for long, however, and this is where the controversy occurs. As Danticat writes in *Create Dangerously*:

> Dany was criticized by some Canadian journalists for leaving Haiti after the earthquake. He should have stayed with his people, they said. And I have no doubt that if he were a doctor, he would have, but at that time, his role was to bear witness and he did it beautifully; going on the radio and television and writing his essays of fifteen hundred words or less to

add one more voice to our chorus of bereavement and paralyzing loss, a loss that is echoed in his 2009 novel *L'énigme du retour* (*The Return*).[125]

Right after the earthquake hit the island, Laferrière was faced with the choice of returning to Canada in the midst of destruction and death or staying in Haiti. He chose the former. Danticat defends Laferrière's choice, but her defense is of course subject to debate.

Saint-Eloi's *Haiti: Kenbe la!* also addresses Laferrière's choice, using the same argument as Danticat's. Saint-Eloi reports telling Laferrière that he must leave to bear witness: "La communauté internationale a besoin de ta voix et de ta parole" (The international community needs your voice and your words).[126] In *Le tremblement* (*The Tremor*), Martin also justifies Laferrière's decision to leave:

> Dany et Rodney s'interrogent: où est leur place, où est l'urgence? Car les pompiers l'affirment: l'aide nationale arrive massivement. . . . Dans ces conditions, rester pour quoi faire? Mieux vaut peut-être agir de l'étranger, témoigner, tirer profit de sa notoriété pour entretenir le feu d'une empathie précaire . . .

> (Dany and Rodney question themselves: where should they be, what is most pressing? Since the firefighters confirm: massive national aid is on its way. . . . Under those circumstances, what is the use of staying? Taking action from abroad might be better, bearing witness, benefiting from his notoriety to keep the story alive given the precariousness of empathy . . . )[127]

One of Martin's facts is wrong, however. It is not "Dany and Rodney" who questioned whether they should leave or stay in Haiti. Rodney had no choice but to stay; as a non-Canadian citizen, he could not benefit from the plane offered by the Canadian embassy. Martin is therefore misinformed when he writes, "Dany and Rodney ont pris leur décision: regagner le Canada pour agir" (Dany and Rodney made up their mind: go back to Canada to act there).[128] The situation with Rodney makes a significant difference to the context of the decision. Here is Laferrière's version of events:

> Il y a un départ vers 13 heures à partir de l'ambassade. Il faut vite prendre sa décision. Saint-Eloi ne peut pas partir car il n'a pas encore la citoyenneté canadienne. Pas question de partir sans Saint-Eloi. Je demande aux gens d'attendre un moment. On se retire sous un arbre pour discuter de

la chose. Partir ou rester? Toujours le même dilemme. J'ai rejoint, après un moment, les gens de l'ambassade pour leur dire que je venais avec eux. . . . Finalement, je me dis que c'est peut-être la dernière fois qu'on me propose un rapatriement.

(There is a departure at 1 p.m. from the embassy. One has to decide quickly. Saint-Eloi cannot leave because he is not yet a Canadian citizen. There is no way I would leave without Saint-Eloi. I ask others to wait a moment. We retreat under a tree to discuss the situation. To leave or to stay? Always the same dilemma. I went back, after a while, to the people of the embassy to let them know that I was leaving with them. . . . After all, I tell myself, it's the last time I may be offered to be repatriated.)[129]

Once again, Laferrière offers no apologies, no altruistic justification for his choice to leave besides his concern that he might not be offered another repatriation after he turns down this one. This episode echoes the one that he experienced at age twenty-three, when his mother had decided to send him to Canada after Gasner's assassination. His first reaction was "Arrête, Maman. Je ne peux pas me sauver seul. Je ne le pourrais tout simplement pas" (Stop, Mom. I cannot escape by myself. I simply couldn't).[130] Those were his words the day he actually left Haiti for good.

In both cases, during the Duvalier regime in 1976 and after the earthquake in 2010, Laferrière had to leave his island. Saint-Eloi writes in his testimonial after the departure of Laferrière:

S'établit une atmosphère lourde, un coup de cafard. Nous avons perdu quelqu'un ou quelque chose qui nous maintenait en vie. . . . Le danger ne peut plus être repoussé. On sent soudain l'imminence de la faille. Une autre faille . . . le premier qui part rompt le cercle de l'illusion.

(A heavy atmosphere fills the air, feeling down. We've lost someone or something that kept us alive. . . . Danger cannot be kept at bay. We suddenly feel the imminence of the problem. Another problem . . . the first to leave breaks the circle of illusion.)[131]

Even though Saint-Eloi, like all others, presents Laferrière's choice as a civic duty, the cost of his departure is painfully felt by the ones left behind. Laferrière's decision is like the diasporic testimonial genre, an uncertain mixture of opportunism ("the last time I may be offered to be repatriated") and remittance ("you must leave and bear witness"). More than the writer, the diasporic testimonial text is the real renegade, half-remittance and half-parasitic text. Back in Montreal, Laferrière becomes like all the others, all of us, a vicarious witness living the aftermath of the earthquake on television. *Tout bouge autour de moi* is a hybrid genre of testimonial: it begins as a firsthand witness testimonial, but it very soon moves on to a virtual witnessing genre.

How, indeed, could Laferrière have written a whole testimonial on barely two days of postearthquake experience in Haiti? From his bed, kept awake by posttraumatic insomnia, Laferrière watches his fellow Haitians on television. He empathizes with their ordeal, tortured by the idea of having lost touch with them. That being said, he is also cognizant of the privilege of his position:

Et ma raison s'est enfuie de mon corps me laissant seul avec cette panique. Que dire alors de ceux pour qui le cauchemar continue toujours? Je parle de tous ceux qui n'ont pas à penser à ce qu'on ressent quand on doit continuer à fouler un sol qui s'est dérobé sous vos pas.

(And my reason left my body, leaving me alone with this panic. What about those for whom the nightmare continues? I'm talking about all those who don't have to think about how it must feel to keep walking on a ground that failed them.)[132]

Writing about how it must feel to be there without having to be there is the best analogy to describe the nature of diasporic testimonial writing. It is all at once an untimely, unhomely, and unwelcomely condition of still feeling right there, at the critical moment of the event, the legs still shaking with the impact of the blow, yet so far away, in a remote and safe place of survival.

# V. S. Naipaul and Jamaica Kincaid

## Rhetoric of National Dis-Allegiance

> The whole of Combray and its surroundings, taking shape and solidity, sprang into being, town and gardens alike, from my cup of tea.
>
> MARCEL PROUST, *A LA RECHERCHE DU TEMPS PERDU*

As Stuart Hall observes, "What we say is always 'in context,' *positioned*."[1] Admittedly, determining the context of the enunciative production is a crucial step in the reception of a statement given that the point of emission helps define the meaning of the enunciation. To that effect, Stuart is right to assert that cultural identities are not a question of essence but of positioning, provided that the idea of *positioning* embraces more than the context of emission. The context of reception is indeed equally important and potentially even more instrumental in producing meaning. Gaston Bachelard famously argued in *La poétique de l'espace* (*The Poetics of Space*, 1964) that writing is always *logée* (housed)[2] in the childhood home. But Bachelard's axiom has yet to be applied to the context of reception. Not enough emphasis in literary scholarship has been put on the residence of the reception, even though reception is undoubtedly, in so many ways, also attached to the birthplace and the childhood home. In instances in which enunciation is determined by geographical distance, the distance will inevitably affect—positively or negatively—the quality of the communication between the migrant enunciator and the home recipient. Many years ago, when a traveler called home, there was often a lot of interference on the telephone line. Because of the technology of the time, it was expected that distance would affect the quality of the call. Even today, some people who get an international call are surprised when they hear the unobstructed voice of the remote caller as though he or she were calling from just next door. Geographical distance is meant, or at least expected, to make communication between the migrant and the home particularly strenuous. The same applies to migrant writing. In English, disturbing noises on the line are commonly referred to as "static," a word that underlines the, ironically, not so static status of the caller. In French, those interferences are called *parasites*. As Michel Serres pointed out in *Le parasite* (*The Parasite*, 1982), the French "parasite" refers to both disruptive noises in communication (phone) and foreign organisms feeding off a body. The French polysemy is interesting because it pinpoints the dual condition of the diasporic writer. Due to distance-induced static (*parasites*), displacement makes it challenging for the writer to come to an understanding with his home community. But also, the migrant writer is herself a parasite, since home, though now foreign to her, still remains the main fodder for creative production.

That being said, an important distinction needs to be kept in mind while addressing parasitic writing. Technically speaking, the migrant writer does not specifically feed off home but rather off the *trouble* with home. Indeed, when there is static on the line, the reaction is not to bring the phone nearer to oneself but rather to keep moving until the communication becomes clear. Likewise for the writer, migrant writing is motivated by the very trouble with reception at home. In that sense, migrant writing is a form of sustainable parasitism feeding on its own migrancy. To put it concisely, the migrant writer is by nature, technically, a troublemaker. The controversial figures of the Trinidad-born writer V. S. (Vidiadhar Surajprasad) Naipaul and the Antigua-born writer Jamaica Kincaid exemplify a genre of migrant writing in which the question of bad reception at home, the native home, is the defining quality of its production.

## England versus North America

V. S. Naipaul was born in 1932 in Trinidad, and Jamaica Kincaid was born in 1949 on the island of Antigua. Both left their islands at an early age. Kincaid left Antigua for Westchester, New York, at the age of sixteen, with the prospect of working as an au pair for an American family. As for Naipaul, he left Trinidad at barely eighteen with a view toward studying in England at Oxford University. Their departures were driven by comparable motivations; their early and irrevocable departures were, in both cases, the consequence of feeling like misfits on their respective islands. But in spite of the fact that they share a common experience of national severance, it needs to be stressed that Naipaul and Kincaid are different types of Caribbean migrant writers. As Patrick French explains in his biography of Naipaul, Naipaul's parents were extremely supportive of their son's education in England. They believed education to be "the route to progress."[3] Naipaul also was adamant about getting a scholarship to England because, for him, a scholarship meant getting off of his doomed island: "By the time I was about twelve,"—French quotes Naipaul as saying—"I had decided to get away, to leave. The scholarship protects you, gives you money for some years. It is protection."[4] Unlike Naipaul, Kincaid suffered from not getting her mother's support for her education. Kincaid mentions in her autobiographical book *My Brother* that her mother removed her from school before she was sixteen for no apparent reason: "She just did it, removed me from school."[5] She would later move to the United States to work as an au pair.

Receiving scholarships from the motherland or a neighboring island in order to achieve greater success abroad is something that has been amply depicted by Caribbean writers such as Zobel, Walcott, Hall, and Condé. The scholarship was often the colonial *passage obligé* for higher education and the only route to scholarly progress, as Naipaul's parents insisted. Compared to Naipaul, Kincaid has followed what was for Naipaul's generation an unconventional path, not only because of her lack of scholarships abroad but also because she chose to move to North America instead of the motherland. What separate Naipaul from Kincaid are essentially gender, age, and social class. As discussed earlier, Carine M. Mardorossian addresses these differences in her book *Reclaiming Difference*, indicating that the first generation of Caribbean writers were mostly men going to Europe for their education, whereas the second generation were mostly female Caribbean migrants leaving home for America with the purpose of earning money as blue-collar workers. As Mardorossian points out, the first generation of European-oriented and -educated migrants were perceived, semantically, as *exiles*, while the second generation are considered *immigrants*. Naipaul's type of migration—namely, his uteral move to the motherland—speaks to the old colonial center-margin dialectic. As such, Naipaul's move calls to be read within Ashcroft, Griffiths, and Tiffin's *The Empire Writes Back*, the influential study of postcolonial discourse that famously argued that the metropolitan center is meant to be the main "target" of reception for the commonwealth writer. Naipaul belongs to a postcolonial discursive trend that takes for granted that the motherland is always the destination of migration and often the source of the migrant's (oppositional or endorsing) statement.

Naipaul's position of migrant enunciation arches back to the old Deleuzian and Guattarian rhetoric of minor literatures in which the minor voice is assumed to position itself either against or within, but always *in regards to*, the metropolitan center.

Kincaid, on the other hand, represents a visionary aptitude for the Caribbean diasporic writer to think outside the colonial paradigm. By choosing North America as a context of production, Kincaid has engaged in a transnational discourse that does not necessarily assume that the European center is her predestined target of reception. In the context of literary production, Kincaid is neither an immigrant nor an exile, but rather a second-generation diasporic writer who is defined by a process of uprootedness (*deterritorialization*) from her colonial history. By pitching her voice in North America, Kincaid has avoided the common paradigmatic—the West and the Rest—discursive position of the Commonwealth writer. Her voice is hence part of, as Stuart Hall calls it, the New World Presence, the *Présence Américaine*,[6] a terra incognita of self-expression.

That being said, even though the context of displacement in Naipaul's and Kincaid's lives largely differs, both writers have been subject to a comparable controversial reception among "their home people," broadly defined here as the Caribbean and Third World communities. When Naipaul and Kincaid, as exile and second-generation diasporic writers, speak about home, they inevitably also speak to home in the dual sense of addressing and calling upon home, as any writer addressing a lost home does. But with the notion of "calling upon" (home)—namely, to convene—often comes a connotation of agreeability. To convene, from the Latin *convenire*, means to come together upon convenience and suitability. Yet, when Naipaul and Kincaid call upon home in their writing, their intention is not to be agreeable. On the contrary, those writers challenge the assumption of migrant writing as an act of convening by emphasizing the very inconvenience of coming together, of reuniting. Their enunciation is nonagreeable precisely because it offers no apologies for its displacement and shows no intention of going back home, and yet, it keeps calling on home.

## Home

If one accepts, as Bachelard suggests, that the main residence of writing is always the childhood home, then diasporic writing, more than any other genre, calls for a positioning in relation to or in contrast to the lost birthplace. But the fact that Bachelard defines his poetics of space in terms of topophilia feeds on a Proustian nostalgic poetic that does not necessarily apply to the second-generation diasporic writing. Bachelard's topophilia is based on the debatable assumption that writers carry an infallible love for the lost home of innocence and that they yearn to imaginatively go back to the house of their formative years. But many would agree that the thought of the happy childhood place, infused with the Combray moment of the *madeleine*, is the wealth of the privileged, which is not to say the "Western" privileged. When the Trinidad-born Naipaul received the Nobel Prize in Literature in 2001, his acceptance lecture opened and closed with reflections on Marcel Proust. While Proust, as Naipaul says, is "a master of happy amplification,"[7] Naipaul, in contrast, is very down-to-earth. The Trinidadian writer comes across as coldly and methodically accurate in his vision of the world and his position in it. In his lecture, Naipaul makes it clear that his childhood house did not look anything like Proust's happy space. Talking about the restricted walls of his childhood home in Trinidad, Naipaul says:

> So as a child I had this sense of two worlds, the world outside that tall corrugated-iron gate, and the world at home—or, at any rate, the world of my grandmother's house. . . . The world outside existed in a kind of darkness; and we inquired about nothing.[8]

How miraculous—as Naipaul apparently wants his audience to see—that a writer like him, given the obstructive and limiting nature of his upbringing, flourished to the extent of becoming one day a Nobel Prize winner. Naipaul's recollection of home is meant to show where he comes from and how far he has gone, both figuratively and literally. After quoting Proust—"talent is like a sort of memory which will enable them finally to bring this indistinct music closer to them"—Naipaul adds dryly as a closing remark to his lecture, "Talent, Proust says. I would say luck, and much labour."[9] Naipaul hereby readjusts Proust's words to fit his humble abode. No wonder Naipaul once said, "I was born there [Trinidad], yes. I thought it was a great mistake."[10]

Some have taken offense at the fact that Naipaul thanked Britain and India in his Nobel lecture, but the Trinidadian-born and -raised author did not thank Trinidad. This intended omission adds to the numerous disgraceful attitudes Naipaul has displayed toward his home place. Though not a topophobia per se, Naipaul's relation to his childhood island sounds like innate estrangement, a condition that is incidentally unrelated, at least partially, to his exile status. Naipaul experienced a sense of estrangement very early on in his life. Milan Kundera defines the German *Entfremdung* as a process of geographical estrangement—namely, a feeling of newly acquired unfamiliarity with the location of one's origin—which is a phenomenon that the exile is bound to experience upon returning home after a long absence. In Naipaul's case, the *entfremdung* cannot be said to be the result of a *process*. His feeling of estrangement with the home place has always been there, even when he was a child, even while living in Trinidad. Naipaul says about his early days in Trinidad, "I just felt I was in the wrong place."[11] Trinidad apparently never spoke to him, which, however, did not stop Naipaul from speaking to the island once he became a writer in England. He spoke to, or rather misspoke of, his island in *The Middle Passage*, a 1962 travel narrative about the Caribbean in which Naipaul wrote comments that have been detrimental to the image of his home place. In his biography of Naipaul, French suggests that Naipaul has been perceived as a traitor for bad-mouthing or ignoring his island. But what, exactly, makes Naipaul a traitor? Had Naipaul remained in Trinidad and been just as vocal about the limitations of his island, would he have been anathemized all the same?

A similar question applies to Jamaica Kincaid, a successful Antigua-born writer living and writing in North America who never shied away from criticizing her native island in her various writings. Kincaid notoriously speaks of Antigua and its people with a mixture of shame and resentment. In her memoir *My Brother*, where Kincaid recounts her return to Antigua after a long absence, Kincaid writes, "I only understand why it is that people lie about their past . . . why anyone would want to feel as if he or she belongs to nothing, comes from no one, just fell out of the sky, whole."[12] Like Naipaul, Kincaid writes from the position of an immigrant writer experiencing detachment from the native land. The context of enunciation is also one of *Entfremdung*. But again, as with Naipaul, it is an innate kind of *Entfremdung*. She left the island at an early age with determination and with no intention of ever moving back. In *A Small Place* (1988), Kincaid deems Antigua a small place—"small" referring not only to the size of the island but also to its limitations:

> It is as if, then, the beauty . . . were a prison, and as if everything and everybody inside it were locked in and everything and everybody that is not inside it were locked out. And what might it do to ordinary people to live in this way every day. . . . It is just a little island.[13]

Kincaid's description echoes Naipaul's words about his childhood home; both immigrant writers emphasize the physical and simultaneously intellectual limitations of being born and raised in a small (post)colonial island. Naipaul's and Kincaid's travel narratives subvert the exotic preconception in favor of an "inotic" vision of the island. In *Essay on Exoticism*, Victor Segalen writes that the prefix *exo-* in *exoticism* refers to "everything that lies outside the sum total of our current, conscious everyday events."[14] In contrast, *inoticism* bears the weight of the ordinary and the daily, and somehow the underwhelming. By nature, travel narratives deal with locations *outside* the travelers' familiarity and thus with what should be un-mundane spots. Yet, even though they use the travel narrative format, Kincaid and Naipaul manage to offer interior and inotic visions of their islands that unabashedly show the imperfect burgeoning skin of their recently or newly independent national territory. In 1996, Stuart Hall notices "interrogation marks which have begun to cluster thick and fast around the question of 'the postcolonial.'"[15] Since the 1990s, there has indeed been a tendency among scholars to question whether postcolonial writers are "cultural brokers" (Hall) or "comprador intelligentsia" (Appiah) who are making a profit off the "ubiquitous academic marketability"[16] of the postcolonial. Graham Huggan spoke of the "postcolonial exotic" as "the global commodification of cultural difference."[17] But postcolonial exoticism is not what Naipaul and Kincaid sell. On the contrary, the in-otic is their postcolonial currency.

## Persona Non Grata and Ungratefulness

Various Caribbean writers have attributed their productivity and creativity to the benefits of geographical displacement. The Guadeloupean Maryse Condé has always been vocal about her lack of creativity in Guadeloupe in comparison to her noticeable productivity in North America. The Haitian René Depestre in *Le métier à métisser* (*Racial Jenny*) wrote that his nomadic identity— what he refers to as his "identité banian" ("banyan" being a rhizome tree with multiple branches in Asia)—has been instrumental to his literary production. As he wrote, "Mon identité multiple se nourrit à la fois du *chez-soi insulaire* de Jacmel (Haïti) et du *chez l'autre hexagonal* de Lezignan-Corbières (France)" (My multiple identity feeds both on my insular sense of home in Jacmel [Haiti] and the hexagonal other's home in Lezignan-Corbières [France]).[18] There is no doubt that Naipaul's decision to become a writer has been determined by his life outside of his native island of Trinidad, as he has often publicly argued. But beyond his creative freedom, migrancy has also granted Naipaul a sense of freedom in his private life. It is no secret today that, during the early decades of his marriage to Pat Hale, Naipaul visited prostitutes. Naipaul was a "prostitute man," as he told the *New Yorker* in a 1994 interview with Stephen Schiff. The kinship between the French word *péripapéticienne* and the adjective *peripatetic* is not coincidental. *Péripapéticienne* refers to a prostitute, while *peripatetic* alludes to the notion of vagrancy and traveling (from Aristotle's itinerant philosophy). The prostitute is known to pace the street in order to attract potential clients, hence the traveling connotation in *péripapéticienne*. Inversely, *peripatetic* is linked to the *péripapéticienne* because vagrancy is transgressive, like prostitution.

When it comes to Naipaul, his peripatetic life, in the bilingual sense of traveling and going to prostitutes, speaks to both his digressive *and* his transgressive natures. From the Greek *perpateîn*, the French *péripapéticienne* calls attention to the negative and dirty connotation of the vagrant. The French almost seems to suggest that migrancy is what leads to transgression. In *Loiterature*, Ross Chambers explores the ideology of loitering, a peripatetic expression. The author says that loitering is directly associated with the notion of the trivial: "trivial comes to us from the Latin *trivialis*, meaning having the character of a three-way crossing (and of those who frequent three-way crossings)."[19] For Chambers, three-way-crossings are the epitome of a location for loiterers, and because of its loiterly nature, this location is "associated with bad people, places, and practices of ill repute."[20] As Chambers points out, the three-way hangout often brings to mind people of bad intent because loafing and digression are more often than not, for the nonloiterers, seen as part of disorderly conduct. In Naipaul's situation, the emphasis is obviously not on the three-way crossing; Naipaul is not that kind of loiterer. But there is indubitably a sense of disorderly conduct in Naipaul's vagrant life and in his unapologetic peripatetic lifestyle.

Naipaul uses the same candor and crude honesty to confess his disloyalty toward his birth nation as in talking about his wife. About his birthplace, Naipaul admits:

> I just wanted to go to a prettier place. I didn't like the climate. I didn't like the quality of the light. I didn't like the heat; I didn't like the asthma that it gave me. I didn't like a lot of the racial tensions around me. These were connected as much with Africans as with Europeans. I wanted to be free of all that. I didn't like the music; I didn't like the loudness.[21]

This is only one example of Naipaul's common and infamous rants against his native island. Naipaul never seems to miss a chance to address the dreadfulness of living in Trinidad. That being said, Naipaul is just as brutal about his intimate life. During his marriage to Pat, his love life, to paraphrase Chambers on *trivialis*, forked out in two directions. Pat was aware of Naipaul's twenty-year affair with the Anglo-Argentine Margaret Gooding but did not expect the news to be publicized. As Naipaul admits, he did not think about the context of reception before speaking:

> I gave an interview to the *New Yorker*, to a nice man, Stephen Schiff, and I mentioned things I really never thought would come back to the house. I remember making a decision to tell Stephen Schiff about it. A simple decision. It all occurred in my head the moment it was happening.[22]

Once Naipaul realized the magnitude of the story and the impact it could have on home, the concerned husband tried to shield his wife from reading the story in the *New Yorker*, to no avail. Naipaul would later admit that Pat never recovered from the devastation of the news. The humiliation and betrayal were lethal. Naipaul said later that his revelations killed his wife.

Again, Naipaul's indiscretions are to be understood in the double sense of his extramarital/extrageographical life and his undue telling about it. Naipaul's indiscretions define him as a migrant writer and, ultimately, as a persona non grata. Even though Naipaul allegedly did not think of the reception at home when he went public with his relationship with prostitutes, his story is nonetheless defined by that reception or, more specifically, by the *prospective* reception at home. His account in the *New Yorker* is indeed proleptically determined. Its real momentum lies not in the telling but rather in the wife receiving the news at home and ultimately dying from it. As French writes, "Two of his sentences ran around the world, chased by Tina Brown's publicity machines: 'So I became a great prostitute man, which, as you know, is highly unsatisfactory. It's the most unsatisfying form of sex.'"[23] What most gave dramatic meaning to his revelation is that he was a married man and that his wife stood on the receiving end. The very public disloyalty to his wife echoes his very public disloyalty to his native island. This is where the amalgam between his *péripapéticienne* and peripatetic life comes into play. Publicly castigating one's birthplace and childhood place is a rather uncommon practice for a migrant writer, particularly when the writer comes from a small postcolonial nation. It is assumed that, again as Gilles Deleuze and Félix Guattari have argued, small nations or communities rely on "active solidarity" and "collective responsibility,"[24] even more so when the subject leaves the group and relates to the group from a distance. But for Naipaul, national loyalty at all costs seems overrated next to true honesty.

No matter the intended ideological context of production, migrant writers are inevitably recalled by their communities and brought back to their unwilling role of national spokespersons. They speak for their countries, which, however, does not mean that they have to speak well of their countries. As Kincaid says in an interview, people do not like to hear the truth about themselves, and not all truths are good to tell: "People do not like it—Antiguans, especially the ones living here, will say: 'It's true, but did she have to tell everybody?'"[25] Kincaid has said that for a long time, she only wrote for one reader—what she calls the "perfect reader."[26] This reader happens to be William Shawn, her father-in-law at the time and the editor of the *New Yorker* from 1952 to 1987. Since she never felt at home in her native Antigua, it is not surprising that Kincaid's perfect reader is American, from her chosen world of the *New Yorker*'s[27] white American elite. But as much as Kincaid's intended context of reception is her adopted country, her native home is never far behind. Like Naipaul, once Kincaid left her country, she partially interrupted her communication with home. In her autobiographically inspired novel *Lucy*, Kincaid recounts the story of an alter ego leaving the Caribbean to work as an au pair in the United States. Kincaid writes about Lucy leaving Antigua: "eventually she had to cross the sea, where the Devil couldn't follow her, because the Devil cannot walk over water."[28] Kincaid gives the impression that the water separating herself from her native island is a protective fluid that keeps her at peace and her native island at bay. Kincaid always had a conflictual relationship with her mother and with Antigua. Anger with the motherland is Kincaid's leitmotif in her writing, from *Annie John* (1985), to *A Small Place* (1988), *Lucy* (1990), and *My Brother* (1997). In *Lucy*, Kincaid describes the real story of her experience as an au pair cutting all epistolary ties with her mother, refusing to open the letters from her mother in Antigua, until she is forced one day to open them and to find out belatedly about the death of her father. Her head-in-the-sand attitude summarizes her relationship with home. Her family continues to have an impact on her despite her unwillingness to address them.

When her brother was diagnosed with AIDS, Kincaid says she had been in a phase of not being in contact with her mother, which happened occasionally in their difficult relationship. When the phone eventually rang, the writer says she was "absorbed" with her own "wellbeing"[29] of herself in the comfortable life that she was sharing with her husband and children in Vermont. The relationship between the context of enunciation and the context of reception is nowhere better illustrated than in the image of the call from home. As absorbed as the writer may have been in the comfort of her immigrant life, home calling is the haunting background that threatens the fixity of her actual here and now. The call is that which eventually forces the writer to address home. As much as Kincaid's books speak about Antigua, they also speak to Antigua.

And Antigua talks back to her. The call from home sidetracks the intended context of reception (William Shawn) and diverts the enunciation back home. The call *from* home announcing the news of her brother's disease eventually transformed itself into a book *about* home, *My Brother*.

*My Brother* is a valuable literary accomplishment due to its unique angle on the question of static and reception at home. The memoir tells the story of Devon, Kincaid's younger brother in Antigua who is dying of AIDS, while Kincaid, the sister, interrupts her life in Vermont in order to care for him in his final days. In the memoir recounting the death, Kincaid creates a subtle analogy between the virus eating Devon to death and Kincaid's family sucking her blood like parasites. Both the virus and the family are portrayed as feeding on otherwise healthy bodies. The parasite carries a twofold meaning in Kincaid's memoir. *Parasite* first refers to Kincaid's family in Antigua. These are people who, contrary to what she would have liked, heavily depend on her for survival. And *parasite* carries also a French connotation in that it calls to mind static (Serres) on the line, an interference that makes the communication between Kincaid and her family challenging. Reestablishing phone contact with her family in Antigua only reminds Kincaid of how much she wants to have nothing to do with them. If only Devon could die quickly so she could resume her life in Vermont sooner: "It would be so nice if he would just decide to die right away, and get buried right away and the whole thing would be done right away and that would be that."[30] Devon dying of AIDS adds an extra layer to the question of parasites, since the acquired immunodeficiency syndrome virus is itself a parasite that does not let go of Kincaid. AZT, the drug used to treat AIDS, was not available in Antigua, so Kincaid, a resident of the United States, obtained the medication for her brother. Kincaid is the go-between; through her remittance role, she becomes the migrant responsible for Antigua's subsistence and literally for its survival. Kincaid is aware of the benefits that her migrant status offers to Antigua. Her self-addressed question, where she wonders what would happen to Antigua if the people there "did not have a sister who lived in the United States"[31] to provide for them, says it all. *My Brother* is pervaded by a "what-if" atmosphere precisely because Kincaid is very clear about her reluctance to provide for her family in Antigua.

As mentioned in chapter 2, the critic Kezia Page came to the defense of the controversial Kincaid in an article about *My Brother* and Kincaid's remittance toward her native island. Her defense, though very pertinent, does not address the context of Kincaid's remittance. Kincaid is indeed a remitter, yet of a reluctant kind, which is an aspect of Kincaid's personality as a migrant and a writer that cannot be overlooked. Relying on Belinda Edmondson's distinction between exile and migrant status, Page argues that Kincaid's assistance to her native Antigua, albeit not always given with good grace, makes her not only a financial but also a cultural benefactress. According to Edmondson, while the migrant is an economic provider, the exile is a provider whose role is to culturally give back to the native country. In that regard, *My Brother*, according to Page, functions on both levels: "One, it tells the story of the author maintaining her family, specifically her sick brother, with cash and kind from abroad. Two, *My Brother* is written outside of the geographical location of the Caribbean, outside of Antigua, then sent home to Antigua."[32] However, disregarding the importance of Kincaid's unwillingness as a benefactress gives an inaccurate picture of her migrant status. More than a migrant and an exile, Kincaid is a renegade who disclaims allegiance with her birth nation. A renegade, in the migrant context, is a reluctant remitter shamelessly voicing his or her wish to be un-indebted to the native land. In *My Brother*, Kincaid, who uses AIDS and her brother dying of it as a parable for her relationship with her home country, explicitly says that she would not want Antigua—and the kind of suffering that only happens there—to contaminate her life in North America. About her brother, she confesses that she would not have wanted to bring "this strange, careless person into the hard-earned order of [her] life."[33] Kincaid had a chance to cover her presumed individualistic tracks. She could have blamed her unwillingness on the prohibitive immigration policies for AIDS-infected patients. Yet, Kincaid is known for provocatively telling the unwanted truth, and the truth is that she sees Antigua as a nuisance to her American life.

Kincaid's trademark is to put herself in the enunciative context of the persona non grata, of someone unwilling to give back to her home community and who defiantly fashions her literary persona on her very unwillingness to remit. Kincaid relies on a contrarian style of writing initially based on her relationship with William Shawn, her perfect reader (now deceased). She writes, "One of the ways I became a writer was by telling my husband's father [Shawn] things he didn't want me to tell him but was so curious about that he would listen to them anyway."[34] The intended reception of Kincaid's writing is akin to a reading technique depicted by Roland Barthes in *Le plaisir du texte* (*The Pleasure of the Text*, 1975). Barthes distinguishes two kinds of reading: one that sticks to the text and one that skips anything deemed superfluous. By skipping the superfluous, the reader aims for a quick fix that goes straight to the anecdotal. As a reading strategy, the goal of skipping is to prioritize in terms of what is most relevant content-wise. By skipping, the reader goes directly to what is pleasurable, thus abstaining from the unpleasantly lengthy. Interestingly enough, with Kincaid, the anecdotal is precisely the unpleasant. When it comes to the autobiographical genre, Kincaid's writing style is very much anecdotal, building a metanarrative made of a concatenation of incidental events that usually go unnoticed—what she refers to as "the small event that cannot be seen by you."[35] As she says in *My Brother*, at Shawn's funeral, she wished she could have told the deceased Shawn "what it was like when he died, all the things that happened what people said, what they did, how they behaved."[36] Her intention is voyeuristic, almost gossipy. She confesses that Shawn would not have liked to know, and yet, he could not have refrained from listening, which is typical of gossip. Ross Chambers in "Gossip and the Novel" mentions the self-reflexive "I shouldn't tell you this, but. . . ."[37] nature of the gossip genre. Gossip relies on the announcement of an undue telling and on an affected breach of trust, the breach being the enticing part of the gossip. Octave Mannoni titled his famous essay on disavowal in *Clefs pour l'imaginaire* (*Keys to the Imaginary*), "Je sais bien mais quand même." This paradoxical phrase—translated as "I know I shouldn't, but still" or "I should know better, but nevertheless"—goes back to the fundamentals of confliction and is the conflicted context of reception that Kincaid also expects from her readers. In a nutshell, Kincaid is, oxymoronically, an enticing persona non grata. Like abjection, an affect that Julia Kristeva in *Pouvoirs de l'horreur* (*Powers of Horror*, 1982) compares to the gagging reflex (an experience of both insertion and repulsion), Kincaid's provocative writing often manages to both attract and repel her readers at the same time. Kincaid is an unwilling remitter in her role as a migrant and a writer; she expects her readers to be equally unwilling to receive her.

Odile Cazenave and Patrica Célérier recently called attention to the growing number of modern African writers who seem to perceive the old tradition of national commitment as a burden. Doing away with *engagée* literature, those contemporary writers want to be "identified as writers rather than as people from a specific national, cultural, or geographical origin."[38] The ultimate goal of Cazenave and Célérier's book is to question the permanence of the equation between Francophone African literature and the idea of commitment. But what needs to be stressed is that the tradition of national commitment in Francophone African literature is directly linked to the question of remittance. The Senegalese Ousmane Sembene's *La noire de . . .* (*Black Girl*, 1975), the Senegalese Fatou Diome's *Le ventre de l'Atlantique* (*The Belly of the*

*Atlantic,* 2006), the Cameroonian Leonora Miano's *L'intérieur de la nuit* (*Dark Heart of the Night,* 2010), and the Congolese Alain Mabanckou's *Bleu-blanc-rouge* (*Blue White Red,* 2013), all attest to the long-standing tradition of remittance that has been weighing on African migrants in France.[39] We have seen that modern Caribbean literature, both English and French, is undergoing a similar trend of disengagement. The burden of financial and, even more importantly, cultural remittance is being renegotiated so that migrant writers can learn to travel light. In a 1971 interview, Naipaul says about his duty as a migrant writer, "A man must write to report his whole response to the world; not because it would be nice to do something for the prestige of the country."[40] Migrant writers struggle with their own ambivalence toward their native country; their work is often a product of conflicted emotions. They feel culturally indebted and pressured to give back to the country—with nice words, love, money, or AZT—and yet they are so eager and so eloquent in their writing to express their reluctance to remit.

## Home Talks Back with a Vengeance

When Derek Walcott defended English (although to the detriment of the Creole language) in his autobiographical essay "What the Twilight Says," some criticized his remarks, but they were said under extenuating circumstances. As the St. Lucian poet Jane King explains in her article "A Small Place Writes Back," Walcott should have gotten into much more trouble for dismissing the Creole language, but he "did not get the absolute condemnation that it is fashionable still to visit upon Naipaul for his supposed demeaning of things Caribbean."[41] To King, the reason for the leniency is not only due to the year in which Walcott made his statement (in the 1970s the Creole language was, for most, not commonly perceived as a language in its own right) but also, and mostly, because of Walcott's location of enunciation. As King says, "[Walcott] lived and worked and produced his plays in the Caribbean and as a Caribbean person was deemed to have the right to comment on Caribbean people." Naipaul, on the other hand, "forfeited that right by becoming English."[42] The suggestion that proximity grants critical privilege and that only local national criticism carries redeeming qualities is food for thought. This logic invites us to conclude that distant enunciation has a duty to be "agreeable"—in the sense of coming together. Yet, is not distance precisely the epitome of inconvenience and therefore disagreeability? Is it not, after all, the nature of the migrant writer to be disagreeable to the native community for the mere fact of not being back, of not convening with the home community? It seems that the migrant's unwillingness to return home precisely accounts for his or her disagreeability. Strictly speaking, the difference between the traditional diasporic subject and the second-generation diasporic subject lies in the question of individual will. As this book posits, traditional diaspora refers to forced and massive human displacement, while second-generation diaspora is motivated by the individual will. Kincaid and Naipaul are in that regard second-generation diasporic writers; their work addresses the challenge of writing *agreeably* about home when one's motivation for leaving was exactly that: to leave.

A sort of chiasmic inversion occurs with Naipaul and Kincaid: it cannot be said that the two are unwilling migrants, for they are rather happy to live outside the native land. Instead, they are migrants unwilling to return—"return" in the sense of returning home but also in the sense of providing for home. Naipaul and Kincaid, as migrants unwilling to return, can be said to embody the static that prevents easy communication between abroad and home. As addressed in the introduction, this book takes its main figure, the renegade, after the Trinidadian C.L.R. James's book *Mariners, Renegades, and Castaways*. In it, James offers a unique perspective on Herman Melville's *Moby-Dick*. James does not focus on Ahab or the whale; instead, he brings to the forefront a side story—namely, the oft-overlooked crewmembers on Ahab's boat. Melville chose to make Ahab's crewmembers islanders, and, as the title suggests, all renegades and all from different continents. Melville calls them *isolatoes*. In a Noah's Ark kind of way, each *isolato* is made to represent his own continent— "a separate continent of his own."[43] As James writes, the expatriate author is stranded on Ellis Island awaiting deportation for a visa violation. Alone, stranded, James himself is an *isolato* but with an added value: the deportation. This forced return is symbolic of the second-generation diasporic voice ineluctably made to return home, to represent home, whether the enunciator wants it or not. Like C.L.R. James's deportation, what matters the most is not whether Kincaid and Naipaul return but rather how willing or unwilling those two writers are to be in the position of the returnee and the provider.

The Guyanese scholar of Indo-Caribbean studies, Frank Birbalsingh, once said that Naipaul was "a picaroon" motivated by his "unscrupulous and unprincipled self-interest."[44] Birbalsingh's aggressive reaction against the Trinidadian writer is not uncommon among postcolonial scholars. Derek Walcott, once an admirer of Naipaul, has himself been involved in a public feud with him. The ongoing feud has culminated in Walcott making a very public attack against Naipaul during the 2008 Calabash Literary Festival in Jamaica.

At the festival, Walcott read a still unpublished poem against Naipaul titled "Mongoose," which is a reference to an animal imported from India during the English Colonial Empire. The poem accuses Naipaul of having lost steam as a writer and deems the old mongoose a worthless writer. Walcott's slander speaks volumes about the degree of resentment attached to Naipaul, particularly from postcolonial writers.

Many postcolonial writers look at Naipaul today as a sellout, a once gifted writer who sold himself to the Western Hemisphere. As French says in his biography of Naipaul, "If you reject the land that formed you, as Naipaul began to do actively in his thirties, you become defined by that rejection."[45] What French does not say however, is that being defined by that rejection also entails having the rejected define you. Edward Saïd once said that "one of the ways of getting hold of the commonest post-colonial debate is to analyse not its content, but its form, not what is said so much as how it is said, by whom, where, and for whom."[46] This statement is very pertinent to Naipaul's situation. Naipaul as a Trinidadian renegade has fashioned his persona not so much on what he has provocatively said about his home community but rather on the reaction that his words have had on his people. The Naipaul case pinpoints how much the context of reception often prevails over the context of production in diasporic writing. It comes to a point where the controversy Naipaul stirs says more about the writer than what he actually wrote.

One of the best-known examples of this extrapolative phenomenon is the infamous quotation from *The Middle Passage*, in which Naipaul claims that Trinidad is a "society that produced nothing."[47] Critics often refer to this quotation to summarize Naipaul's up-to-date legacy, thus illustrating Naipaul's art of rubbing the Third World the wrong way. Naipaul's initial provocative statement from *The Middle Passage* has since come in all sorts of shapes and targets. In a 1979 interview, Naipaul not only said, "Africa has no future,"[48] but about the Indians, he told Hardwick, "I do not write for Indians who . . . in any case do not read. My work is only possible in a liberal, civilized country. It is not possible in primitive societies."[49] Two years later, in another interview, Naipaul claimed that "Africa is a land of bush, again, not a very literary land."[50] In the same interview, he also posited that "Asiatics do not read, of course; they are a non-reading people."[51] Naipaul has been very clear about his intended readership. The Trinidadian writer does not write for his people (Trinidadians, Africans, Indians, Asiatics) because he deems these people, in terms of literacy and literature, backward. Naipaul's essential argument is that Third World writers are made to produce for an outside readership, simply because their people are nonreaders. This argument leads him to conclude that literary outsourcing is not about the writer but about the local audience, or the lack thereof. As he says in an interview with Adrian Rowe-Evans about the Nigerian writer Chinua Achebe:

> Of course there are good writers who are African. Chinua Achebe is a grand writer by most people's standards, but he is not published in his own country. His work needs the blessing of the foreign market, and for a very good reason: because the local society doesn't have any body of judgment as yet; it can't trust itself yet to make its own appraisals.[52]

The question remains, does literary outsourcing necessarily lead to selling out? Why is Naipaul repeatedly accused of being a "neocolonial apologist for European colonialism,"[53] when the equally outsourced Achebe is not?

Selwyn Reginald Cudjoe has brought attention to the fact that Naipaul is perceived differently depending on whether one comes from the First or the Third World. She writes:

> Controversy in interpreting Naipaul's work arises from the almost opposite manner in which the Third World and First World critics interpret it. The preponderance of critiques of Naipaul's work from the First World and their generally favorable responses can be opposed to the generally unfavorable responses of Third World critics.[54]

Naipaul shows a clear tendency of choosing the Third World as his main target, which explains the volume of negative criticisms that he gets in return from the Third World, because, obviously, the injured will strike back. The Third World's retaliative response is part of a dialogic rhetoric to be addressed later. Literary feuds are common among peers in minor literary fields (Richard Wright, James Baldwin, Raphaël Confiant, Aimé Césaire, to name a few). One of the reasons for the feuding trend is that the minor is often challenged, space-wise; the retaliative rhetoric comes then as a negotiation of space. When Walcott read his antagonistic poem "Mongoose" at the Calabash Literary Festival, the poem against Naipaul was indeed said to be retaliation against an earlier attack. The year before, Naipaul had very subtly suggested in a published review on Walcott that the Saint Lucian poet was a deflated writer no longer at the prime of his career. Walcott could have ignored Naipaul, since the Signifying Monkey Naipaul is known for his antagonizing semantics. Yet, the lion Walcott took it upon himself to fight back for all to see. Given that the poem "Mongoose" was read in Jamaica and that it involves two internationally known Caribbean Nobel Prize winners at war with each other, there was definitely a sense of reclaiming one's space in this intertextual public feud. In Walcott and Naipaul's case, it is clear that literary outsourcing did not prevent feuding among peers, and it may have even exacerbated the need for retaliation.

Homi Bhabha talks about taking "the measure of one's dwelling,"[55] which is a necessary critical endeavor when the subject is, as Bhabha explains, in a state of mutual contamination between home and the outside world. But it needs to be added that the diasporic enunciation is a dwelling measurer for both the diasporic enunciator *and* the home recipient. The reason is that when the diasporic enunciator speaks, the enunciation also impacts his or her native home, and even more so when the enunciation is of an offensive nature. In *Excitable Speech*, Judith Butler addresses the effects of offensive illocutionary speech acts on the recipient. Talking about the performativity of insults, Butler writes:

> To be injured by speech is to suffer a loss of context—that is, not to know where you are. Indeed, it may be that what is unanticipated about the injurious speech act is what constitutes its injury, the sense of putting its addressee out of control.[56]

The loss of control mentioned by Butler echoes Bhabha's "unhomely"—what the author describes as "a displacement, the borders between home and world becom[ing] confused."[57] In a diasporic offensive statement, distance adds to injury. Offenses from afar make home feel particularly displaced and disfigured (*Enstellung*), which causes home to lose touch with its sense of self and place. As Butler explains, with the insult "one can be 'put in one's place' by such speech, but such place may be no place."[58] As it were, there is a very thin line between being put in one's place and being put in no place. The diasporic offensive statement lays stress on the fragility of one's sense of place or, as Butler puts it, on "the volatility of one's 'place.'"[59] Consequently, the diasporic writer insults twice, first by leaving home and second by insulting the home left behind. Due to the double insult, the home recipient is forced to redetermine the validity of his or her home place. It makes no difference whether the home recipient lives at home or abroad. In Walcott's case, Naipaul's offense touched home, wherever Walcott was.

In 1985, Edward Saïd attended a panel discussion at Skidmore College on "The Intellectual in the Post-Colonial World." The panel discussed Saïd's lecture of almost same title, "Intellectuals in the Post-Colonial World." In his lecture, Saïd had accused Naipaul of being "a witness for the Western prosecution."[60] The Palestinian-born academic had also criticized Naipaul for being, among other writers of his kind, a sort of Third World Uncle Tom. Here is Saïd talking about Naipaul (and others):

> In presenting themselves as members of courageous minorities in the Third World, they are in fact not interested at all in the Third World—which they never address. . . . [61]

In response to those attacks on Naipaul, two panel participants, American professor Robert Boyers and Irish politician and academic Conor Cruise O'Brien, challenged Saïd's view. Even though they outnumbered Saïd in their defense of Naipaul, Saïd did not back down. The clear divide between Boyers/O'Brien and Saïd left the discussion at a standstill, so much so that O'Brien concluded the panel discussion with "Obviously we're not going to agree on much of this."[62] This confirms Cudjoe's assertion as to "the almost opposite manner in which the Third World and First World critics interpret"[63] Naipaul. It is debatable whether, as Saïd argues, Naipaul provides a kind of enunciation aimed to comfort the First World in its preconception of the Third World. What is certain, however, is that Third World critics put Naipaul back in his place as a way to reaffirm their own space. To paraphrase Bhabha, it can be said that the retaliative technique "retakes" the measure of one's dwelling. As Butler suggests, only the injured calls for a counteroffensive, which explains the Third World—including Birbalsingh, Walcott, and Saïd's—reception of Naipaul.

For Cudjoe, the misreadings of Naipaul are mainly due to the fact that "critics do not seem to understand that the text always arrives accompanied, 'determined,' as it were, by the existence of other works, which can belong to different areas of production."[64] It needs to be stressed that Naipaul's offensive enunciation is *proleptically* determined, which means that it is not defined by what comes before but rather what comes after the enunciation reaches home. In other words, the offense feeds on the anticipated reaction of the offended. Naipaul's enunciation carries the perlocutionary effect[65] of, literally and figuratively speaking, hitting home, and as such, it always already prompts a retaliative answer from home. Patrick French, in his biography of Naipaul, has addressed a local Caribbean practice, "playing ole mas," referring to someone "masquerading and making trouble for [one's own] entertainment."[66] French says that the Barbadian George Lamming used that expression in regards to Naipaul's attitude. In Trinidad, as French notes, the "picong," from the French *piquant*, meaning "spicy" or "stinging," is like "playing ole mas," an enunciative practice, half jesting and half truthful, meant to sting the recipient. "Picong" *pokes* fun, in the figurative and literal sense of the term. The stinging effect of the poking cannot leave the poked unmoved. There will inevitably be a reactive gesture on the part of the poked.

The diasporic Caribbean literary genre of Naipaul, and also of Kincaid, takes after the "picong" tradition. Like Naipaul, Kincaid is known for telling the unpleasant truth to people's faces. And like Naipaul's infamous assertion that Trinidad is a society that produced nothing, Kincaid has said about Antigua in *A Small Place* that it is an island that comes from nothing and means nothing:

> They [the Antiguans] have nothing to compare this incredible constant with, no big historical moment to compare the way they are now to the way they used to be. No Industrial Revolution, no revolution of any kind, no Age of Anything, no world wars, no decades of turbulence balanced by decades of calm. Nothing, then, natural or unnatural, to leave a mark on their character. It is just a little island.[67]

*A Small Place* is to Kincaid what *The Middle Passage* was to Naipaul. They are both travel books shedding a negative light on the Caribbean. Because they are natives turned migrants, it is easy to imagine how Naipaul's and Kincaid's critical perceptions of the Caribbean sound treacherous to some.

But Kincaid, though equally anathematized by her home community, rejects the comparison with Naipaul. In a 1996 interview, Kincaid said about Naipaul:

> But I would say that the difference between Naipaul and myself is that I am not ashamed either of anything that has happened in the place I come from, or of the things that have been done by the people I come from. I suppose the most vivid thing I remember from *The Middle Passage* is how Naipaul despised the black people getting on the train, going toward Southampton to take the boat, he even used the shape of a black man's bottom to denounce him.[68]

The way Kincaid touches on the subject of race in her disclaiming of Naipaul is historically determined. It is because Naipaul is not of African descent that he is alleged to be condescending to the black race. Naipaul is the grandchild of indentured laborers who migrated to Trinidad from Eastern India. Being of East Indian descent, Naipaul represents the population that is said to have sold out to the colonial system in the Caribbean. After the emancipation of the African slaves, East Indians were brought to the Caribbean to replace the blacks. But as a docile substitute workforce, the newcomers divested the emancipated slaves of their leverage to negotiate with plantation owners. In the above quotation, Kincaid surreptitiously addresses the archaic resentment of the *Bossale* (African slave) for East Indians. As George Lamming explains, what happened between East Indians and African emancipated slaves has had a long-lasting impact on the Caribbean community:

> If the newly freed African labour was going to sabotage anything, they could not do it because of this new force. So that kind of challenge could be set up between them, and it continued to be used long afterward.[69]

That said, portraying Naipaul as an ancestral traitor to the Afro-Caribbean cause is an oversimplification of Kincaid's resentment toward him. It is undeniable that, being an East Indian Caribbean, Naipaul is, as Charles Michener put it, "twice displaced,"[70] but it is ultimately his own identity and his individual voice that make Naipaul come across as a deserter to the anticolonial picket line. By Naipaul's own admission, the writer does not believe in an Afro-Caribbean cause. This is why, as Naipaul told Bharati Mukherjee and Robert Boyers, he meant to use the phrase "the illiterate black man shouting for racial redemption" in *The Middle Passage* as a criticism of "racialist politics."[71]

But since Naipaul rejects his whole West Indian identity and not just the Afro-Caribbean cause, it would be erroneous to apply a purely racialist dimension to his national betrayal. Naipaul once switched publishers after a publishing house labeled him a "West Indian Writer" in its catalog. "West Indian is a political word," he argued, "It's all the things I reject. It's not me."[72] As a case in point, *An Area of Darkness*, his travelogue on India, is no less forgiving than *The Middle Passage*. Naipaul may not think as an Afro-Caribbean, but he does not identify either with the West Indian or the East Indian. Kincaid says that the only people who have nice things to say about Naipaul are "Western people, right-wing people. I don't want to say 'white.'"[73] As aforementioned, the First World—not to say the "White World"—seems indeed more prone to endorse Naipaul, but it remains to be proven that this endorsement is race motivated. In "A Small Place Writes Back," the St. Lucian poet Jane King builds the same kind of race-based argument. She posits that, unlike for Naipaul, if Kincaid seems to have retained her right to comment on the Caribbean people, it is either because she is a woman or because she is of African descent (like Walcott). That she has retained the right to criticize her native land at all is debatable. But this debate aside, nothing in Naipaul or Kincaid allows us to conclude that race, or gender for that matter, plays a role in their right to tell or not to tell.

What essentially differentiates Kincaid from Naipaul is not race but location. *A Small Place* differs from *The Middle Passage* mainly because, unlike Kincaid's view from her North American location, Naipaul offers a European critical perspective on the Caribbean. Kincaid's work on the Caribbean has been produced from a North American observatory, so to speak. Starting with *Lucy* in 1990, the geographical context of observation of the native land becomes very visible in Kincaid's work. *Lucy* is an autobiographically inspired novel about a Caribbean protagonist's first time in America, which focuses on the elusive moment of facing the new in the country. Very early on in the novel, the newly migrated Lucy says, "In the past, the thought of being in my present situation had been a comfort, but now I did not even have this to look forward to, and so I lay down on my bed and dreamt I was eating a bowl of pink mullet and green figs cooked in coconut milk."[74] Lucy looks back on her native island with a perception already altered by her short stay in America. The new having lost its luster, Lucy is able to reinvest in her fantasized projections onto the native land in lieu of the prospective land. This is only the beginning for Lucy; she has just made it to North America, and she is free to adjust and readjust her position between the old and the new country as she pleases. For now she feels melancholy for the home country, but there is room to grow and the possibility of national resentment as time progresses.

The same applies to Kincaid. Kincaid's freedom from geographical contextualization allows her to autonomously reassess the measure of her dwelling. If the story and Kincaid's migrant life had taken place in England, the migrant perception would be bound to carry a colonial-impacted rhetoric with either an assimilationist or an anticolonial framework. Kincaid is very aware of having something that Naipaul does not have, which is a terra incognita context of enunciation. As she says in an interview with Birbalsingh, "I think that if there is anything different about me, it is that I do not have to, or want to, please an English audience or an English colonial audience."[75] Her privileged location from which to tell about home is the reason why Kincaid can propose a vision of America as a site of creative freedom where criticizing home is a personal affair and not necessarily a (post)colonial historicized endeavor. North America provides Kincaid with some kind of enunciative defiance, a unique, politically divested standpoint. This is also the reason why in *Lucy* the protagonist is able to talk about the colonial native home with such disengagement. Lucy says, "If only we had been ruled by the French: they were prettier, much happier in appearance, so much more the kind of people I would have enjoyed being around."[76] The protagonist makes it sound as though it would be good if one could choose a colonial home as one would pick a new dress: superficially, only for the effect of it, with no historical strings attached.

What is most interesting in Kincaid's geographical position of enunciation is that she has been able to shift the postcolonial discussion from a question of language to a question of location. In *A Small Place*, Kincaid repeats almost word for word what Jean-François Lyotard wrote in *The Differend*, published two years prior to *A Small Place*. Lyotard defines *differend* as follows:

A Martinican is a French citizen; he or she can bring a complaint against whatever impinges upon his or her rights as a French citizen. But the wrong he or she deems to suffer from the fact of being a French citizen is not a matter of litigation under French law. It might be under private or international law, but for that to be the case it would be necessary that the Martinican were no longer a French citizen. But he or she is. Consequently, the assertion according to which he or she suffers a wrong on account of his or her citizenship is not verifiable by explicit and effective procedures.[77]

In *A Small Place*, Kincaid defines the wrong in the following manner:

For, isn't it odd that the only language I have in which to speak of this crime is the language of the criminal who committed the crime? When I say to the criminal, "This is bad, and this other deed is bad, and this one is also very very bad," the criminal understands the word "wrong" in this way: It is wrong when "he" doesn't get his fair share of profits from the crime just committed.[78]

Even though she never mentions Lyotard, Kincaid is obviously very familiar with the predicament of the "Caribbean wrong" as depicted by Lyotard. But for Kincaid, the "crime scene"—namely, England—is far behind. Not only does she not speak *in the land of* the criminal, but she also does not speak back *to* the criminal. Even though Kincaid can only speak in the language of her criminal, she does not have to speak in the location of the criminal. Instead, from a North American context of enunciation, she speaks to her home (Caribbean) community, which in return, speaks back to her. By following a trajectory away from the metropolitan center, Kincaid depoliticizes and disengages her voice, keeping it purely individual. This brings us back to what the

Haitian-born and -naturalized Canadian Dany Laferrière said about moving to Montreal instead of France: "Je n'entends parler de colonialisme que quand je suis invité dans un colloque en Europe. . . . La seule façon de l'éviter, c'est de ne jamais vivre dans un pays qui vous a colonisé" (I hear about colonialism only when I am invited to a conference in Europe. . . . The only way to avoid it is never to live in a country that colonized you).[79]

There is no real answer as to whether publicly criticizing home is necessarily an act of treason in diasporic writing. What is certain, however, is that no matter the geographical context of production, postcolonial writers are inevitably recalled by their communities. For Kincaid, the context of reception, even more than that of production, remains the defining quality of the Caribbean diasporic voice. Kincaid may have shed an extra pound of responsibility by relocating her voice to North America, but the relocation does not mean that she is now out of reach of all supervision. On the contrary, as Jane King's "A Small Place Writes Back" clearly shows, Kincaid's enunciation anticipates, expects, and calls for home's reception and retaliation. In other words, her enunciation is invested and defined by home's reception, which means that the second-generation diasporic writer is, in spite of all, indebted to home.

Talking about Kincaid's location of production, King writes, "I can only reply to her [Kincaid] that it is simply much harder to be published, since we don't have magazines like the *New Yorker* ready to publish writers from fashionable minorities."[80] King is writing from Saint Lucia and her voice speaks for, and from the location of, the Caribbean. King seems to feel resentment not necessarily because Kincaid has migrated to North America but more precisely due to the fact that Kincaid has become an *ungrateful successful* migrant. This brings us back to what French wrote about Naipaul's lack of remittance: "For a *successful immigrant* [my italics] writer to take such a position was seen as a special kind of treason."[81] One of the capital rules of migration is that success and migration should equate to remittance, not defiance. King suggests between the lines that Kincaid has made it in North America precisely because she is a Caribbean migrant (a "minority"), and yet she is unable to give back to her community *as a migrant*.

King's "A Small Place Writes Back" adds a crucial layer to the question of the postcolonial ripostive genre. As mentioned in the introduction, in the last few years, an emerging trend in African studies has attempted to shift the critical focus of postcolonial studies initiated by Ashcroft, Griffiths, and Tiffin's influential *The Empire Writes Back* (1989). Exactly twenty years after the publication of *The Empire Writes Back*, Evan Mwangi publishes *Africa Writes*

*Back to Self* (2009), a study that focuses on what the author names the African "self-reflexive fiction," a locally produced African literature addressing local issues and by extension writing to no one but itself. Odile Cazenave and Patrica Célérier's 2011 *Contemporary Francophone African Writers and the Burden of Commitment* recently joined Mwangi's voice in addressing an African literature no longer politically or (post)colonially engaged. This scholarship, however, raises an obvious question, mostly when it comes to Mwangi's phrasing. In Mwangi's Africa that is writing back to itself, to what is *back* referring? Why does postcolonial literature necessarily have to write *back*? And if this literature is in fact a retort, what is the nature of the initial statement? It seems that the postcolonial genre is assumed to be always ripostive even when it is self-directed, as if to say that the postcolonial voice always owes and has to give back, even if it means giving back to itself.

In Mwangi's case, the writing back is an obvious reference to first Salman Rushdie and second Ashcroft, Griffiths, and Tiffin. Salman Rushdie's influential 1982 article from the *Times of London*, "The Empire Writes Back with a Vengeance," jump-started a trend in postcolonial studies that considered the Western center no longer the main context of enunciation but rather the target of reception, the Empire having become the new enunciator. The problem with this new direction, however, is that the notion of writing *back* assumes that the Empire is still accountable to Europe in its enunciation, even and particularly so in its discourse of resistance. The adverb "back" remains the enunciative traffic controller determining the trajectory of the margin and the center. The figure of the Creole renegade complicates the question of postcolonial decentralizing. In a modern Caribbean diasporic context, the local has incidentally become the new center from which individual diasporic voices are breaking free. The figure of the Creole renegade proceeds past the "writing back to the (local) self" model in order to question the very meaning of "center," not only simply as a metropolis but also today as the native colonial place. If the diasporic subject can be said to be writing *back*, it is because the adverb "back" has become proleptic in nature: "back" refers to the future retort from home (the native land), the one that the diasporic subject anticipates and calls for. To complicate matters, if home answers back to the migrant, it is precisely because the migrant has failed to give *back* to home; the expectation of retribution from home gives its full meaning to the word *background*. The home recipient calls on the diasporic writer for having failed to remit. Individual migrancy offers thus a deceptive sense of autonomy to the migrant subject. The modern Caribbean migrant is twice deterritorialized—first collectively in the slave trade and then individually in the move from the Caribbean to North America. The center has accordingly been displaced as well. What was once the margin has become the center; the native Caribbean is now for the Caribbean diasporic subject the new center. The Creole renegade—as the one who left the new center and failed to answer back to what he or she left behind—lives in the bliss of failure but also in the failure of bliss.

# Creole versus *Bossale* Renegade

## "Turfism" in the Black Diaspora of the Americas

Espèce de isalop mal-cochon chien makak, ich Man banse et ich kône.

PATRICK CHAMOISEAU, *CHRONIQUE DES SEPT MISÈRES*

Questioning the role of individualism in diasporic cultures seems like a suitable way to close a book on the Creole renegade. The shift from the collective to the individual experienced by the black diaspora of the Americas has been mostly unaccounted for in studies about modern black displacement. There is a need to question whether individualism has a role to play in black diasporic cultures, given that the idea of particularism clashes with the old concept of diaspora traditionally defined as forced human dispersion. The fact that the black diasporic subject in the Americas is no longer (necessarily) associated with a collective experience contradicts the very notion of diaspora as evocative of community and solidarity. Yet, it should be added that this contradiction is precisely what defines the diasporic experience. Bear in mind that the Atlantic slave trade is not only about the displacement of peoples but also about the survival of the fittest—namely, the individual struggle to be among those who survive the Middle Passage. In that sense, the *bossale* roots of the Creole subject should not be ignored; they call upon the survival instinct and basic needs of the single African slave shipped to the New World. The word *bossale*, as opposed to the Creole subject who is born in the Americas, refers to a New World slave born in Africa, so the *bossale* carries along with her or him the experience of the Middle Passage. Next to the chronotope of the generic slave ship, which Paul Gilroy sees as the ultimate bonding experience in the history of the black diaspora,[1] the *bossale* refers to the *individual* experience in the triangular trade. The *bossale*, the ancestor and one of the forefathers of the Creole culture, conveys what is all too human about the history of creolization: basic survival. In addition to the slave ship, in *The Black Atlantic*, Gilroy uses also the rhetoric of the chronotope to illustrate the diversity of the black diasporic people. For Gilroy, the black Atlantic tells the story of a move from the chronotope of the road to the chronotope of the crossroads, which accounts for a change from "Africa, authenticity, purity" to "the Americas, hybridity, creolisation, and rootlessness."[2] However, from a historiographical point of view, it seems that stressing the multiple and hybrid nature of the Creole experience has resulted, in Caribbean studies, in muting the voice of the individual *bossale* amidst the deafening chatter of discourses on creolization. Where does the individual stand in the overwhelming praise of (Creole) hybridity and multiplicity?

The subject's claim for individualism, in a slavery-impacted diasporic society, is a *bossale* vestige. So far, this study of Creole renegadism has consisted of looking at instances of individuals finding their voices away from their overbearing birthplace. Yet, the Creole subject does not necessarily have to step out of his or her community to become a renegade. Before spreading to other parts of the continent, the seed of individual contestation against what Gilroy calls "cultural insiderism" germinates at home. "Cultural insiderism," as defined in *The Black Atlantic*, refers to cultural/ethnic entitlement and protectionism that are inclined to foster claims of "national belonging."[3] In a specifically Caribbean context, cultural insiderism comes close to cultural inbreeding in spite of the (too) common connection between diasporic cultures and diversity. Preserving to the excess the idea of "Antillean domiciliation" (*Eloge de la Créolité*) and Creole identity is what runs the risk of territorializing what was once a diasporic culture. In Creole culture, it seems that diversity is often taken for granted, since Creoleness is said to be inherently diverse. Edouard Glissant has even argued that the discourse of heterogeneousness that Gilles Deleuze and Félix Guattari had expressed at the level of the "le fonctionement de la pensée" (functioning of thought)[4] already existed as an organic phenomenon in Creole culture. Likewise, Celia M. Britton pointedly summarized Glissant's philosophy as "the irreducible difference of the Other."[5] But Glissant also sensed that, to be true to its diverse nature, Creoleness needed to be experienced from a perspective wider than the Caribbean context. In 1997, the French publishing house Gallimard took over Glissant's scholarship initially published by Seuil; for the relaunching, Gallimard chose to relabel most of Glissant's work under the serial collection *Poétique (I–V)*, which overshadowed the political activism of Glissant's earlier work such as *Le discours antillais* (1981). Chris Bongie argues that the visible emphasis on poetics rather than politics in Glissant's later work is mainly due to Gallimard's marketing strategy of presenting the author's extensive work as a *Poétique* series. But there is more to Glissant's later work than a question of repackaging. Unquestionably, Glissant's more recent poetics of diversity[6] indicates a growing interest in poetics rather than politics. But more importantly, unlike *Le discours antillais*, Glissant's later work shows an increasing awareness of the global, of what exceeds the local (Caribbean) frontiers of Creoleness. Glissant's *chaos-monde* (chaos world) perspective invites the newly territorialized diasporic culture to expand, reach out, and resist the natural inclination toward cultural insiderism.[7] Glissant's poetics of Creoleness is a call for regeneration, not only against "cultural erosion," as Glissant calls it, but also against cultural inbreeding.

Admittedly, Glissant's global perspective starting in the late 1980s coincides with the moment when he started living in North America, teaching first at LSU and then at CUNY (Graduate Center). In comparison, his fellow countrymen Raphaël Confiant and Patrick Chamoiseau have been more "local" in their literary production early in their career,[8] as they live and write mainly in Martinique. This could explain why Confiant, specifically, shows a particular kind of *bossale* survival attitude in his early work, an attitude of wanting to make it against all odds within the local restricted space of Martinique.[9] Confiant is known for antagonistic impulses that he exhibited early in his career. The writer engaged in feuds that are incidentally part of a larger black diasporic tradition including African-Americans and referred to as "Signifying" or the "Dozens." The feeling of belonging to a minor restricted space has triggered turf wars among writers who have infamously battled it out publicly through open letters and other types of published work. This intertextual antagonistic exchange reached its peak in the Martinique of the late 1980s and early 1990s, at the same time that Antillean literature was attracting wider attention on the French literary scene and in American universities. The new postcolonial trend meant that writers whose work fit into the hyped category of Postcolonial Studies jockeyed for space among themselves to get a piece of that recognition. A similar phenomenon had already occurred in African-American literature of the 1950s and 1960s, where so-called minor writers such as James Baldwin and Ralph Ellison engaged in a literary dozens, a war of words, as a way to make room for themselves in the well-respected, albeit too small and congested, space of *black American literature*. However destructive this antagonism may have been in the history of the black Diaspora of the Americas, it had the benefit of creating

dialogical chaos, a sort of intertextual repartee where antagonistic participants create difference through communicating their *differend* (difference of
opinion).

## The "Dozens"

In *The Signifying Monkey*, Henry Louis Gates defines vernacular as a language whose characteristic is to challenge the official word by adding a semantic difference. Within an African-American context, vernacularizing is
a racially connoted practice using black revision as a way to subvert white
language. From the Latin *verna*, meaning "slave born in his master's house,"[10]
vernacularizing signifies making oneself at home in the master's house. In
North America, the vernaculazing practice is referred to as "signifying" or
"signifyin'," the word being stripped of its last consonant as an indication of
change. As Gates argues, the signifying tradition conveys the need in African-
Americans to single out their voice and to articulate their difference in the
most imperceptible ways. "Whereas black writers most certainly revise texts
in the Western tradition," Gates writes, "they often seek to do so 'authentically,' with a black difference, a compelling sense of difference based on the
black vernacular."[11] Through the practice of signifying, black speakers are in a
way adding their family portraits to the master's house. The signifying tradition arches back to the plantation society, when slaves resorted to innovative
strategies to bootleg forbidden truths. Nick Nesbitt refers to those clandestine
strategies as "split signifiers." Nesbitt thus returns to the origins of signifying,
placing it in a literal context of the master-slave dialectic:

> In the context of the plantation, where rare moments of open contes-
> tation are rapidly and violently suppressed, hidden revolt becomes the
> daily medium of resistance, and often this takes the form of a play of
> ambiguity in which a subaltern person hides his or her revolt behind a
> split signifier.[12]

What makes Nesbitt's theory particularly poignant within the context of slavery is his emphasis on the question of indirection. Being by nature "contestatory,"[13] the split signifier[14] seeks to add an interracial difference that will
circumvent white sovereign rule. The goal of the split signifier is therefore
to sidetrack the word of the white master in order to pave the way for a new
subversive meaning derived from the established one. As it were, the word
*signifying* itself is a direct reference to the practice of indirection.

The expression *signifying* comes from the African folkloric tale "The Signifying Monkey," which recounts the adventures of a cheeky monkey who wants to antagonize a lion but does not want to do it himself. The monkey goes to the elephant and tells the elephant that the lion has badmouthed him. A subsequent fight arises between the elephant and the lion, in which the monkey rejoices, since his mischievous plot has succeeded. The link between the act of signifying that Gates discusses in his book and the story of the monkey is based on what Claudia Mitchell-Kernan calls "indirection," which occurs when "the correct (referential) interpretation or signification of the utterance cannot be arrived at by a consideration of the dictionary meaning of the lexical items involved and the syntactic rules for their combination alone."[15] Mitchell-Kernan presents signifying as an intentional malapropism that forces the white semantic rule out of its comfort zone. But through the story of the "Signifying Monkey," it is also apparent that the semantic disfiguration is based on a culture of ruse and cheekiness, which is incidentally an essential feature of the plantation society. The monkey, albeit not as noble and proud as the lion, is nonetheless much quicker and more cunning.

From the plantation era on, disguise and cunning indirection have been essential qualities of the black diasporic culture of the Americas. As Maryse Condé explains in her book *La civilisation du bossale* (*Bossale Civilization*), the *bossale* culture is essentially a culture of ruse. Due to the transplantation and hostile living conditions in the New World, the *bossale* subject belongs to an adaptive culture that, according to Condé, had to rely on "ruse" and "dissimulation"[16] in order to survive. Condé presents the *bossale* society as "a civilization of make-believe":[17] the slave fakes docility in front of his master while mocking the master's gullibility behind his back. The *bossale* experience is obviously the foundation of the Creole culture, a resilient culture born out of repression and subjection and yet able to find coping mechanisms in order to survive in bondage. Today, the Creole culture still shows *bossale* characteristics, particularly in its inclination toward semantic indirection, ruse, and dissimulation. As Glissant also says, not only the culture but also the Creole language is an expression of indirection and ruse: "Le camouflage. C'est là une mise en scène du Détour. La langue créole s'est constituée autour d'une telle ruse" (Camouflage. Here is a mise-en-scène of Detour. The Creole language developed around such a ruse).[18] The correlation between the Creole language of ruse and the African-American vernacular is easily noticeable: both use social and semantic detours as a mode of adaptation in order to cope with inadequate conditions of living. Condé applies a slightly negative twist to the *bossale* culture of ruse, but Edouard Glissant has made a point of praising this adaptive culture, proud as he is to belong to a "peuple rusé, connaisseur, à la patience délibérée" (cunning and witty people with deliberate patience).[19]

Vernacularizing, indirection, and signifying belong to a slave-inherited and black diasporic culture that is used to staging conflict in order to create a public outlet for self-expression. The best example of this public staging is found in the African-American practice of the dozens, a ritualistic mode of address shared among African-American adolescents and sometimes adults, in which, with a mixture of playfulness and aggressiveness, two antagonists exchange insults in the presence of an audience. Though at times the exchange can lead to real fights, the dozens remains a game demanding performance and verbal skills. As Jemie Onwuchekwa says in *Yo' Mama!*, while signifying focuses on the opponent, the "dozens broadens the attention to his family, and especially the mother."[20] Accordingly, among its many names (*joining, joning, sounding, screaming, woofing, wolfing, cracking*), the dozens is also referred to as "talkin' 'bout yo' mamma."[21] It is assumed that the tradition is an African diasporic idiosyncrasy that initially developed in the Americas through the *bossale* culture. Onwuchekwa traces back its roots to the African continent, in particular western and southern Africa (Senegal, Niger, Kenya). Several interpretations have been proposed as to the social role this game may carry within the African-American community. John Dollard's contribution is particularly interesting because it situates the roots in plantation culture. Dollard proposes to look at the dozens as a game of indirection where the real target of the insults would not be the black fellow player but the untouchable white figure:

> Dozens is an in-caste pattern. It does not countenance jeering openly at white people, but it confines aggressiveness within Negro society. The reason for this limitation seems obvious, i.e., the punishing circumstances which come into play when Negroes display direct hostility for whites.[22]

Tracing back the origins of the dozens to slavery concurs with the speculation by some scholars that the name "dozens" actually comes from the slave market, where African slaves were bargained for and sold by the dozens. The dehumanizing effect of being sold by the dozens would then account for the self-demeaning spirit of the dozens. For the scholar Roger D. Abrahams, the dozens involves a coming-of-age initiation of the young black man. One of the biggest challenges for the black male in America is finding a sense of masculinity because "not only is he a black man in a white man's world, but he is a male in a matriarchy."[23] Here is Abrahams' logic: the young black man needs to cut the strangling umbilical cord that connects him to his mother, but out of respect for her, he cannot directly attack his mother, so he attacks the opponent's mother, knowing very well that the opponent will retaliate by insulting his own. Even though the origins of the "dozens" are still being debated, most studies agree that the dozens and signifying are retaliative tactics against an overbearing environment (born in the master's house); those games of indirection account for the dire need in young black men to stage conflict as a palliative for the various types of subordination they face.

## The Initial Literary Dozens: James Baldwin

James Baldwin belongs to a distinct group of black American writers who chose to live in Paris in the 1950s at a time when North America was perceived as too racially prejudiced for a black artist to thrive there. In addition to the intention to avoid prejudice at home, Baldwin's move was motivated by the vision at the time of France as a racial no man's land, the place where writers who happen to be born black in America have the chance to write outside the confines of so-called *African-American literature*. As Baldwin says in an essay, he left America because he wanted to "prevent [himself] from becoming *merely* a Negro; or, even, merely a Negro writer."[24] Baldwin sought to step outside the shadow of African-American literature, even though he had first knocked on the African-American Richard Wright's door to request professional support. In a 1984 *New York Times* interview, Baldwin recollects the circumstances that prompted him to approach Wright. Baldwin says, "By the time I went to see Richard I was committed to the idea of being a writer, though I knew how impossible it was. Maybe I went to see Richard to see if he would laugh at me."[25] Baldwin, however, quickly became Wright's protégé; Wright was in fact instrumental in getting Baldwin the fellowship from the Eugene F. Saxton Memorial Trust Foundation that launched the aspiring writer's career. But four years later, in a surprising turn of events, Baldwin turned against his devoted mentor by publishing a harsh critique of Richard Wright's acclaimed novel *Native Son* in the *Partisan Review*. The article, entitled "Everybody's Protest Novel," meant to deconstruct the protest novel genre, arguing that the books belonging to that genre were "both badly written and wildly improbable."[26] The article targeted in particular Harriet Beecher

Stowe's *Uncle Tom's Cabin* and Richard Wright's *Native Son*. Baldwin was at the threshold of his career when he published this blasphemous article. More than twenty years later, the then established Baldwin would write another article ("Alas, Poor Richard") in commemoration of Wright's death, trying to explain what had pushed him to write the article for which Wright never forgave him. Besides blaming his actions on the fact that he was only twenty, which he considered to be a "carnivorous age," Baldwin said that it was a time in his life when he was "uncertain of himself" and "egotistical";[27] for him, Wright "was a road-block in [his] road, the sphinx, really, whose riddles [he] had to answer before [he] could become [him]self."[28] The Oedipal Baldwin saw Wright as a stifling father figure. As he says, he needed to destroy that "father,"[29] that "idol," because "idols are created in order to be destroyed."[30] Simply put, Wright was the older master to destroy.

Baldwin's article in the *Partisan Review* can be seen as a complicated version of the dozens. Similar to what occurs in the urban dozens, the young man verbally and publicly takes on a black fellow as an indirect way to attack the untouchable master of the house; but unlike the original dozens, in this case the master is double, being both white (the American canon) and black (Richard Wright). Baldwin's staged patricide has to be understood within the context of a black literary puberty; it is the story of a young inexperienced writer under pressure to overcome the master of his "African-American literary" field. This literature is a double-edged vernacular literature that forces younger black writers to leave the house of both the black and the white master for fear of a multilayered type of emasculation.

The question of the *master* overshadowing black literature arches back to the case of Phillis Wheatly, the black slave woman who in 1772 had to prove in front of a white male jury in Boston that she was indeed the author of her intricately beautiful poems. The trial resulted in a white attestation confirming the validity of her black authorship.[31] In the Wheatly case, the defendant was a woman, but since then, there have been various instances in the history of the black diaspora of the Americas where black male writers have been subject to a similar kind of white tutelage. In a French-speaking context, Jean-Paul Sartre's "Orphée noir" ("Black Orpheus") and André Breton's endorsement of Aimé Césaire's *Cahier d'un retour au pays natal* are two examples of the white master famously patronizing newer black writers. ("Black Orpheus" was originally the preface to Léopold Sédar Senghor's *Anthologie de la nouvelle poésie nègre et malgache* [*Anthology of New Black and Malagasy Poetry*].)

Addressing the deplorable tradition of white endorsement, the Martinican author Frantz Fanon vehemently criticized Breton's relationship to Césaire in *Peau noire, masques blancs*.[32] But not to be outdone by the French, North America maintained a similar tradition as well. For example, when the white American author Stanley Edgar Hyman endorsed the African-American Ralph Ellison's *Invisible Man* in a piece entitled "The Folk Tradition," the critic made the faux pas of ambitiously identifying Ellison's book as part of the African folk tradition, thereby unconsciously putting Ellison back in his (black) place.[33]

The black writer is therefore often attacked on all fronts, through white positive yet patronizing reinforcement and through black Oedipal attacks. In the James Baldwin case, we see that instead of imposing his voice against the hegemonic specter of the white literary canon (embodied by the Wheatly jury), Baldwin attacks his own people, just like in the dozens. Some twenty years later, it is the turn of the younger writer Eldridge Cleaver to attack the well-established Baldwin. In 1966, Cleaver publishes "Notes on a Native Son," an essay in which the author infamously says that while Baldwin is "the most honored Negro writer since Richard Wright,"[34] he is deep down a black hater.[35] Cleaver's accusations are very pregnant with meaning within the context of the dozens. Indeed, there is always a self-reflexive dimension in the ambiguous tradition of a young black writer attacking a fellow: whether it is motivated by black hate or self hate, there is no doubt that the young attacker seeks to destroy something from within. Ironically enough, Cleaver repeats the self-reflexive tradition by himself attacking Baldwin, thereby trying to destroy the master of his own field. The self-beheading of African-American literature is clearly evocative of the puberty ritual of the dozens. The literary dozens is an initiation rite that simultaneously acknowledges the elder as the master of the literary field and attempts to take over his position. As Baldwin says about his attack on Wright, "I thought confusedly then, and feel very definitely now, that this was the greatest tribute I could have paid him."[36] Baldwin was evidently caught in the highly specialized and exclusive field of *African-American writers in Paris*.[37] Gilles Deleuze and Guattari have said that, in minor literature, "there are no possibilities for an individuated enunciation that would belong to this or that *master* and that could be separated from a collective enunciation."[38] If minor literatures were not literatures with masters, as Deleuze and Guattari claim they are, why then would Baldwin have tried to ruin a novel and a writer who greatly contributed to the rise of African-American literature?

## Raphaël Confiant and the Creole Literary Dozens

The connection between African-American and Caribbean literature has often been overlooked in Black Diasporic Studies, even though the two minor literatures share a common plantation history of semantic indirection and the Signifying Monkey. The feuds among Baldwin, Wright, and then Cleaver are well known and have been exhaustively discussed in various academic venues. What is less known, however, is that signifying has also been a common practice in Caribbean literature. The Creole version of signifying has involved vernacularizing the white canon by taking European classics and rewriting them within a historical, geographical, and cultural Caribbean context. As we know, William Shakespeare's Caliban from *The Tempest* underwent several Caribbean revisions (Césaire's *Une tempête*, Lamming's *Water with Berries*, Retamar's *Caliban and Other Essays*) and the works of the Brontë sisters as well (Rhys's *Wide Sargasso Sea*, Condé's *La migration des coeurs*). One year after Gates's publication of *The Signifying Monkey*, Bill Ashcroft, Gareth Griffiths, and Helen Tiffin published *The Empire Writes Back*, a work on the significance of minority revision. In their book, Ashcroft and his coauthors bring attention to the ways in which writers from the margin reconstitute "the language of the center, . . . remolding the language to new usages."[39] Their words resonate with those of Gates as they assert that minor appropriation involves bringing the master language "under the influence of a vernacular tongue."[40] Ashcroft, Griffiths, and Tiffin also argue that Creole literature is particularly fit for the work of revision due to the "polyglossic communities of the Caribbean."[41] The title of their book, *The Empire Writes Back*, is a reference to Salman Rushdie's 1982 piece in the *Times of London*, "The Empire Writes Back with a Vengeance,"[42] an article in which Rushdie discusses the decentering influence of Commonwealth writers on English literature. "The language, like much else in the newly independent societies, needs to be decolonized, to be remade in other images,"[43] Rushdie writes. What has made Rushdie's piece so sensational in the history of postcolonial literature is its tone, which is anything but reverential. Rushdie purposely goes on the offensive with "a vengeance." As he goes on to say, "The Empire is striking back."[44] In everyday language, the expression "with a vengeance" is mostly used as a quantitative indication of intensity; it points to an action being performed with much force. Rushdie's use of the expression, however, is quantitative but also qualitative in that it emphasizes the retaliatory nature of Commonwealth literature; the author warns his audience that it is *their* turn to write.

Rushdie's mention of vengeance is something that Ashcroft, Griffiths, and Tiffin left out in their appropriation, opting for a more neutral tone. *The Empire Writes Back* is of a scholarly nature and thus somewhat too coldly and unaffectedly analytical and theoretical to bear the weight of the vengeance. Also, and more importantly, if Ashcroft, Griffiths, and Tiffin did not include the notion of vengeance in their book, it is mostly because the discourse of resistance that they analyze does not itself come across as angry, emotional, or revengeful. Writing back to the center has remained in large part a conservative literary genre that borrows respectfully from the center. Aimé Césaire's *Une tempête*, a revision of Shakespeare's *The Tempest*, which may be the most celebrated work of black revision in Postcolonial Studies, is a good example. In spite of the fact that Césaire transforms Shakespeare's original Caliban, a half-human fishlike beast,[45] into an opinionated colonized black (Caliban tells the colonizer Prospero, "Call me X" [act 1, scene 2]), Césaire's play does not carry the call-to-action revolutionary tone of the legendary Malcolm X. Instead, with its existentialism reminiscent of Jean-Paul Sartre's *Huis clos* (*No Exit*, 1967), Césaire's island in *Une tempête* is meant as a locus of contemplation of the human condition, a sort of Sartrean *pour-autrui* location offering a methodical, articulate, and self-composed reflection on colonialism. All this is to say that, as far as the Caribbean is concerned, the idea of writing back "with a vengeance," with the raw emotions of anger and retaliation that are usually associated with the idea of violence, is not a prevalent theme in the Caribbean approach to revising the canon.

The apparent self-composure of the revisional practice should, however, not lead to the conclusion that Caribbean literature is deprived of antagonistic emotions. Granted, overt antagonistic emotions do not commonly run from the Caribbean margin to the continental center, but they do manifest themselves within the margin. As in the African-American literature of the 1950s and 1960s, French Antillean writers have had a history of fighting among themselves, a tradition of feuding that has also been motivated by a question of space, or lack thereof. French Antillean literature—which is often not seen by the Western literary intelligentsia as French but more as a francophone exotic bird—is a crammed minority space that, due to its subcategory status, offers few seats to its participants. And because of its exiguity, the Antillean space is easily subject to a game of musical chairs. The minor writer fighting against his literary peers (or mentors) for individual recognition is not, strictly speaking, a Creole renegade of the kind previously examined in this book. This contestatory figure is more of a *bossale* renegade confined in the collective space of the slave ship and resisting the overbearing nature of this generic experience. To do so, the writer must single out his or her voice from Martinique as a national, archipelagic, and universal entity embodied by Aimé Césaire, the *nègre fondamental*, as he is often called.

Aimé Césaire, one of the forefathers of the Negritude Pan-African movement and author of the internationally renowned 1939 *Cahier d'un retour au pays natal*, and Frantz Fanon, the widely praised author of the 1952 *Peau noire, masques blancs* and the 1961 *Les damnés de la terre*, put Martinique on the map. As for Edouard Glissant, he was awarded the prestigious French literary distinction the *Prix Renaudot* back in 1958 for his first novel *La lézarde*. His exhaustive study of the French Antilles in *Le discours antillais* (1981) was the first of a series of extensive essays that succeeded in bringing Edouard Glissant to the forefront of modern critical theory. Glissant's growing recognition as a leading voice in Caribbean Studies later prompted the critic Michael Dash to open his book on Edouard Glissant with the following statement: "At present, Edouard Glissant's eminence not only in French Caribbean literature but in Caribbean literature as a whole is undisputed. There is evidence of his emerging status as a theorist whose concepts and terminology have gained widespread acceptance."[46] Astonishingly enough, the three literary figures from the Caribbean who gained a considerable amount of international recognition over the last decades, namely Césaire, Fanon, and Glissant, all happen to come from the same island of Martinique. Their success shows that the exiguity of the island has had no effect whatsoever on the magnitude of its literature. As Lucien Taylor points out, "Martinique boasts an astonishing number of intellectuals—and such a tiny island to produce the likes of Fanon, Césaire, and Edouard Glissant. I've even read that the only *pays* with more degrees per square kilometer than Martinique is Israel."[47] In light of this, François Paré is right to point out, in *Exiguity: Reflections on the Margins of Literature*, that *exiguity* is a more pertinent word than *minority* when addressing the literatures coming from small nations or small communities. As he argues, exiguity holds the benefit of keeping the focus on the size, and not the value.

Going back to the initial point, exiguity and creative magnitude represent an explosive combination, which makes for a volcanic production of ideas bursting with pride and confidence. But the question remains, how to find one's voice in a space already crowded with such internationally praised personalities? The young Martinican writer Raphaël Confiant published his open letter to Aimé Césaire in 1982, only one year after the release of Glissant's famous *Le discours antillais*. Young, fearless, confident like his name (*confiant* is

French for *confident*), the writer was barely thirty when he attacked the senior master of his literary field, the almost seventy-year old Aimé Césaire. Confiant created a polemic with his open letter in order draw attention to himself through the father of the Negritude movement. The letter was entitled "Lettre d'un homme de trente ans à Aimé Césaire" (Letter from a Thirty-Year-Old Man to Aimé Césaire).[48] Even though the letter's heading stresses the age discrepancy between the sender and the recipient, the tone of the letter is defiant. In this letter, Confiant mainly reproaches Césaire for his lack of support for the independence movement and his politics of assimilation in Martinique. He addresses Césaire directly, criticizing him for having "trainé dans la boue les nationalistes-indépendantistes, accabl[é] d'un mépris sardonique et souverain ceux que vous [talking to Césaire] traîtez de manieurs d'insultes et de rodomontades" (dragged the nationalists-separatists in the mud, subjected to your [talking to Césaire] sardonic and sovereign spite those whom you call insult givers and boasters).[49] Confiant was not yet well known when he wrote this letter. The young novelist would rise to national recognition six years later, in 1988, with the publication of *Le Nègre et l'amiral* (*The Negro and the Admiral*), his first novel written in French. In 1993, Confiant reiterated his attacks with the publication of *Aimé Césaire: Une traversée paradoxale du siècle* (*Aimé Césaire: A Paradoxical Journey through the Century*), an ambitious attempt at tarnishing the image of Césaire. There is definitely an Oedipal dimension in Confiant's symbolic decapitation. In a recent address in honor of the release of the new edition of *Aimé Césaire: une traversée paradoxale du siècle*, Confiant was unapologetic regarding his earlier treatment of Césaire, claiming the absolute right of children to criticize their parents.[50] Confiant also praised Western civilization for abolishing respect for the aged and the worship of ancestors.

What Confiant does not mention in his address, however, is the other ancestral tradition that his book questions: allegiance to one's small nation. Due to the relative scarcity of big names belonging to a small place, it is assumed that there is more pressure to protect one's national patrimony in smaller nations than in bigger ones. As the Czech-born novelist Milan Kundera points out:

Quand Nietzsche malmène bruyamment le caractère allemand, quand Stendhal proclame qu'il préfère l'Italie à sa patrie, aucun Allemand, aucun Français ne s'en offense; si un Grec ou un Tchèque osait dire la même chose, sa famille l'anathémiserait comme un détestable traître.

(When Nietzsche handles roughly the German soul, when Stendhal claims to prefer Italy over his own country, no Germans, no French take offense; if a Greek or a Czech would dare say the same thing, their family would banish them as despicable traitors.)[51]

There is such a thing as the pressure of having to stick together in exiguous spaces. Some talk about the pressure of small places, while others see exiguity as a gift. We know that for Gilles Deleuze and Félix Guattari, minority literature involves "active solidarity" and "collective responsibility"[52] within the group, which makes for a precious and unique kind of literature. But again, Deleuze and Guattari do not belong to a minority group and they find poetic beauty in a condition that others would see, from the inside, as a handicap. We may wonder indeed what could be "beneficial," as they phrase it, about belonging to a literature—as mentioned earlier—where "there are no possibilities for an individuated enunciation that . . . could be separated from a collective enunciation?"[53] What is the pleasure of having one's voice inextricably linked to the indivisible Martinican literature without a chance for individuation? Is there any space left for Milan Kundera after Franz Kafka, James Baldwin after Richard Wright, or Raphaël Confiant after Aimé Césaire?

In an article addressing Deleuze and Guattari's book on Kafka, Karim Larose characterizes the two writers' vision of Kafka as "idealistic," "unrealistic," and "incorrect."[54] In his view, "Kafka never *valorized*"[55] his minor condition; the Czech writer publishing in German only tried to make the best out of a challenging situation. As a counterexample, Larose describes the "stifling space" of the Quebecois language, where the minor is "stuck" in his language "without any breathing space"[56] and with a desire to reach a nonoppressive major where there would be more room for maneuver. By pointing to the question of exiguity, suffocation, and lack of breathing space, Larose brings up an important aspect of the minor condition. In their idealized vision of minority, Deleuze and Guattari seem to have overlooked the quantitative aspect of the minor condition, focusing only on the qualitative and creative side. Again, Deleuze and Guattari's assertion that in minor literature there is no "individuated enunciation that would belong to this or that *master*" overlooks the fact that precisely because masters do not abound in minor literature, a single master will overpower any attempts by other writers to become one. In light of this important distinction, Confiant's attack on Césaire seems to be the result of what Harold Bloom calls "poetic influence."

In his book *The Anxiety of Influence*, Bloom defines "poetic influence" as "a disease of self-consciousness" occurring when a less experienced writer feels "inhibited from creativity by an obsessive reasoning and comparing, presumably of one's work to the precursor's."[57] One way to remedy this obsessive feeling of comparison is to develop a revisional technique, what Bloom technically calls the *clinamen*. Bloom writes:

> *Clinamen* . . . is poetic misreading or misprision proper; I take the word from Lucretius, where it means a "swerve" of the atoms so as to make change possible in the universe. A poet swerves away from his precursor, by so reading his precursor's poem as to execute a *clinamen* in relation to it. This appears as a corrective movement in his own poem, which implies that the precursor poem went accurately up to a certain point, but then should have swerved, precisely in the direction that the new poem moves.[58]

The young poet who applies the *clinamen* technique creates an indirection by "swerving" away from the primary text into the direction of the revised version. This technique requires presenting one's work as a correction of the precursor's masterpiece. Like Gates's black revision, the *clinamen* is catachrestic, which means that it purposely misapplies a signifier as a way to create new meaning through redirection. But unlike the rhetorical figure of catachresis, which is by definition apologetic, the *clinamen* carries arrogance and confidence; it does not claim to use redirection for *lack of* a better word but rather *for* a better word.

The *clinamen* technique is syntactically visible in *Eloge de la Créolité* by Raphaël Confiant and his two coauthors Jean Bernabé and Patrick Chamoiseau. Their Creolist manifesto builds on Glissant's *Antillanité*, as it promotes the importance of the Creole culture and language to the Caribbean identity. Unlike *Antillanité*, however, *Créolité* is essentialist in nature, which is an aspect of the literary movement that Glissant openly disapproved. Bernabé, Chamoiseau, and Confiant's manifesto opens with the following statement: "Ni Européens, ni Africains, ni Asiatiques, nous nous proclamons Créoles" (Neither Europeans, nor Africans, nor Asians, we proclaim ourselves Creoles).[59] This statement is exemplary of the Creolists' radical *clinamen* frame of mind. The structure of the sentence is based on an opposition between an incorrect situation and its corrective answer. The corrective strategy is characteristic of the Creolists who tend to first state what they are not in order to then affirm what they are; through contrast, the first negation makes the following affirmation all the more effective. In the manifesto, the three authors also use a corrective approach to retrace the history of Antillean literature. They present the various literary trends that preceded theirs in a negative light (literally speaking, since they use the negation) to finally introduce their own voice with an affirmative statement. The whole history of French Antillean literature is thus presented as an ever-deferred Creole truthfulness. In other words, in their view, Glissant's *Antillanité* (1980s) came as a response to Césaire's *Négritude* (1930s), and the latter was created as a reaction to the *doudouist* literature (late nineteenth / early twentieth centuries), which was in turn a revision of the "mimetic phase" (mid-seventeenth to late nineteenth centuries). This approach makes it easy for the newest generation to present its literary movement as the fulfillment of an ever-deferred achievement. By first presenting how the literary movements preceding *Créolité* were inadequate, they can emphasize, in their final focus the corrective nature of their own literary endeavor.

When it comes to Césaire, the Creolist *clinamen* takes on a whole new dimension. While addressing Césaire's legacy, the authors of *Eloge de la Créolité* claim they do not think of Césaire as an "anti-Creole" but rather as an "ante-Creole,"[60] and they are "à jamais fils d'Aimé Césaire" (forever Aimé Césaire's sons). But by presenting Martinican literature within a Césairian filiation, Confiant and his coauthors draw attention to the Creolists' irrepressible need to situate their own work in relation to the great precursor. Their pre-/post-Césaire chronology makes it sound as if their movement had to go through the old sphinx first in order to be validated. *Créolité* completes the shift that Césaire was unable to fully achieve and thus makes the corrective move that finally puts Martinican literature on the right track. The ephebe must show a strong position, daring to discredit the precursor's well-established work in order to legitimate his own. In that respect, Bloom's use of the atom metaphor ("a swerve of the atoms so as to make room for change"[61]) is one of the most interesting parts of his concept. Bloom presents friction, and therefore conflict, as a vital self-serving ploy for a newcomer. If Confiant wanted to show the public how much his literary path differed from Césaire's failed literary attempt, the young writer had no choice but to heat up the discussion, thus making the atoms move more rapidly and antagonistically. The poetics of Confiant is, in that sense, like the chaos image in the Cuban Antonio Benítez-Rojo's *Repeating Island*, "a metamachine of differences,"[62] whirling and twisting to the point of indecipherability while being very much meaningful in its chaotic difference.

Attacking Césaire is also an indirect tactic for Confiant to aim at France. Friction allows him to reclaim his Caribbean roots and reject French assimilation through an intertextual chaos redolent of Creole heterogeneousness. Because Confiant sees Césaire as "un indécrottable Français" (a hopeless Frenchman),[63] "le plus noir des Français" (the blackest kind of Frenchman),[64] the racially based and vicarious nature of the attack is ultimately what makes Confiant part of the tradition of the literary dozens. Ironically enough, the vicarious tradition of addressing the white canon via a fellow writer is something that Césaire himself initiated. In 1955, Césaire launched an offensive against French poetry using René Depestre as a target. That year, *Présence Africaine* had set up a debate on the future of African and Antillean poetry, during which the Haitian poet Depestre publicly sided with the French poet Louis Aragon regarding his wish to see the return of traditional French prosody. To express his discontent with Depestre, Césaire wrote an open letter to the Haitian poet, "Réponse à Depestre, poète haïtien (Eléments d'un art poétique)" (Answer to Depestre, Haitian Poet [Elements of Poetic Art]).[65] In it, Césaire uses a slavery-based terminology to invite the Haitian poet on an escape route away from Aragon's Western conventions:[66] "marronnerons-nous Depestre, marronnerons-nous?" (Will we maroon Despestres, will we?).[67] Césaire recaptured the marooning tradition from slavery and transformed it into what Glissant calls "intellectual marooning."[68] Interestingly enough, Confiant ends *Aimé Césaire: une traversée paradoxale du siècle* with an invitation to Césaire to run and maroon into the Creole mangrove; the invitation to maroon comes full circle.

By going against the postcolonial trend that consists of praising the *nègre fundamental*, Confiant's dissenting voice stands apart from the cohesive Caribbean "we" suggestive of Gilroy's slave ship chronotope. And by discrediting the one who, in *Cahier d'un retour au pays natal*, had vowed to be "la bouche des malheurs qui n'ont pas de bouche" (the mouth of the sorrows that have no mouth),[69] Confiant comes across as some sort of a renegade in the *bossale* sense of preserving one's individuality against the collective experience of Caribbean-ness or Martinican-ness. Because of its marooning leitmotif, the reference to the plantation culture is more pronounced in the Caribbean than in the African-American literary dozens, and therefore the underlying idea of the *bossale* figure as a survivor who has acquired skills to survive within the (Creole) plantation society is more prevalent. As of yet, the literary dozens has not been accounted for in Creole literature, even though its historical and cultural relevance begs to be unveiled. The Creole literary dozens longs to join its African-American counterpart within a more global black diasporic context. Creole, as a language of indirect contestation, is comparable to the African-

American vernacular. It is a language that has been for a long time forbidden in the master's house. Until a decade ago, speaking Creole was not allowed in many public institutions in the French Antilles, including schools. Because the Creole language has always been used behind the back of whites, it functions like the dozens. As Chamoiseau says in *Chronique des septs misères* (*Chronicle of the Seven Sorrows*, 2003):

> Le créole nous était rigoureusement interdit. . . . Nous apprîmes à pro-noncer le patois zoulou mais nous en gardâmes toujours une espèce de distanciation moqueuse, de sorte que nous ne pouvions formuler une phrase sans sourire en même temps. Le créole devint progressivement l'outil de nos plaisanteries salaces et de nos jurons les plus osés.

> (Creole was rigorously forbidden to us . . . We learned to speak the patois zulu, while keeping a sense of mocking distance from it, so much so that we could not say a sentence without smiling at the same time. Creole became gradually the tool of our most salacious jokes and our most dar-ing swear words.)[70]

Because Creole calls for carnavalesque release, it also means that it is a lan-guage of performance like the dozens. The salacious jokes and the swearing are just a mise-en-scène meant to release the tension of linguistic repression that cannot be overtly released in the master's house.

The origin of the dozens is still undetermined. According to Dollard, it may have originated in Western European culture and then been "refashioned by Negroes in the last one hundred and fifty years,"[71] which suggests a potential lineage between the French and the black diasporic feuding tradition. An-other potential origin suggested by Dollard is again Africa. In that scenario, African-Americans would have later adapted this African tradition to fit their own needs. A third option, according to Dollard, would be that there is no particular origin and that African-Americans merely invented it, an option that sounds less convincing given its African diasporic presence in the new world today. Incidentally, in *Ribbin', Jivin', and Playin' the Dozens*, Herbert L. Foster finds an overwhelmingly large quantity of case studies indicating the presence of ritualistic insults throughout Africa. Going from the Dahomeans and Ashanti natives and to various groups in West Africa, Foster follows a solid African lead that eventually brings him to Louisiana, a place where we know Ashanti slaves were brought"[72] and, coincidentally, a place where black boys would talk about one another's mamas to initiate fights. Given the variety of possible origins of the dozens, one must come to the conclusion that this tradition is part of the slavery-impacted history of the New World, a history combining the French, the African-Americans, and the Creoles.

What sets the Creole dozens apart from its initial African-American manifestation is its blatantly oxymoronic nature, a trait not so present in the African-American dozens. In the collection of essays *Le métier à métisser*, the scholar Jean Jonnassaint defends Depestre's relationship with Aragon, arguing that Despestre sided with Aragon only because they were friends, and friends support each other, no matter the nationality or political affiliation to which they belong.[73] But we could say that the same applies to Césaire. Césaire attacked Depestre precisely because he cared for him. Césaire wanted to have the poet on his side, in his "forêt natale" (native forest),[74] as he says in the poem. Though critical, the tone of Césaire's poem remains hospitable and courteous. Likewise, though Confiant opts for deprecation, his call to Césaire remains, paradoxically enough, an inviting expression. Confiant invites Césaire to elope from French assimilation in order to join him in a Creole expression of diversity in the mangrove, his native forest. In the open letter to Césaire, Confiant claims that insults are the only way to address the desperate situation in which young Martinicans find themselves, even blaming Césaire for having been too polite in his political career: "C'est votre politesse qui nous a tué" (Your politeness killed us).[75] Since Césaire's politeness brought them assimilation, Confiant feels that insults should be the only option left to claim a right to nonassimilation and diversity. Toward the end of the letter, Confiant says to Césaire, "C'est avec fierté que nous revendiquons l'insulte, la hargne, le rejet viscéral de cette francité empoisonnée que vous avez contribué à nous fourguer sous couvert de Négritude" (It is with pride that we claim insults, spite, and the visceral rejection of this poisoned Frenchness that you contributed to pass onto us in the guise of Negritude).[76]

Insolence, resentment, and emphatic rejection are exactly what Confiant will use against Césaire in the years to follow. In *Aimé Césaire: une traversée paradoxale du siècle*, Confiant's attacks against Césaire are even harsher than in the open letter. Confiant criticizes Césaire for being too much of a Frenchman, for thinking like a mulatto, for being a "petit-bourgeois nègre" (little Negro bourgeois)[77] for always wearing a suit and a tie, for never having danced like Mandela, for never speaking Creole like his own people, for being an alumnus from an elite French school, and for not treating Creole as an endangered language. It is ironic that *Eloge de la Créolité*, the manifesto that Confiant cowrote with Bernabé and Chamoiseau, contains the word *éloge* (praise), when in real life these writers are far from being known for their ability to praise. Because of their infamous use of insults, intolerance, and aggressiveness toward others, the Creolists have even been accused of "intellectual terrorism" and of being "Ayatollahs."[78]

In an interview with Bernabé, Chamoiseau, and Confiant, Lucien Taylor gives a page-long list of insults that the Creolists have exchanged with other writers and critics. Taylor mentions an incident when "Guy Cabort-Masson, a former comrade-in-arms of yours, once referred to *Créolité* as 'but a little runt of francophony,'" to which Bernabé responded by calling him "a disjointed jumping jack, inebriated with himself, thirsting after a recognition he's always been denied."[79] Taylor also describes another incident "when the distinguished man of letters Roland Suvélor took issue with your defense of the anti-Semite Pierre Davidas," to which Confiant responded by describing him as "a loyal mulatto soul menaced with senility . . . Frenchified to the tips of his toenails."[80] Taylor quotes many other incidents involving the Creolists, ending his list with Chamoiseau's misogynist attack against the French writer and critic Annie Lebrun:

> Finally, when Annie Le Brun recently described the three of you as a "demolition team" and spoke of your "spite, where dishonesty, vileness, and idiocy play an equal part," Patrick denounced the "inanity of the obscure poetess" and the "quivering of her ovaries" as she read Césaire.[81]

Taylor further asks the three writers whether "repartee and riposte, stamping on others, the ritualized dance of boasting and humiliation"[82] is characteristic of Creole culture. Even though he claims not to personally operate this way, Bernabé concedes that insults are "a colonial phenomenon. You know, the brothers tearing themselves apart. Because one of them wants to be the representative of the Father."[83] Aside from one incident (quoted above with Roland Suvélor) in which Bernabé engaged in a verbal joust with an opponent, Bernabé admittedly comes across as less aggressive than his notoriously foul-mouthed comrades. For example, when Bernabé was asked by Confiant to write the afterword to *Aimé Césaire: une traversée paradoxale du siècle*, while complying with Confiant's wishes, Bernabé added in the afterword that he could not blindly approve of the author's offensive manners toward Césaire. Interestingly enough, Bernabé is the only one of the three Creolists not known for his insults, and yet he is the only one acknowledging the role of insults in the Creole culture. Chamoiseau, on the other hand, asserts that there is "nothing particularly Creole about [their] polemics."[84] But in "Creole in the French Caribbean Novel of the 1990s," the Creole expert Marie-Christine Hazaël-Massieux argues otherwise. Her chart detailing the different uses of the Creole language in novels by Chamoiseau and Confiant shows that insults are a frequent part of Creole expression.[85] As Hazaël-Massieux concludes, "What remains typical in both Chamoiseau and Confiant[86] is the context of production in which Creole is used: it appears only to express insults or very coarse emotions, or else to speak in very crude terms of facts relating to sexuality."[87]

Reflecting upon the agenda of Antillean literature, Confiant once said, "La littérature est souvent l'expression d'une situation, ou la réponse à cette même situation" (Literature is often the expression of a situation, or the answer to this situation).[88] "Situation" suggests the idea of a problem to be resolved. Césaire was the problem, and he became, unbeknownst to him, the instigator of a defiant and very assertive literature. In "Créolité is/as resistance," Ronnie Scharfman uses the expression "resistance-as-residence" or "domiciliated resistance"[89] to discuss Confiant's and Chamoiseau's relationships to their local Antillean identity. What the authors of the *Créolité* pamphlet call their "interior vision" is undoubtedly a question of domiciliation; it is a call to do away with both the French metropolis and the ancestral Africa: "L'Européanité et l'Africanité" (Europeanity and Africanity).[90] When it comes to a postcolonial discourse of resistance, the question of domiciliation is indeed an important feature of Confiant's and Chamoiseau's literature, but "domiciliation" or "residence" is too soft a word to describe what is really at stake in the *Créolité* movement. More than "domiciliation," Confiant and Chamoiseau have created a *territorial* literature, not in the sense of Gilles Deleuze and Félix Guattari's *territorialization* and *deterritorialization*, which they define in terms of major versus minor,[91] but rather in the intramural sense of minor versus minor.

A territorial literature is a turf literature; it is a literature under the influence of a master and coveted by minor fellows. For the sake of clarity, one should avoid the term *territorialism* and have recourse instead to the neologism *turfism*, since *turfism* is precisely the opposite of the deterritorialization applauded by Deleuze and Guattari for participating in "active solidarity."[92] *Turfism* is a condition of Oedipal dissension within one community resulting from anxiety of influence. "A minor literature doesn't come from a minor language," Deleuze and Guattari assert. "It is rather that which a minority constructs within a major language."[93] Confiant would agree with Deleuze and Guattari, since he has explicitly positioned his voice within a postcolo-nial discourse of resistance, further admitting that Creole has allowed him to go "on the offensive" against the French language.[94] Yet, beneath the surface, Confiant's real discourse of resistance is not only against "extériorités"[95] but also against the resident, the one who occupies the Antillean space. The post-colonial discourse of resistance landmarked by Rushdie's "The Empire Writes Back with a Vengeance" as well as Ashcroft, Griffiths, and Tiffin's *The Empire Writes Back* has famously looked at the postcolonial discursive genre whose role was to answer to the metropolitan center. But what has been overlooked in Postcolonial Studies is the self-reflexive writing back with a vengeance that aims at the minor residence and, more specifically, at the master inhabiting the minor residence. Like the Creole renegade, the *bossale* renegade ques-tions the impact that local residence may have on individual expression. How much does one have to step out, even if it means stepping out while remaining within the local space, in order to produce an emancipated literature? How much betrayal of one's own kin is involved in minor literary production?

The anxiety of influence is not a new phenomenon and is not necessarily specific to minor literatures. What Confiant experienced with Césaire is com-parable to the territorial dispute that led to a rift in the French 1930s between the pope of surrealism André Breton and the philosopher Georges Bataille.[96] Following the *clinamen* tradition, the young and unknown Bataille used in-tertextual feuding to produce a corrective swerve that presented his emerg-ing philosophy, *Hétérologie*, as a revised and improved version of Breton. The noteworthy detail in this infamous exchange lies in the connection to be made between the intertextual nature of the feuding and the development of a phi-losophy based on the notion of diversity. Just as Confiant introduced his liter-ary agenda (leading to the *Créolité* movement) by attacking Césaire, Bataille used Breton to introduce his philosophy also based on the idea of difference.[97] It is certainly not a coincidence that Confiant's and Bataille's philosophies have become two of the most important expressions of diversity and difference in the history of modern French thought.

Bataille and Confiant form a trend of underdog writers who have experi-enced a differend (différend) as a means to reach difference. They have used public conflict as a communicative platform that lets them raise their voices from anonymity. A *differend*, as Jean-François Lyotard explains, occurs when the victim is divested of the means to argue. In most cases, the victim is in-capable of speaking for herself due to the fact that the perpetuator is in sole possession of discursive power. Martinique is an appropriate example:

A Martinican is a French citizen; he or she can bring a complaint against whatever impinges upon his or her rights as a French citizen. But the wrong he or she deems to suffer from the fact of being a French citizen is not a matter of litigation under French law. It might be under private or international law, but for that to be the case it would be necessary that the Martinican were no longer a French citizen. But he or she is. Consequently, the assertion according to which he or she suffers a wrong on account of his or her citizenship is not verifiable by explicit and effective procedures.[98]

The differend is primarily a matter of narratology, a question of determining how identities are being recounted and accounted for while localizing the source and recipient of the telling. As the Haitian scholar Michel-Rolph Trouillot argues, when looking at world history, one should first and foremost track the "exercise of power that makes some narratives possible and silences others."[99] Historiographical power lies just as much in the access to telling as in the power to silence. Lyotard and Trouillot offer theoretical concepts applicable to all underdog conditions. Access (or lack thereof) to the telling of a story is an issue prevalent in both major-versus-minor and minor-versus-minor contexts. The differend, the inaccessibility of the *Geschichteschreibung*, will gag whoever feels deprived of a platform to present his or her case. In Martinique, some aspiring writers felt divested of their means to be heard given that Césaire occupied so much of their minor literary space. They had to come up with innovative strategies, such as the *clinamen*, to tell their stories outside of the master's shade. Recourse to the *clinamen* is by no means an indicator of having been deemed unworthy. As said before, the *clinamen* only addresses a question of discursive space, not of discursive quality. By applying a very public corrective swerve (through an open letter and a book), Confiant successfully pitched his voice away from that of the master and yet still within his field.

There is no doubt that the question of minor space has had a significant impact on the local production of black literature in the Americas, and particularly so in black Creole literature. Why continue writing within one's minor space when residential writing has proven to be so antagonistic for the minor writer? As the previous chapters have shown, a new wave of black diasporic writers have made a point of pitching their voices outside the community precisely to avoid the rivalry inherent in minor communities. The black Pan-American trend of antagonistic rhetoric explains why some writers have more recently started pitching their voices far from their local residence. In so doing, they have created more room for themselves and a more autonomous kind of literature, yet a literature that is often perceived by the community back home as too individualistic and disengaged. Betraying the master to better belong to the minor field is a thing of the past. A growing number of minor writers now prefer moving away from the community, a move that has incidentally introduced a new form of betrayal.

# Notes

## Introduction: The Second-Generation Caribbean Diaspora

1. Lamming, "George Lamming: Concepts of the Caribbean," 9.

2. Braziel and Mannur, *Theorizing Diaspora*, 2.

3. Hall, "Cultural Identity and Diaspora," 438.

4. Gilroy, "Diasporas," 207.

5. Braziel and Mannur, *Theorizing Diaspora*, 4.

6. Gilroy, "Diasporas," 310.

7. Arendt, *The Origins of Totalitarianism*, 271.

8. Brathwaite. *The Development of Creole Society in Jamaica*, 309.

9. In her article, Scharfman looks at the *Créolité* movement as a discourse of resistance to French assimilation. Her main argument is built around the notion of "interior vision" and "domiciliation," one of the main concepts from *Eloge de la Créolité*.

10. In *Pays sans chapeau*, Laferrière stages the writing of his novel in Haiti. That being said, it is difficult to determine whether Haiti is only a diegitic staging in the book or if it is the actual location of production.

11. Benítez-Rojo, *The Repeating Island*, 4.

12. Paré, "Edouard Glissant: A Poetics of Shorelines," 267.

13. For more on the German concept "die Entfremdung," see Milan Kundera's *Les testaments trahis* (*Testaments Betrayed*, 1996), 117.

14. Lionnet and Shih, *Minor Transnationalism*, 3.

15. Rushdie, "The Empire Writes Back with a Vengeance," 8.

16. Ashcroft, Griffiths and Tiffin, *The Empire Writes Back*, 33.

17. See Mwangi, *Africa Writes Back to Self: Metafiction, Gender, Sexuality*, 6.

18. James, *Mariners, Renegades, and Castaways*, 18.

19. Ibid.

20. Melville, *Moby-Dick*, 160.

21. Hall, "Cultural Identity and Diaspora."

22. Ibid., 223.

23. Fabre and Benesch, *African Diasporas in the New World*, xviii.

24. On Edouard Glissant's groundbreaking literary movement, *Antillanité*, see *Le discours antillais*, 421–39.

25. Scharfman, "'Créolité' Is/As Resistance: Raphaël Confiant's *Le nègre et l'amiral*," 126. In her article, Scharfman looks at the *Créolité* movement as a discourse of resistance to French assimilation. Her main argument is built around the notion of "interior vision" and "domiciliation," which is one of the main concepts from *Eloge de la Créolité* by Jean Bernabé and his coauthors.

26. Bernabé, Chamoiseau, and Confiant, *Eloge de la Créolité*, 13.

27. Clifford, *Routes*, 247.

28. Danticat, *Create Dangerously*, 50.

29. Kincaid, *My Brother*, 196.

30. Dash, "Fictions of Displacement," 40.

31. Noxolo and Preziuso, "Postcolonial Imaginations," 168.

32. Brathwaite, *The Development of Creole Society in Jamaica*, xv.

33. Glissant, *Le discours antillais*, 44.

34. Benítez-Rojo, *The Repeating Island*, 11.

35. On *différance*, see Jacques Derrida's *Writing and Difference*.

36. Clifford, *Routes*, 3.

37. Labat, *Voyage aux îles*, 51.

38. Ibid.

39. Ibid.

40. Brathwaite, *The Development of Creole Society in Jamaica*, 249.

41. Price, *Maroon Societies*, 22.

42. Craton, *Testing the Chains*, 65.

43. Ibid.

44. Ibid., 64.

45. As Richard explains in *Maroon Societies*, "They were carefully codified rules regulating the sharing of one woman by more than one man" (19).

46. Glissant, *Le discours antillais*, 104.

47. As Condé shows in *Ségou*, the British ended up not keeping their part of the bargain. They either killed the maroons by making dogs attack them or sent them to Nova Scotia.

48. Pfaff, *Entretiens avec Maryse Condé*, 78.

49. Butel, *Histoire des Antilles françaises*, 173.

50. Brathwaite, *The Development of Creole Society in Jamaica*, 248.

51. Dash, "Fictions of Displacement," 141.

52. Danticat, *Create Dangerously*, 33.

53. Chamoiseau, *L'esclave vieil homme et le molosse*, 42.

54. Condé, "Order, Disorder, Freedom, and the West Indian Writer," 153.

55. Benali and Simasotchi-Bronès, "Le rire créole," 20.

56. Laferrière, *Je suis fatigué*, 87.

57. Ibid.

58. Dash, *The Other America*, 135.

59. Fanon, *Peau noire, masques blancs*, 14.

60. Lyons and Danticat, "An Interview with Edwidge Danticat," 189.

61. In "An Interview with Edwidge Danticat," Danticat is quoted as saying, "We have a Creole proverb that says, 'Pale franse pa vle di gen lespri.' This means, 'Just because you speak French doesn't mean you're smart.' I think that says a lot." Ibid., 190.

62. Britton, *Edouard Glissant and Postcolonial Theory*, 119.

63. Hall, "Cultural Identity and Diaspora," 233.

64. Ibid., 235.

65. Coates and Laferrière, "An Interview with Dany Laferrière," 916.

66. Ibid.

67. Benali and Simasotchi-Bronès, "Le rire créole," 22.

68. Phillips, *Dancing in the Dark*, 214.

69. Birbalsingh, "Jamaica Kincaid: From Antigua to America," 139.

70. Ibid., 143.

71. Boisseron and Condé, "Intimité," 145.

72. Danticat, *Create Dangerously*, 162.

73. Fanon, *Peau noire, masques blancs*, 51.

74. Schoelcher is to Martinique and Guadeloupe what the black revolutionaries Jean-Jacques Dessalines, Henri Christophe, and Toussaint L'Ouverture are to Haiti, the embodiment of emancipation. But because of the 1804 Haitian revolution—hence the early independence of formerly known Saint-Domingue—the master-slave dialectic and the Schoelcherian cry for revenge against the white master (and his daughter) are not predominant features in Haitian literature. "Haïti, où la négritude se mit debout pour la première fois" (where Negritude stood up for the first time) (Césaire) did not wait to be granted its independence; instead, this proud nation snatched it away from its oppressor.

## Chapter 1. Anatole Broyard: Racial Betrayal and the Art of Being Creole

1. Harris, *Patterns of Race in the Americas*, 56.

2. Nelson, "Racial Definition," 319.

3. Hollinger, "Amalgamation and Hypodescent," 168.

4. In *La couleur comme maléfice*, Jean-Luc Bonniol offers an interesting genealogical study of race and racial passing in Creole cultures. In particular, he addresses "le caractère perpétuellement 'en situation' de l'ethnicité" (29) (the perpetual character "in situation" of ethnicity) of the passing Creole subject.

5. Broyard, *One Drop*, 16.

6. Ibid., 339.

7. Ibid.

8. Ibid., 42.

9. Bernabé, Chamoiseau, and Confiant, *Eloge de la Créolité*, 61.

10. Garraway, *The Libertine Colony*, 20.

11. Hall, *Africans in Colonial Louisiana*, 60.

12. Ibid.

13. Domínguez, *White by Definition*, 14.

14. Dubois and Melançon, "Creole Is, Creole Ain't," 240.

15. Domínguez, *White by Definition*, 102.

16. Ibid., 125.

17. Ibid., 143.

18. "Sans en être originaire" (not originating from), as Bernabé, Chamoiseau, and Confiant put it in *Eloge de la Créolité*, 61.

19. Bernabé, "De la négritude à la créolité," 25.

20. Buisseret, *Creolization in the Americas*, 7.

21. Bauer and Mazzotti, *Creole Subjects in the Colonial Americas*, 4.

22. Gates, "White Like Me," 68.

23. Ibid., 67.

24. Broyard, *One Drop*, 437.

25. Ibid., 390.

26. Gates, *The Signifying Monkey*, xxii.

27. Ibid., 6.

28. De Certeau, *L'invention du quotidien 1*, 61.

29. Kein, *The History and Legacy of Louisiana's Free People of Color*, xiii.

30. Garraway, *The Libertine Colony*, 22.

31. Brathwaite, *The Development of Creole Society in Jamaica*, 296.

32. Ibid., 303.

33. Larsen, *Passing*, 161.

34. Ibid.

35. Ibid., 24.

36. According to Sigmund Freud, *unheimlich* (uncanny) is the moment—quick as a flash—when one becomes aware that they have mistaken a doll for a living human being. The doll is about to revert to its inanimate perception, but right before its exposure, it stands in an interstitial moment of being neither entirely alive nor entirely dead, neither human nor quite entirely inanimate, nor even both.

37. "The Figure in the Carpet" is a 1896 novella by Henry James about a literary critic who, after being told by the author Vereker that there is a secret in his story yet to be found, takes it upon himself to unravel the secret, "the thing for the critic to look for . . . the thing for the critic to find" (282). He soon shares with his fellow critic George Corvick the exciting news about the mysterious secret in Vereker's writing, "like a complex figure in a Persian carpet" (289).

38. Racial passing also works like Nathaniel Hawthorne's black veil in his 1836 parable "The Minister's Black Veil." The black veil represents a secret. We know it does not necessarily hide a secret, but, more important, we also know that if there is a secret, it must be of a sexual nature. In the story, when Reverend Hooper decides to cover his face with a black veil that will never be lifted, even after his death, people naturally believe he is trying to hide something. Yet, the supposed secret is never revealed, and readers are slowly led to suspect that there was never a secret to be exposed, even though they—just as the characters in the story—keep looking for it.

39. That Irene pushed Clare from the balcony is only one possible explanation for Clare's accidental death. Clare could have also committed suicide or had an accidental fall after her husband found out she was black.

40. A more developed version appeared a year later in Gates's book *Thirteen Ways of Looking at a Black Man*.

41. Gates, "White Like Me," 66.

42. Broyard, *One Drop*, 108.

43. In his introduction to *Thirteen Ways of Looking at a Black Man*, Gates writes, "Broyard presented the challenge of writing about someone I could never meet, a circumstance that turned out to have advantages as well as disadvantages" (xxiii).

44. Broyard, *One Drop*, 109.

45. Gates writes, "Broyard told his sister Lorraine that he had resolved to pass so that he could be a writer, rather than a Negro writer" ("White Like Me," 67–68), which is exactly, word for word, what James Baldwin said about himself in an article. Baldwin said that he left America because he wanted to "prevent [himself] from becoming merely a Negro; or, even, merely a Negro writer" ("The Discovery of What It Means to Be an American," 171).

46. Broyard, *One Drop*, 109.

47. Ibid.

48. Ibid., 110.

49. Ibid.

50. Carr, "Paranoid Interpretation," 294n9.

51. McDowell, "Introduction," xxvi.

52. Ibid., xvi.

53. Ibid., xvii.

54. The fact that Irene's suspicions are said to be unfounded ("the classic unreliable narrator, Irene is confused and deluded about herself, her motivations, and much that she experiences," xxiv) is debatable.

55. Butler, *Bodies That Matter*, 277.

56. Ibid., 275.

57. Freud, "The Uncanny," 241.

58. Carr, "Paranoid Interpretation," 283.

59. Vian, *J'irai cracher sur vos tombes*, 212.

60. Ibid., 19.

61. Ibid., 48.

62. Roth, *The Human Stain*, 38.

63. Ibid., 26.

64. Gates, "White Like Me," 70.

65. Ibid., 77.

66. Ibid., 74.

67. Broyard, *One Drop*, 444.

68. Gates, "White Like Me," 71.

69. Ibid.

70. Ibid.

71. Freud, "The Unconscious," 191.

72. Boyarin, "What Does a Jew Want?" 276.

73. Bhabha, *The Location of Culture*, 122.

74. Ibid., 216.

75. "The ambivalence between origin and *Entstellung*, discipline and desire, mimesis and repetition" (*The Location of Culture*, 152).

76. Bhabha, *The Location of Culture*, 105.

77. Butler, *Bodies That Matter*, 341.

78. Ibid., 341–42.

79. Ibid., 346.

80. Gates, "White Like Me," 70.

81. Ibid.

82. Barthes, *Le plaisir du texte*, 17.

83. "Like in a Looking-Glass," 146.

84. Rhys, *Wide Sargasso Sea*, 87.

85. Ibid., 67.

86. Ibid., 534.

87. In "Ghosts in the Mirror," Adlai Murdoch looks at Charlotte Brontë's *Jane Eyre* and George Sand's *Indiana*, two nineteenth-century classics worthy of attention for the unusual presence of a Creole figure in each of them. Murdoch argues that in both cases, the Creole figure symbolizes the unstable counterpart of the continental white protagonist. As such, the Creoleness of Brontë's Bertha and Sand's Noun is meant to disrupt the fixed identity of, respectively, Jane Eyre and Indiana. As Murdoch explains, "Despite their differences, both France and Britain as European colonial powers came to represent the Creole as the unnamable third, the impossible indeterminacy excluded by the colonial binary's neither/nor dyad" (1).

88. Murdoch, "Ghosts in the Mirror," 2.

89. Prasad, "Intimate Strangers," 10.

90. Phillips, *Dancing in the Dark*, 212.

## Chapter 2. Maryse Condé's *Histoire de la femme cannibale:* Coming Out in the French Antilles

1. *The Empire Writes Back: Theory and Practice in Post-Colonial Literature*, by Bill Ashcroft, Gareth Griffiths, and Helen Tiffin, is a 1989 groundbreaking theoretical work on the role that the postcolonial text plays in deconstructing the Western canon and the English language.

2. Bongie, *Friends and Enemies*, 303.

3. Ibid., 303–4.

4. "Coloniality is the condition of what we might ungenerously call comprador intelligentsia: of a relatively small, Western-style, Western-trained, group of writers and thinkers, who mediate the trade in cultural commodities of world capitalism at the periphery. In the West they are known through the Africa they offer; their compatriots know them both through the West they present to Africa and through an Africa they have invented for the World, for each other and for Africa" ("The Postcolonial and the Postmodern," 119).

5. Mardorossian, *Reclaiming Difference*, 29.

6. See *Maryse Condé: une nomade inconvenante* (2002), edited by Madelaine Cottenet-Hage and Lydie Moudileno.

7. Condé, "Cherchons nos vérités," 305.

8. Condé, "Liaison dangereuse," 206.

9. Boisseron and Condé, "Intimité," 145.

10. Ibid., 146.

11. Fanon, *Peau noire, masques blancs*, 15.

12. Fanon, *Black Skin, White Masks*, 19.

13. Mabanckou, *Bleu-blanc-rouge*, 40.

14. In his book, the author uses the word *débarqué*, which he italicizes, hereby suggesting that it is a borrowed usage from assumingly Fanon's original use:

> "Bien sûr ceux qui sont de notre sérial me traiteront de poltron, de blanc-bec, de *débarqué*." (16)
>
> (Of course, those who are from our series will call me a coward, a whitey, a *débarqué*.)

15. For more on Mabanckou's new returnee, see Dominic Thomas, "Fashion Matters: La Sape and Vestimentary Codes in Transnational Contexts and Urban Diasporas."

16. Fanon, *Peau noire, masques blancs*, 18.

17. Ibid., 19.

18. Condé, "Liaison dangereuse," 212.

19. Condé, "Cherchons nos vérités," 308.

20. Like Condé, Edouard Glissant has been spending part of the year in New York as a distinguished professor at CUNY since the early 1990s, but unlike Condé, the writer still mainly comes across in his writing as an Antillean-in-residence.

21. In *Chronique des sept misères* (*Chronicle of the Seven Sorrows*), Chamoiseau elegiacally recounts the last days of the "djobeur," an old traditional profession in the Creole market that consisted in making oneself useful—for example, transporting goods in wheelbarrows for merchants.

22. Fanon, *Peau noire, masques blancs*, 19.

23. The novel tells the story of a psychiatrist specializing in the alienation disorders of *negropolitans*. Delsham's protagonist takes after Fanon, who was also a psychiatrist specializing in colonial alienation disorders.

24. Frantz Fanon's doctoral thesis "Essai pour la désaliénation du Noir" was later published as *Peau noire, masques blancs*.

25. Delsham, *Négropolitains et Euro-blacks*, 40.

26. Condé, "Cherchons nos vérités," 306.

27. "Erosion" is one of Edouard Glissant's main concerns in *Le discours antillais*. As he says:

> "Nous n'en finissons pas de disparaître, victimes d'un frottement du monde." (15)
> (We keep disappearing as victims of world friction.)

28. Murray, "Laws of Desire?" 163.

29. Noxolo and Preziuso, "Postcolonial Imaginations," 168.

30. Laplanche, *Life and Death in Psychoanalysis*, 35.

31. Fanon, *Peau noire, masques blancs*, 146n44.

32. Fanon, *Black Skin, White Masks,* 180n44.

33. The first one took place right after the war, when he studied for his baccalauréat in Martinique under Aimé Césaire's guidance, and the second one was in 1951, when he worked as a substitute physician in Colson Psychiatric Hospital in Martinique. In both cases, the biographer Alice Cherki uses the adjective "disappointing" and mentions "the close-mindedness" of the people to describe Fanon's experience back home and his hasty return to metropolitan France: "In 1951, after defending his thesis, Fanon accepted a temporary position as a substitute physician at Colson, in the Antilles. The experience proved disappointing, and he returned to France complaining of the close-mindedness and lack of awareness he found there" (Cherki, *Frantz Fanon: A Portrait*, 19).

34. Cherki, *Frantz Fanon: A Portrait*, 15.

35. Murray, "Laws of Desire?" 166.

36. Spear, "Carnivalesque jouissance," 11.

37. Murray, "Laws of Desire?" 166.

38. Hayes, "Looking for Roots among the Mangroves," 470.

39. Boisseron and Condé, "Intimité," 149.

40. Pépin, *Cantique des tourterelles*, 55.

41. Condé's novel is also based on a mysterious story of inbreeding.

42. Condé, *Célanire cou-coupé*, 288.

43. Boisseron and Condé, "Intimité," 150.

44. Ibid., 149.

45. Condé, "Postface," 241.

46. Boisseron and Condé, "Intimité," 150.

47. Condé, *Histoire de la femme cannibale*, 271.

48. Ibid., 311.

49. Ibid., 273.

50. Baldwin, *Giovanni's Room*, 305.

51. Ibid., 315.

52. Dash, *The Other America*, 4.

53. Doris Garraway explains that it is in the seventeenth century that the indigenous peoples in the Caribbean "began to use the term *Carib* to describe themselves, a fact that is amply demonstrated in the French ethnographic record" (*The Libertine Colony*, 42).

54. Lamming, "George Lamming: Concepts of the Caribbean," 2.

55. Fulton, "A Question of Cannibalism," 88.

56. Chambers, *Untimely Interventions*, 29.

57. Condé, *Histoire de la femme cannibale*, 352.

58. Rosello, "Post-Cannibalism in *Histoire de la femme cannibale*," 42.

59. Sansavior, "Entretien avec Maryse Condé," 17.

60. Ibid.

61. Bérard, "Entretien avec Maryse Condé," 122.

62. An epitext is an element outside the book contributing to the relationship between author and reader. A paratext refers to an element inside the book such as inscription and title influencing the reading of the text. For further information on paratext, epitext, and peritext, see Gérard Genette's *Seuils*.

63. Rosello, "Post-Cannibalism in *Histoire de la femme cannibale*," 42.

64. Lachman, Simek, and Broichhagen, "A Conversation at Princeton with Maryse Condé," 26.

65. Boisseron and Condé, "Intimité," 151.

66. Ibid., 147.

67. Lachman and Broichhagen, "A Conversation at Princeton with Maryse Condé," 3.

68. For a psychoanalytical study of the Caliban figure, see Octave Mannoni's *Psychologie de la colonisation*.

69. In "'Something Rich and Strange': Caliban's Theatrical Metamorphoses," Virginia Mason Vaughan explains:

> Since Caliban's first appearance in 1611, Shakespeare's monster has undergone remarkable transformations. From drunken beast in the eighteenth century, to noble savage and missing link in the nineteenth, to Third-World victim of oppression in the mid-twentieth, Caliban's stage images reflect changing Anglo-American attitudes toward primitive man. Shakespeare's monster once represented bestial vices that must be eradicated; now he personifies noble rebels who symbolize the exploitation of European imperialism. (390)

70. Derrida, "Freud and the Scene of Writing," 92.

71. Schneebaum, *Keep the River on Your Right*, 50.

72. Ibid., 110.

73. Here is how the author describes the rite immediately preceding the cannibalistic act:

> [One of the brothers] walked to the man beside me who was himself half erect, and touched the ends of their penises together, then moved in a counter-clockwise fashion from one to another, pressing slightly on each penis with his own, ending up with mine, and re-entering the circle at my side. (102)

74. Condé, *La vie scélérate*, 24.

75. Ibid.

76. Ibid., 32.

77. Ibid., 62.

78. Ibid., 63.

79. Condé, *La migration des coeurs*, 41.

80. *Histoire de la femme cannibale*, 19.

81. Ibid., 31–32.

82. See in particular Bakhtin's *Problems of Dostoevsky's Poetics*.

83. Condé, "O Brave New World," 5.

84. None of her stories take place exclusively in Guadeloupe with the exception of *Victoire: les saveurs et les mots* (*Victoire, My Mother's Mother*), the story of Condé's grandmother from Marie-Galante who moved to the main island of Guadeloupe. Yet again, this book is a true memoir, not a novel.

85. The group TLC used the expression in their song "Creep" ("Just keep it on the down low / said nobody is supposed to know"), and R. Kelly made the expression famous with his song "Down Low (Nobody Has to Know)."

86. Keith Boykin reports the following statistics in his book *Beyond the Down Low*: "Of the 7,000 black female AIDS cases in 2003, only 118 reported sex with a bisexual male as the method of exposure. . . . Only 1.6 percent of black women diagnosed with AIDS reported sex with a bisexual male, but nearly 100 percent of the public discussion about AIDS in the black community focused on the down low" (vii).

87. Boykin, *Beyond the Down Low*, 20.

88. Kincaid, *My Brother*, 161.

89. Noxolo and Preziuso, "Postcolonial Imaginations," 170.

## Chapter 3. Edwidge Danticat and Dany Laferrière: Parasitic and Remittance Diaspora

1. Hallward, *Damming the Flood*, xxxiv.

2. Braziel, *Duvalier's Ghosts*, xxi.

3. Ibid., xxx.

4. Ibid., xxiii.

5. Ibid., xxiv.

6. Nesbitt, *Voicing Memory*, 204.

7. Page, "What If He Did Not Have a Sister?" 37.

8. Braziel, *Duvalier's Ghosts*, xxi.

9. Nesbitt, *Voicing Memory*, 207.

10. Munro, *Exile and Post-1946 Haitian Literature*, 207.

11. Danticat, *Create Dangerously*, 33.

12. Laferrière, *L'énigme du retour*, 134.

13. Danticat, *Create Dangerously*, 19.

14. Nesbitt, *Voicing Memory*, 203.

15. Bongie, *Friends and Enemies*, 325.

16. Ibid., 326.

17. Ibid., 326–27.

18. Laferrière, *L'énigme du retour*, 144.

19. Laferrière, *Cette grenade*, 19.

20. Ibid., 331.

21. Edmondson, *Making Men*, 141.

22. Ibid.

23. Ibid.

24. Mardorossian, *Reclaiming Difference*, 115.

25. Ibid., 121.

26. Laferrière, *Je suis fatigué*, 52.

27. Lamming, "George Lamming: Concepts of the Caribbean," 9.

28. Lyons, "An Interview with Edwidge Danticat," 190.

29. Ibid.

30. Danticat, *Create Dangerously*, 159.

31. Ibid., 49.

32. Ibid., 50.

33. Ibid., 50.

34. Dash, "Fictions of Displacement," 40.

35. Saint-Eloi, *Haïti: Kenbé la!*, 96.

36. Dominique, *Mémoire errante*, 168.

37. Césaire, *Cahier d'un retour au pays natal*, 42.

38. Danticat, *Create Dangerously*, 50.

39. Ibid., 53.

40. Laferrière, *Le cri des oiseaux fous*, 67.

41. Ibid.

42. Danticat, *Create Dangerously*, 160.

43. Laferrière, *Je suis fatigué*, 42.

44. Laferrière, *Je suis un écrivain japonais*, 16.

45. Ibid., 14.

46. Laferrière, *L'énigme du retour*, 141.

47. Bongie, *Friends and Enemies*, 326–27.

48. Danticat, *Create Dangerously*, 28.

49. *Comment faire l'amour* (1985), *Eroshima* (1987), *Cette grenade* (1993), *Chronique de la dérive douce* (1994).

50. *L'odeur du café* (1991), *Le goût des jeunes filles* (1992), *Le charme des après-midi sans fin* (1997), *La chair du maître* (2000).

51. Dash, "Fictions of Displacement," 1.

52. Nesbitt, *Voicing Memory*, 130.

53. Laferrière, *Tout bouge autour de moi*, 77–78.

54. Ricoeur, *Histoire et vérité*, 26.

55. Trouillot, *Silencing the Past*, 99.

56. Laferrière, *Le cri des oiseaux fous*, 32.

57. Ibid., 113.

58. Dash, "Fictions of Displacement," 33.

59. Glissant, *Le discours antillais*, 20.

60. Dash, "Fictions of Displacement," 33.

61. Laferrière, *Le cri des oiseaux fous*, 113.

62. Ibid., 114.

63. Ibid., 40.

64. Danticat, *Create Dangerously*, 6.

65. *L'odeur du café* (1991), *Le goût des jeunes filles* (1992), *Pays sans chapeau* (1996), *Le charme des après-midi sans fin* (1997), *La chair du maître* (2000).

66. Laferrière, *J'écris comme je vis*, 118.

67. "J'ai donc connu mon premier exil à l'âge de cinq ans" (I experienced my first exile at the age of five) (*Le cri des oiseaux fous*, 53).

68. Laferrière, *L'odeur du café*, 216.

69. Laferrière's particularity is to find poetic beauty in the simplest moments of life:

> Tiens, un oiseau traverse mon champ de vision. J'écris: oiseau. (*Pays sans chapeau*, 14)
>
> (Here, a bird crosses my field of vision. I write: bird.)

70. Laferrière, *Le cri des oiseaux fous*, 42.

71. Bhabha, *The Location of Culture*, 2.

72. Ibid.

73. Ibid.

74. "Je suis sur-déterminé de l'extérieur" (I am over-determined from the outside) (*Peau noire, masques blancs*, 93).

75. Danticat, *Create Dangerously*, 159.

76. Laferrière, *Je suis un écrivain japonais*, 198.

77. Chambers, *Untimely Interventions*, 19.

78. Ibid., 16.

79. Ibid.

80. Danticat, *Create Dangerously*, 162.

81. Kincaid, *My Brother*, 7.

82. Ibid., 152.

83. Chambers, *Untimely Interventions*, 20.

84. Rosello, *Postcolonial Hospitality*, 33.

85. Laferrière, *L'énigme du retour*, 157.

86. Kincaid, *My Brother*, 180.

87. Ibid., 146.

88. Ibid., 162.

89. Chambers, *Untimely Interventions*, 16.

90. Kincaid, *My Brother*, 196.

91. Page, "What If He Did Not Have a Sister?" 51.

92. Lyons, "An Interview with Edwidge Danticat," 190–91.

93. Danticat, *Create Dangerously*, 158.

94. Page, "What If He Did Not Have a Sister?" 51.

95. Danticat, *Create Dangerously*, 94.

96. Danticat, however, would promise only not to use her aunt's or cousin's real names. Marius is a pseudonym.

97. Danticat, *Create Dangerously*, 95.

98. Chambers, *Untimely Interventions*, 31.

99. Ibid., 43.

100. Laferrière, *Tout bouge autour de moi*, 50.

101. Ibid., 51.

102. Ibid.

103. Chambers, *Untimely Interventions*, 6.

104. Danticat, *Create Dangerously*, 157.

105. Laferrière, *Tout bouge autour de moi*, 156.

106. Ibid.

107. Danticat, *Create Dangerously*, 113.

108. Dash, "Fictions of Displacement," 35.

109. Sontag, *Illness as Metaphor*, 176.

110. Baudrillard, "The Spirit of Terrorism."

111. The first part of *Haiti parmi les vivants* brings together testimonials by Michel Le Bris, Dany Laferrière, and Lyonel Trouillot posted immediately following the earthquake on the *Le Point* Web site.

112. Yannick Lahens offers a testimonial on the earthquake in Failles. She is not included in the list because she was in Haiti but not staying at Hotel Karibe, since she is a Haitian resident.

113. Laferrière, *Tout bouge autour de moi*, 12.

114. Martin, *Le tremblement*, 26.

115. Saint-Eloi, *Haiti: Kenbé la!* 52.

116. The suitcase is filled with books published by Mémoire d'encrier, one of the two publishing houses that will eventually publish *Tout bouge autour de moi*, Laferrière's testimonial on the Haitian earthquake.

117. Spear, "Point of View," 35.

118. Laferrière, *Tout bouge autour de moi*, 31.

119. Laferrière, *L'énigme du retour*, 180.

120. Ibid., 199.

121. Ibid.

122. Danticat, *Create Dangerously*, 169.

123. Laferrière, *Tout bouge autour de moi*, 65.

124. Ibid., 55.

125. Danticat, *Create Dangerously*, 161.

126. Saint-Eloi, *Haiti: Kenbé la!* 137.

127. Martin, *Le tremblement*, 68.

128. Martin, *Le tremblement*, 77.

129. Laferrière, *Tout bouge autour de moi*, 76.

130. Laferrière, *Le cri des oiseaux fous*, 46.

131. Saint-Eloi, *Haiti: Kenbé la!* 138.

132. Laferrière, *Tout bouge autour de moi*, 92.

## Chapter 4. V. S. Naipaul and Jamaica Kincaid: Rhetoric of National Dis-Allegiance

1. Hall, "Cultural Identity and Diaspora," 222.

2. Bachelard, *La poétique de l'espace*, 31.

3. French, *The World Is What It Is*, 55.

4. Ibid., 57.

5. Kincaid, *My Brother*, 75.

6. Hall, "Cultural Identity and Diaspora," 235.

7. Naipaul, "Two Worlds: The 2001 Nobel Lecture," 10.

8. Ibid., 7.

9. Ibid., 10.

10. Levin, "V. S. Naipaul: A Perpetual Voyager," 93.

11. Ibid.

12. Kincaid, *My Brother*, 13.

13. Kincaid, *A Small Place*, 79–80.

14. Segalen, *Essay on Exoticism*, 16.

15. Hall, "When Was the 'Post-Colonial'?" 242.

16. Dirlik, "The Postcolonial Aura," 109.

17. Huggan, *The Postcolonial Exotic*, vii.

18. Depestre, *Le métier à métisser*, 210.

19. Chambers, *Loiterature*, 7.

20. Ibid.

21. Levin, "V. S. Naipaul: A Perpetual Voyager," 93.

22. French, *The World Is What It Is*, 459.

23. Ibid., 459.

24. Deleuze and Guattari, *Kafka: Toward a Minor Literature*, 17.

25. Birbalsingh, "Jamaica Kincaid: From Antigua to America," 146.

26. Kincaid, *My Brother*, 198.

27. As we see, the *New Yorker* is a recurrent submotive in *Creole Renegades*. The magazine is at the heart of Henry Louis Gates's outing of Anatole Broyard, Naipaul's revelations of his sexual indiscretions, and Kincaid's writing career, which shows the intimate relationship between mainstream media and the "comprador intelligentsia" of postcolonial literature.

28. Kincaid, *Lucy*, 21.

29. Kincaid, *My Brother*, 7.

30. Ibid., 90.

31. Ibid., 36.

32. Page, "What If He Did Not Have a Sister?" 51.

33. Ibid., 49.

34. Kincaid, *My Brother*, 180.

35. Kincaid, *See Now Then*, 154

36. Kincaid, *My Brother*, 179.

37. Chambers, "Gossip and the Novel," 213.

38. Cazenave and Célérier, *Contemporary Francophone African Writers*, 5.

39. For further reading on the question of remittance in francophone literature, see Thomas, "Fashion Matters," and Boisseron, "Potlatch transnational dans *Bleu-blanc-rouge* d'Alain Mabanckou."

40. Rowe-Evans, "V. S. Naipaul: A Transition (Interview)," 29.

41. King, "A Small Place Writes Back," 891.

42. Ibid.

43. James, *Mariners, Renegades, and Castaways*, 18.

44. Birbalsingh, "Jamaica Kincaid: From Antigua to America," xv.

45. French, *The World Is What It Is*, xiii.

46. Saïd, "Intellectuals in the Post-Colonial World," 46.

47. Naipaul, *The Middle Passage*, 42.

48. Hardwick, "Meeting V. S. Naipaul," 49.

49. Ibid., 45.

50. Mukherjee and Boyers, "A Conversation with V. S. Naipaul," 77.

51. Ibid., 76.

52. Rowe-Evans, "V. S. Naipaul: A Transition (Interview)," 57.

53. Hardwick, "Meeting V. S. Naipaul," 45.

54. Cudjoe, *V. S. Naipaul: A Materialist Reading*, 6.

55. Bhabha, *The Location of Culture*, 13.

56. Butler, *Excitable Speech*, 4.

57. Bhabha, *The Location of Culture*, 13.

58. Butler, *Excitable Speech*, 5.

59. Ibid.

60. Saïd, "Intellectuals in the Post-Colonial World," 53.

61. Ibid.

62. Ibid., 81.

63. Cudjoe, *V. S. Naipaul: A Materialist Reading*, 6.

64. Ibid., 6.

65. For a detailed discussion on perlocutionary and other speech acts, see J. L. Austin, *How to Do Things with Words*, and Jacques Derrida, *Limited Inc.*

66. French, *The World Is What It Is*, xi.

67. Kincaid, *A Small Place*, 79–80.

68. Birbalsingh, "Jamaica Kincaid: From Antigua to America," 140.

69. Lamming, "George Lamming: Concepts of the Caribbean," 11.

70. Michener, "The Dark Visions of V. S. Naipaul," 63.

71. Mukherjee and Boyers, "A Conversation with V. S. Naipaul," 13.

72. Michener, "The Dark Visions of V. S. Naipaul," 68.

73. Winokur, "The Unsparing Vision of V. S. Naipaul," 121.

74. Kincaid, *Lucy*, 7.

75. Birbalsingh, "Jamaica Kincaid: From Antigua to America," 139.

76. Kincaid, *Lucy*, 1356.

77. Lyotard, *The Differend*, 27.

78. Kincaid, *A Small Place*, 31–32.

79. Laferrière, *Je suis fatigué*, 81.

80. King, "A Small Place Writes Back," 904.

81. French, *The World Is What It Is*, x.

## Chapter 5. Creole versus *Bossale* Renegade: "Turfism" in the Black Diaspora of the Americas

1. Gilroy defines the chronotope of the slave ship as "a living, micro-cultural, micro-political system in motion" (*The Black Atlantic*, 4).

2. Gilroy, *The Black Atlantic*, 199.

3. Ibid., 3.

4. Glissant, *Introduction à une poétique du divers*, 59.

5. Britton, *Edouard Glissant and Postcolonial Theory*, 11.

6. See, in particular, Glissant, *Poétique de la relation* and *Introduction à une poétique du divers*.

7. Let us keep in mind that Glissant, since the late 1980s, had been living in North America, first teaching at LSU and then at the CUNY Graduate Center.

8. In his more recent work, Chamoiseau has adopted a more global perspective that is reminiscent of Glissant's. See, for example, *L'empreinte à Crusoé* (2012), a rewriting of Robinson Crusoe reflecting on the absence of origins, the potential for a new beginning of civilization, and the tabula rasa of identity (due to amnesia).

9. In his more recent work, Confiant mentions again, through his protagonist, the smallness, in every sense, of insular life:

> J'ai en permanence une mappemonde sur mon bureau. C'est là une garantie ab-solue contre cette dérive, propre aux insulaires, qui consiste, pour peu qu'on ne soit pas sorti depuis quelques mois, à oublier qu'il existe quelque chose en-dehors de la petite calebasse où l'on marine. (*Black Is Black*, 112)
>
> (I always have a globe on my desk. It is an absolute guarantee against drifting, specific to islanders, which consists, if one did not get out for a while, in forgetting that there is something out there, outside the small calabash where we soak.)

10. Gates, *The Signifying Monkey*, 6.

11. Ibid., xxii.

12. Nesbitt, *Voicing Memory*, 51.

13. Ibid., 53.

14. Nesbitt explains "signifying" as follows: "In this manner, through parody and irony, the slave appropriates a signifier that has been imposed through the master's discourse, colonizing it and evacuating it of its traditional meaning, then reinvesting it with a new, contestatory sense" (53).

15. Mitchell-Kernan, "Signifying, Loud-Talking and Marking," 326.

16. Condé, *La civilisation du bossale*, 32.

17. Ibid.

18. Glissant, *Le discours antillais*, 50.

19. Ibid., 67.

20. Onwuchekwa, *Yo' Mama!*, 46.

21. Because of the emphasis on the mother, *motherfucker* is a common address in the dozens (Mitchell-Kernan, "Signifying, Loud-Talking and Marking," 326).

22. Dollard, "The Dozens: Dialectic of Insult," 291.

23. Ibid., 304.

24. Baldwin, "The Discovery of What It Means to Be an American," 17.

25. Lest, "James Baldwin—Reflections of a Maverick," 1.

26. Baldwin, "Everybody's Protest Novel," 31.

27. Baldwin, "Alas, Poor Richard," 182.

28. Ibid., 184.

29. Ibid.

30. Ibid., 189.

31. See Henry Louis Gates discussing the Phillis Wheatly case in "Writing Race and the Difference It Makes."

32. Fanon, *Peau noire, masques blancs*, 54.

33. Ralph Ellison was rightfully furious at his white friend Stanley Edgar Hyman when the latter wrote a piece on *Invisible Man* that exclusively focused on the influence of African folklore in Ellison's book. In an open letter, Ellison publicly castigated Hyman for trying to find a purely African-American and African idiosyncrasy in his work instead of going beyond the author's color and appreciating *Invisible Man* as a personal or simply American work. The title of Ellison's open letter, "Change the Joke and Slip the Yoke," is a snappy sentence purposely reminiscent of the dozens. Ellison invites Hyman to a game of black repartee, thereby establishing superiority over his white friend who is incognizant of the black semantic rules. By using an inside joke, Ellison stresses the subtleties of one's cultural idiom, thus suggesting that Hyman may not be culturally equipped to accurately read African diasporic idiosyncrasy in *Invisible Man*. That said, the problem with the nature of Ellison's open letter lies in the fact that it somehow leads us to the conclusion that the black writer needs to revert to an African-American idiosyncratic language in order to take back his voice from the white text (Hyman). In other words, Hyman eventually succeeds in confining Ellison to the role of the *African-American writer*, which is one of the perverted consequences of the literary dozens.

34. Cleaver, "Notes on a Native Son," 352.

35. Cleaver writes, "A rereading of *Nobody Knows My Name* cannot help but convince the most avid of Baldwin's admirers of the hatred for blacks permeating his writings" (*Black Expression*, 341).

36. Baldwin, "Alas, Poor Richard," 197.

37. A few weeks before his death in November 1960, Wright gave a lecture addressed to the students and members of the American Church in Paris entitled "The Situation of the Black Artist and Intellectual in the United States." In it, the moribund writer comes to the conclusion that the overpowering American government is responsible for creating friction within the community. He says:

> It is a deadly fight in which brother is set against brother, in which threats of mystical violence are hurled by one black against the other, where vows to cut or kill are voiced. . . . My speaking of it has its aim: perhaps I can make you aware of the tragic tensions and frustrations which such a system of control inflicts upon Negro artist and intellectuals. (*The Unfinished Quest of Richard Wright*, 518)

Among other incidents, Wright cites Baldwin's infamous attack against him. Though governmental pressures may have played a role in the frustration of some black intellectuals, it cannot fully account for the motivation behind the *Partisan Review* article.

Wright's magnanimous gesture of holding the government responsible for Baldwin's actions clearly overlooks Baldwin's personal predicament. Though he left his country to become independent, Baldwin was ineluctably brought back to his black roots through Wright's mentorship.

38. Deleuze and Guattari, *Kafka: Toward a Minor Literature*, 17.

39. Ashcroft, Griffiths, and Tiffin. *The Empire Writes Back*, 38.

40. Ibid., 39.

41. Ibid., 45.

42. Salman Rushdie's *Times* article, "The Empire Writes Back with a Vengeance," argues that literature from the Empire has put an end to the monological and hegemonic nature of English literature.

43. Rushdie, "The Empire Writes Back with a Vengeance," 7.

44. Ibid.

45. Aside from Aimé Césaire's revision, for a detailed study of the transformation of Shakespeare's Caliban over the centuries, see the work of Virginia Mason Vaughan, "'Something Rich and Strange': Caliban's Theatrical Metamorphoses" and (with Alden T. Vaughan) *Shakespeare's Caliban: A Cultural History*.

46. Dash, *Edouard Glissant*, 1.

47. Taylor, "Mediating Martinique," 262.

48. Confiant's open letter was originally published on June 1, 1982, in *Antilla* 19. Confiant published the letter again in his book *Aimé Césaire: une traversée paradoxale du siècle*.

49. Ibid., 319–20.

50. See *Aimé Césaire* on the online chronicle *Tribune des Antilles*.

51. Kundera, *L'ignorance*, 227.

52. Deleuze and Guattari, *Kafka: Toward a Minor Literature*, 17.

53. Ibid.

54. Larose, "Major and Minor: Crossed Perspectives," 4.

55. Ibid., 40.

56. Ibid., 42.

57. Bloom, *The Anxiety of Influence*, 29.

58. Ibid., 14.

59. Bernabé, Chamoiseau, and Confiant, *Eloge de la Créolité*, 7.

60. Ibid., 18.

61. Bloom, *The Anxiety of Influence*, 14.

62. Benítez-Rojo, *The Repeating Island*, 18.

63. Confiant, *Aimé Césaire*, 321.

64. Ibid.

65. The open letter was later republished in Césaire's *Oeuvres complètes* under the title "Le verbe marronner" (The marooning verb).

66. Césaire compares black authenticity with the native forest and wonders if Depestre's lack of it is due to his exile (in Brazil):

Vaillant cavalier du tam-tam
est-il vrai que tu doutcs dc la forêt natale

...

Se peut-il que les pluies de l'exil
Aient détendu la peau de tambour de ta voix. (223)

67. Confiant, "Lettre d'un homme de trente ans à Aimé Césaire," 225.

68. Glissant, *Le discours antillais*, 67.

69. Césaire, *Cahier d'un retour au pays natal*, 42.

70. Chamoiseau, *Chronique des sept misères*, 167.

71. Dollard, "The Dozens: Dialectic of Insult," 290.

72. Foster, *Ribbin,' Jivin,' and Playin' the Dozens*, 225.

73. In "Le nomade enraciné," Jonassaint writes:

Dans sa fragilité d'exilé, le poète tient plus à des amitiés particulières au-delà des espaces et idéologies qu'à des mots d'ordre. Son ralliement à la proposition d'Aragon d'un retour à l'alexandrin que Césaire critique bellement dans un poème "Le verbe marronner" est de cet ordre. Il veut communiquer. Il interpelle. Il est reconnaissant. Il connaît le prix de l'amitié, et multiplie épigrammes, clins d'oeil, dédicaces, hommages, remerciements. Autant de marques de reconnaissance. (240)

(Weakened by his exile, the poet holds on more to his particular friendships beyond places and ideologies than to decrees. His rallying to Aragon's side on the proposition to return to the alexandrine, which Césaire beautifully criticized in his poem "The Marooning Verb," is of that sort. He wants to communicate. He calls out. He is grateful. He knows the price of friendship, and multiplies epigrams, winks, dedications, homage, and thanks. So many signs of gratitude.)

74. Depestre, *Le métier à métisser*, 223.

75. Confiant, *Aimé Césaire*, 321.

76. Ibid.

77. Ibid., 100.

78. Taylor, "Créolité Bites," 156.

79. Ibid., 157.

80. Ibid.

81. Ibid.

82. Ibid.

83. Ibid.

84. Ibid.

85. The three books used for Marie-Christine Hazaël-Massieux's study are Chamoiseau's *Chronique des sept misères* and *Chemin d'école*, and Confiant's *L'allée des soupirs*.

86. *Eloge de la Créolité* depicts the Creole language as a "véhicule originel de notre moi profound" (the original vehicle of our deepest self) (43). For close to ten years, Confiant

wrote all of his books in Creole. In 1979, Confiant published his first work in Creole, a collection of short stories entitled *Jik dèyè do Bondyé* with the publishing house *Grif An tè*, and only in 1988 did he start publishing in French, his first book being *Le nègre et l'amiral*.

87. Hazaël-Massieux, "Creole in the French Caribbean Novel of the 1990s," 97.

88. Elte and Ludwig, "En guise d'introduction," 6.

89. Scharfman, "Créolité Is/As Resistance," 126.

90. Bernabé, Chamoiseau, and Confiant, *Eloge de la Créolité*, 18.

91. "[Domiciliation is] a deterritorialized language, appropriate for strange and minor uses" (*Kafka: pour une littérature mineure*, 17).

92. Ibid.

93. Ibid.

94. Taylor, "Créolité Bites," 139.

95. Bernabé, Chamoiseau, and Confiant, *Eloge de la Créolité*, 18.

96. When Bataille first met Breton, he was not a known writer, having published only one obscure book, *Notre-Dame de Rheims*. Breton, on the other hand, had already published the (first) *Le manifeste du surréalisme* (*Manifesto of Surrealism*). We know from Michel Surya's biography of Bataille that the year Bataille met Breton, the former was "sick of his empty life, with no reputation or means; so envious of the authentic life these recognized writers embodied" (*Georges Bataille: An Intellectual Biography*, 76). As the underdog, Bataille was the first to throw a punch at the master Breton, which initiated a long intertextual feud between the two rivals. The exchange eventually culminated in Bataille writing an open letter to Breton, in which the young writer questioned Breton's philosophy while introducing his own. Like Confiant's, Bataille's open letter lacks the light and mundane tone that one usually ascribes to the epistolary genre. Judging by the pattern of their dispute, it seems that Bataille viewed the epistolary dialectic of insults as a way to make room for his voice in the tight-knit Surrealist community.

97. By the 1950s, Bataille will begin addressing the concept of *Hétérologie* with the term *Souveraineté*.

98. Lyotard, *The Differend*, 27.

99. Trouillot, *Silencing the Past*, 25.

# Bibliography

Abrahams, Roger D. "Playing the Dozens." *Journal of American Folklore* 75 (1962): 209–20.

Appiah, Kwame Anthony. "The Postcolonial and the Postmodern." *In My Father's House: Africa in the Philosophy of Culture*. New York: Oxford University Press, 1992: 137–57.

Arendt, Hannah. *The Origins of Totalitarianism*. New York: Harvest Books, 1973.

Ashcroft, Bill, Gareth Griffiths, and Helen Tiffin. *The Empire Writes Back: Theory and Practice in Post-Colonial Literatures*. London: Routledge, 2002.

Austin, J. L. *How to Do Things with Words*. Oxford: Oxford University Press, 1962.

Bachelard, Gaston. *La poétique de l'espace*. Paris: Presses Universitaires de France, 1961.

Bakhtin, Mikhail. *The Dialogic Imagination*. Austin: University of Texas Press, 1981.

———. *Problems of Dostoevsky's Poetics*. Minneapolis: University of Minnesota Press, 1984.

Baldwin, James. "Alas, Poor Richard." *Nobody Knows My Name*. New York: Dial Press, 1961: 181–89.

———. "Everybody's Protest Novel." *The Price of the Ticket: Collected Nonfiction 1948–1985*. New York: St. Martin's Press, 1985: 27–33.

———. *Giovanni's Room. Early Novels and Stories*. New York: Library of America, 1997: 221–360.

———. "The Discovery of What It Means to Be an American." *The Price of the Ticket: Collected Nonfiction, 1948–1985*. New York: St. Martin's Press, 1985: 171–76.

Barthes, Roland. *The Pleasure of the Text*. Translated by Richard Miller. New York: Hill and Wang, 1975.

Bataille, Georges. "Dossier sur l'hétérologie." *Oeuvres complètes, vol. II*. Paris: Gallimard, 1970: 147–64.

———. *Notre-Dame de Rheims. Oeuvres complètes I*. Paris: Gallimard, 1970.

Baudelaire, Charles. "Le serpent qui danse." *Les fleurs du mal*. Paris: Hatier, 2003: 286.

Baudrillard, Jean. "The Spirit of Terrorism." Translated by Rachel Bloul. *Le Monde*, November 2, 2001. http://www.egs.edu/faculty/jean-baudrillard/articles/the-spirit-of-terrorism/.

Bauer, Ralph, and José Antonio Mazzotti, eds. *Creole Subjects in the Colonial Americas: Empires, Texts, Identities*. Chapel Hill: University of North Carolina Press, 2009.

Benali, Zineb Ali, and Françoise Simasotchi-Bronès. "Le rire créole: entretien avec Maryse Condé." *Littérature* 154 (2009): 13–23.

Benítez-Rojo, Antonio. *The Repeating Island: The Caribbean Perspective and the Postmodern Perspective*. (2nd ed.) Translated by James Maraniss. Durham, N.C.: Duke University Press, 1996.

Bérard, Stéphanie. "Entretien avec Maryse Condé, Petit-Bourg, Guadeloupe, juillet 2002." *Women in French Studies* 12 (2004): 119–29.

Bernabé, Jean. "De la négritude à la créolité: éléments pour une approche comparée." *Etudes Françaises* 28 (1992): 23–38.

Bernabé, Jean, Patrick Chamoiseau, and Raphaël Confiant. *Eloge de la Créolité*. Paris: Gallimard, 1989.

Bhabha, Homi. *The Location of Culture*. London: Routledge Classics, 1994.

Birbalsingh, Frank. "Jamaica Kincaid: From Antigua to America." *Frontiers of Caribbean Literature in English*. Edited by Frank Birbalsingh. New York: St. Martin's Press, 1996: 138–51.

Bloom, Harold. *The Anxiety of Influence: A Theory of Poetry*. New York: Oxford University Press, 1973.

Boisseron, Bénédicte. "Potlatch transnational dans *Bleu-blanc-rouge* d'Alain Mabanckou." *Dalhousie French Studies* 84 (Fall 2008): 113–19.

Boisseron, Bénédicte, and Maryse Condé. "Intimité: entretien avec Maryse Condé." *International Journal of Francophone Studies* 13.1 (June 2010): 131–53.

Bongie, Chris. *Friends and Enemies: The Scribal Politics of Post/Colonial Literature*. Liverpool: Liverpool University Press, 2008.

Bonniol, Jean-Luc. *La couleur comme maléfice: une illustration créole de la généalogie des Blancs et des Noirs*. Paris: Albin Michel, 1992.

Boyarin, Daniel. "What Does a Jew Want?; or, The Political Meaning of the Phallus." *The Masculinity Studies Reader*. Edited by Rachel Adams and David Savran. Malden, Mass.: Blackwell, 2002: 274–90.

Boykin, Keith. *Beyond the Down Low: Sex, Lies, and Denial in Black America*. New York: Carroll and Graf, 2005.

Brathwaite, Edward. *The Development of Creole Society in Jamaica 1770–1820*. Oxford: Clarendon, 1971.

Braziel, Jana Evans. *Duvalier's Ghosts: Race, Diaspora, and U.S. Imperialism in Haitian Literatures*. New York: Palgrave Macmillan, 2007.

Braziel, Jana Evans, and Anita Mannur, eds. *Theorizing Diaspora: A Reader*. Malden, Mass.: Blackwell, 2003.

Breton, André. "Second manifeste du surréalisme." *La révolution surréaliste* (December 15, 1929): 1–17.

———. *Les manifestes du surréalisme*. Paris: Sagittaire, 1955.

Britton, Celia. *Edouard Glissant and Postcolonial Theory: Strategies of Language and Resistance*. Charlottesville: University of Virginia Press, 1999.

Brontë, Charlotte. *Jane Eyre*. London: Penguin, 2006.

Broyard, Bliss. *One Drop: My Father's Hidden Life—A Story of Race and Family Secrets*. New York: Little, Brown, 2007.

Broyard, Chandler. *Who Walk in Darkness*. New York: Herodias, 2000.

Buisseret, David. *Creolization in the Americas*. College Station: Texas A&M University Press, 2000.

Bullo, Alain. "Entretien avec Raphaël Confiant." *Caribana* 5 (1996): 39–49.

Burton, Richard. *Le roman marron: études sur la littérature martiniquaise contemporaine*. Paris: Harmattan, 1997.

Butel, Paul. *Histoire des Antilles françaises: XVIIe–XXe siècle*. Paris: Perrin, 2002.

Butler, Judith. *Excitable Speech: A Politics of the Performative*. New York: Routledge, 1997.

———. "Gender Is Burning: Questions of Appropriation and Subversion." *Bodies That Matter: On the Discursive Limits of Sex*. New York: Routledge, 1993: 121–40.

———. "Passing, Queering: Nella Larsen's Psychoanalytic Challenge." *Bodies That Matter: On the Discursive Limits of Sex*. New York: Routledge, 1993: 167–85.

Carr, Brian. "Paranoid Interpretation, Desire's Nonobject, and Nella Larsen's *Passing*." *PMLA* 119.2 (2004): 282–95.

Cazenave, Odile, and Patrica Célérier. *Contemporary Francophone African Writers and the Burden of Commitment*. Charlottesville: University of Virginia Press, 2011.

Césaire, Aimé. *Cahier d'un retour au pays natal*. Paris: Présence Africaine, 1986.

———. "Nègrerie: jeunesse noire et assimilation." *Légitime Défense* 1 (March 1935): 3.

———. *Une tempête*. Paris: Seuil, 1969.

Chambers, Ross. "Gossip and the Novel: Knowing Narrative and Narrative Knowing in Balzac, Mme de Lafayette and Proust." *Austrian Journal of French Studies* 22–23 (1985–86): 212–33.

———. *Untimely Interventions: AIDS Writing, Testimonial, and the Rhetoric of Haunting*. Ann Arbor: University of Michigan Press, 2004.

Chamoiseau, Patrick. *Chemin d'école*. Paris: Gallimard, 1993.

———. *Chronique des sept misères*. Paris: Gallimard, 1986.

———. *L'empreinte à Crusoé*. Paris: Gallimard, 2012.

———. *L'esclave vieil homme et le molosse*. Paris: Gallimard, 1997.

Cherki, Alice. *Frantz Fanon: A Portrait*. Translated by Nadia Benabid. Paris: Seuil, 2000.

Cisneros, Sandra. *The House on Mango Street*. London: Bloomsbury, 2004.

Cleaver, Eldridge. "Notes on a Native Son." *Black Expression: Essays by and about Black Americans in the Creative Arts*. Edited by Addison Gayle Jr. New York: City College of the University of New York, 1969: 339–49.

Clifford, James. *Routes: Travel and Translation in the Late Twentieth Century*. Cambridge, Mass: Harvard University Press, 1997.

Coates, Carrol F., and Dany Laferrière. "An Interview with Dany Laferrière." *Callaloo* 22.4 (1999): 910–21.

Condé, Maryse. *Célanire cou-coupé*. Paris: Laffont, 2000.

———. "Cherchons nos vérités." *Ecrire la parole de la nuit*. Edited by Ralph Ludwig. Paris: Gallimard, 1994.

———. *Desirada*. Paris: Laffont, 1997.

———. *En attendant la montée des eaux*. Paris: Lattès, 2010.

———. *Heremakhonon*. Paris: Union Générale d'Éditions, 1976.

———. *Histoire de la femme cannibale*. Paris: Mercure, 2003.

———. *La belle Créole*. Paris: Mercure, 2001.

———. *La civilisation du bossale: réflexion sur la littérature orale de la Guadeloupe et de la Martinique*. Paris: Harmattan, 1978.

———. *La migration des coeurs*. Paris: Laffont, 1995.

———. *La vie scélérate*. Paris: Seghers, 1987.

———. "Liaison dangereuse." *Pour une littérature-monde*. Edited by Michel Le Bris and Jean Rouaud. Paris: Gallimard, 2007: 205–16.

———. *Moi Tituba sorcière . . . Noire de Salem*. Paris: Mercure, 1986.

———. "O Brave New World." *Research in African Literatures* 29.3 (Fall 1998): 1–8.

———. "Order, Disorder, Freedom, and the West Indian Writer." *Yale French Studies* 83 (1993): 121–35.

———. *Penser la Créolité*. Paris: Karthala, 1995.

———. "Postface." *La culture vue d'ici et d'ailleurs*. Edited by Thomas C. Spear. Paris: Karthala, 2002: 241–48.

———. *Ségou: les murailles de terre*. Paris: Laffont, 1984.

———. *Traversée de la mangrove*. Paris: Mercure, 1989.

———. *Victoire: les saveurs et les mots*. Paris: Mercure, 2006.

Confiant, Raphaël. *Aimé Césaire: une traversée paradoxale du siècle*. Paris: Écriture, 2006.

———. *Black Is Black*. Monaco: Alphée, 2008.

———. *L'allée des soupirs*. Paris: Grasset, 1994.

———. *Le nègre et l'amiral*. Paris: Grasset, 1988.

———. "Lettre d'un homme de trente ans à Aimé Césaire." *Aimé Césaire: une traversée paradoxale du siècle*. Paris: Écriture, 2006: 319–22.

Craton, Michael. *Testing the Chains: Resistance to Slavery in the British West Indies*. Ithaca, N.Y.: Cornell University Press, 2009.

Cudjoe, Selwyn Reginald. *V. S. Naipaul: A Materialist Reading*. Amherst: University of Massachusetts Press, 1988.

Danticat, Edwidge. *Breath, Eyes, Memory*. New York: Vintage Books, 1998.

———. *Brother, I'm Dying*. New York: Alfred A. Knopf, 2007.

———. *Create Dangerously: The Immigrant Artist at Work*. Princeton, N.J.: Princeton University Press, 2010.

———. *The Dew Breaker*. New York: Alfred A. Knopf, 2004.

————. *The Farming of Bones*. New York: Penguin, 1998.

————. *Krik? Krak!* New York: Soho Press, 1991.

Dash, Michael J. *Edouard Glissant*. Cambridge: Cambridge University Press, 1995.

————. "Fictions of Displacement: Locating Modern Haitian Narratives." *Small Axe* 27 (2008): 32–41.

————. *The Other America: Caribbean Literature in a New World Context*. Charlottesville: University of Virginia Press, 1998.

De Certeau, Michel. *L'invention du quotidien 1. Arts de faire*. Paris: Gallimard, 1990.

Delbo, Charlotte. *Auschwitz et après: aucun de nous ne reviendra*. Paris: Éditions de Minuit, 1970.

Deleuze, Gilles, and Félix Guattari. *Kafka: Toward a Minor Literature*. Minneapolis: University of Minnesota Press, 1986.

Delpech, Catherine, and Maurice Roelens. *Société et littérature antillaises aujourd'hui: actes de la rencontre de novembre 1994 (Université de Perpignan)*. Perpignan: Presses Universitaires de Perpignan, 1997.

Delsham. Tony. *Négropolitains et Euro-blacks*. Schoelcher: MGG, 2000.

Denizet-Lewis, Benoit. "Double Lives on the Down Low." *New York Times*, August 3, 2003.

Depestres, René. *Le métier à métisser*. Paris: Stock, 1998.

Derrida, Jacques. "Freud and the Scene of Writing." *Yale French Studies* 48 (1972): 74–117.

————. *Limited Inc*. Evanston, Ill.: Northwestern University Press, 1988.

————. *Writing and Difference*. Chicago: University of Chicago Press, 1978.

Dirlik, Arif. "The Postcolonial Aura: Third World Criticism in the Age of Global Capitalism." *Dangerous Liaisons: Gender, Nation, and Postcolonial Perspectives*. Edited by Anne McClintock, Aamir Mufti, and Ella Shohat. Minneapolis: University of Minnesota Press, 1997.

Dollard, John. "The Dozens: Dialectic of Insult." *Mother Wit from the Laughing Barrel: Readings in the Interpretation of Afro-American Folklore*. New York: Garland, 1981: 277–94.

Domínguez, Virginia. *White by Definition: Social Classification in Creole Louisiana*. New Brunswick, N.J.: Rutgers University Press, 1994.

Dominique, Jan J. *Mémoire errante*. Montreal: Mémoire d'Encrier, 2008.

Dracius, Suzanne. *Lumina Sophie, dit 'Surprise' 1848–1889*. Paris: Desbel, 2005.

Dubois, Sylvie, and Megan Melançon. "Creole Is, Creole Ain't: Diachronic and Synchronic Attitudes toward Creole Identity in Southern Louisiana." *Language in Society* 29.2 (June 2000): 237–58.

Edmondson, Belinda. *Making Men: Gender, Literary Authority, and Women's Writing in Caribbean Narrative*. Durham, N.C.: Duke University Press, 1999.

Ellison, Ralph. "Change the Joke and Slip the Yoke." *Shadow and Act*. New York: Random House, 1953: 45–59.

Elte, Ottmar, and Ralph Ludwig. "En guise d'introduction: points de vue sur l'évolution de la littérature antillaise: entretiens avec les écrivains martiniquais Patrick Chamoiseau et Confiant, Raphaël." *Lendemains* 17.67 (1992): 6–16.

Erwin, Lee. "'Like in a Looking-Glass': History and Narrative in *Wide Sargasso Sea.*" *A Forum on Fiction* 22.2 (Winter 1989): 143–58.

Fabre, Geneviève, and Klaus Benesch, eds. *African Diasporas in the New World: Consciousness and Imagination*. Amsterdam: Rodopi, 2004.

Fabre, Michel. *The Unfinished Quest of Richard Wright*. Translated by Isabel Barzun. Chicago: University of Chicago Press, 1973.

Fanon, Frantz. *Black Skin, White Masks*. Translated by Charles Lam Markmann. New York: Grove Press, 1967.

———. *Black Skin, White Masks*. Translated by Richard Philcox. New York: Grove Press, 2008.

———. *Les damnés de la terre*. Paris: Maspero, 1961.

———. *Peau noire, masques blancs*. Paris: Gallimard, 1991.

Ferguson, James. "Return of the Creole." *Caribbean Beat* 39 (September–October 1999): 48–52.

Foster, Herbert L. *Ribbin', Jivin', and Playin' the Dozens: The Unrecognized Dilemma of Inner City Schools*. Cambridge, Mass.: Ballinger, 1974.

French, Patrick. *The World Is What It Is*. New York: Alfred A. Knopf, 2008.

Freud, Sigmund. "The Uncanny." *The Standard Edition of the Complete Psychological Works of Sigmund Freud Vol. 22*. London: Hogarth, 1953: 159–215.

———. "The Unconscious." *The Standard Edition of the Complete Psychological Works of Sigmund Freud Vol. 14*. London: Hogarth, 1953: 240–54.

Fulton, Dawn. "A Question of Cannibalism: Unspeakable Crime in Histoire de la femme cannibale." *Feasting on Words: Maryse Condé, Cannibalism, and the Caribbean Text*. Edited by Kathryn Lachman, Nicole Simek, and Vera Broichhagen. Princeton, N.J.: PLAS Program in Latin American Studies, Princeton University, 2006.

Garraway, Doris. *The Libertine Colony: Creolization in the Early French Caribbean*. Durham, N.C.: Duke University Press, 2005.

Gates, Henry Louis, Jr. "White Like Me. African American Author Anatole Broyard." *New Yorker*, June 17, 1996, 66–81.

———. "The Passing of Anatole Broyard." *Thirteen Ways of Looking at a Black Man*. New York: Random House, 1997: 180–214.

———. *The Signifying Monkey: A Theory of African-American Literary Criticism*. Oxford: Oxford University Press, 1988.

———. "Writing Race and the Difference It Makes." *Critical Inquiry* 12.1 (Autumn 1985): 1–20.

Genette, Gérard. *Seuils*. Paris: Seuil, 1987.

Gilroy, Paul. "Diasporas." *Paragraph* 17.3 (November 1994): 207–12.

———. *The Black Atlantic: Modernity and Double Consciousness*. Cambridge, Mass.: Harvard University Press, 1993.

Glissant, Edouard. *Introduction à une poétique du divers*. Paris: Gallimard, 1995.

———. *La lézarde*. Paris: Gallimard, 1997.

———. *Le discours antillais*. Paris: Seuil, 1981.

———. *Poétique de la relation*. Paris: Gallimard, 1990.

———. *Tout-monde*. Paris: Gallimard, 1993.

Griffin, John Howard. *Black Like Me*. Boston: Houghton Mifflin, 1961.

Hall, Gwendolyn Midlo. *Africans in Colonial Louisiana: The Development of Afro-Creole Culture in the Eighteenth Century*. Baton Rouge: Louisiana State University Press, 1992.

Hall, Stuart. "Cultural Identity and Diaspora." *Identity, Community, Culture, Difference*. Edited by Jonathan Rutherford. London: Lawrence and Wishart, 1990: 222–237.

———. "When Was the 'Post-Colonial'? Thinking at the Limit." *The Post-Colonial Question*. Edited by Ian Chambers and Lidia Curti. London: Routledge, 1996.

Hallward, Peter. *Damming the Flood: Haiti, Aristide, and the Politics of Containment*. London: Verso, 2010.

Hardwick, Elizabeth. "Meeting V. S. Naipaul." *Conversations with V. S. Naipaul*. Edited by Feroza Jussawa. Jackson: University Press of Mississippi, 1997: 45–49.

Hardwick, Louise. "J'ai toujours été une personne un peu à part." *International Journal of Francophone Studies* 9.1 (2006).

Harris, Marvin. *Patterns of Race in the Americas*. Westport, Conn.: Greenwood Press, 1980.

Hawthorne, Nathaniel. "The Minister's Black Veil." *The Novels and Tales of Nathaniel Hawthorne*. New York: Modern Library (Random House), 1937: 872–82.

Hayes, Jarrod. "Looking for Roots among the Mangroves: Errances enracinées and Migratory Identities." *Centennial Review* 42.3 (1998): 459–74.

Hazaël-Massieux, Marie-Christine. "Creole in the French Caribbean Novel of the 1990s: From Reality to Myth?" *The Francophone Caribbean Today. Literature, Language, Culture, Studies in Memory of Bridget Jones*. Edited by Gertrud Aub-Buscher and Beverley Ormerod Noakes. Kingston, Jamaica: University of the West Indies Press, 2003: 82–101.

Hollinger, David A. "Amalgamation and Hypodescent: The Question of Ethnoracial Mixture in the History of the United States." *American Historical Review* 108.5 (December 2003): 1363–90.

Huggan, Graham. *The Postcolonial Exotic: Marketing the Margins*. London: Routledge, 2001.

James, Cyril Lionel Robert. *Mariners, Renegades, and Castaways: The Story of Herman Melville and the World We Live In*. (2nd ed.) Hanover, N.H.: University Press of New England, 1978.

James, Henry. "The Figure in the Carpet." *The Complete Tales of Henry James Vol. 9 (1882–1898)*. Edited by Leon Edel. London: Rupert Hart-Davis, 1964: 273–315.

Jonassaint, Jean. "Le nomade enraciné." *Le métier à métisser*. Paris: Stock, 1998: 137–47.

Kanor, Fabienne. *D'eaux douces*. Paris: Gallimard, 2003.

Kein, Sybil. *The History and Legacy of Louisiana's Free People of Color*. Baton Rouge: Louisiana State University Press, 2000.

Kincaid, Jamaica. *A Small Place*. New York: Farrar, Straus and Giroux, 1988.

———. *Lucy*. New York: Macmillan, 2002.

————. *My Brother*. New York: Farrar, Straus and Giroux, 1997.

————. *See Now Then*. New York: Farrar, Straus and Giroux, 2013.

King, Jane. "A Small Place Writes Back." *Callaloo* 25.3 (Summer 2002): 885–909.

Kundera, Milan. *L'ignorance*. Paris: Gallimard, 2000.

————. *Les testaments Trahis*. Paris: Gallimard, 1996.

Labat, Jean-Baptiste. *Voyage aux îles: chronique aventureuse des Caraïbes*. Paris: Phébus Libretto, 1993.

Lachman, Kathryn, Nicole Simek, and Vera Broichhagen, eds. "A Conversation at Princeton with Maryse Condé (December 3, 2003)." *Feasting on Words: Maryse Condé, Cannibalism, and the Caribbean Text*. Princeton, N.J.: PLAS Program in Latin American Studies, Princeton University, 2006: 1–27.

Laferrière, Dany. *Cette grenade dans la main du jeune nègre est-elle une arme ou un fruit?* Paris: Serpent à Plumes, 2002.

————. *Chronique de la dérive douce*. Montreal: VLB, 1994.

————. *Comment faire l'amour avec un nègre sans se fatiguer*. Montreal: VLB, 1985.

————. *Eroshima*. Montreal: VLB, 1987.

————. *J'écris comme je vis. Entretien avec Bernard Magnier*. Outremont: Lanctôt, 2000.

————. *Je suis un écrivain japonais*. Paris: Grasset, 2008.

————. *Je suis fatigué*. Vincennes: Librairies Initiales, 2000.

————. *La chair du maître*. Outremont: Lanctôt, 1997.

————. *Le charme des après-midi sans fin*. Outremont: Lanctôt, 1997.

————. *Le cri des oiseaux fous*. Paris: Serpent à Plumes, 2000.

————. *L'énigme du retour*. Paris: Grasset, 2009.

————. *Le goût des jeunes filles*. Montreal: VLB, 1992.

————. *L'odeur du café*. Montreal: VLB, 1991.

————. *Pays sans chapeau*. Paris: Serpent à Plumes, 1999.

————. *Tout bouge autour de moi*. Paris: Grasset, 2011.

————. *Vers le sud*. Paris: Grasset, 2006.

Lahens, Yannick. *Failles*. Paris: Sabine Wespeiser, 2010.

Lamming, George. "George Lamming: Concepts of the Caribbean." *Frontiers of Caribbean Literature in English*. Edited by Frank Birbalsingh. London: Macmillan Caribbean, 1996. 1–14.

————. *Water with Berries*. New York: Holt, Rinehart, and Winston, 1972.

Laplanche, Jean. *Life and Death in Psychoanalysis*. Translated by Jeffrey Mehlman. Baltimore: Johns Hopkins University Press, 1976.

Larose, Karim. "Major and Minor: Crossed Perspectives." *SubStance* 31.1 (2002): 36–47.

Larsen, Nella. *Passing*. Oxford: Penguin, 1997.

Le Bris, Michel, ed. *Haïti parmi les vivants*. Paris. Actes Sud, 2010.

Lest, Julius. "James Baldwin—Reflections of a Maverick." *New York Times*, May 27, 1984.

Levin, Bernard. "V. S. Naipaul: A Perpetual Voyager." *The Listener*, June 23, 1983, 93–98.

Lionnet, Françoise, and Shu-mei Shih, eds. *Minor Transnationalism*. Durham, NC: Duke University Press, 2005.

Lyons, Bonnie, and Edwidge Danticat. "An Interview with Edwidge Danticat." *Contemporary Literature* 44.2 (2003): 183–98.

Lyotard, Jean-François. *The Differend: Phrases in Dispute*. Translated by Georges Van Den Abbeele. Theory and History of Literature 46. Minneapolis: University of Minnesota Press, 1988.

Mabanckou, Alain. *Bleu-blanc-rouge*. Paris: Présence Africaine, 1998.

Mannoni, Octave. *Psychologie de la colonisation*. Paris: Seuil, 1950.

Mardorossian, Carine M. *Reclaiming Difference: Caribbean Women Rewrite Postcolonualism*. Charlottesville: University of Virginia Press, 2005.

Marshall, Paule. *Brown Girl, Brownstones*. New York: Feminist Press at the City University of New York, 1959.

Martin, Lionel-Edouard. *Le tremblement, Haïti 12 janvier 2010*. Paris: Arléa, 2010.

Mauss, Marcel. *The Gift: Forms and Functions of Exchange in Archaic Societies*. Translated by Ian Cunnisoon. London: Cohen and West, 1966.

McDowell, Deborah E. "Introduction." *Passing and Quicksand*. Nella Larsen. New Brunswick, NJ: Rutgers University Press, 1986: ix–xxxv.

Melville, Herman. *Moby-Dick*. New York: Bantam Dell, 1967.

Michener, Charles. "The Dark Visions of V. S. Naipaul." *Conversations with V. S. Naipaul*. Edited by Feroza Jussawa. Jackson: University Press of Mississippi, 1997: 63–74.

Mitchell-Kernan, Claudia. "Signifying, Loud-Talking and Marking." *Rappin' and Stylin' Out: Communication in Black America*. Edited by T. Kotchman. Urbana: University of Illinois Press, 1972.

Mukherjee, Bharati, and Robert Boyers. "A Conversation with V. S. Naipaul." *Conversations with V. S. Naipaul*. Edited by Feroza Jussawa. Jackson: University Press of Mississippi, 1997: 75–92.

Munro, Martin. *Exile and Post-1946 Haitian Literature: Alexis, Depestre, Ollivier, Laferrière, Danticat*. Liverpool: Liverpool University Press, 2007.

Murdoch, Adlai. "Ghosts in the Mirror: Colonialism and Creole Indeterminacy in Brontë and Sand." *College Literature* 29.1 (Winter 2002): 1–31.

Murray, David A. B. "Laws of Desire? Race, Sexuality, and Power in Male Martinican Sexual Narratives." *American Ethnologist* 26.1 (February 1999): 160–72.

Mwangi, Evan. *Africa Writes Back to Self: Metafiction, Gender, Sexuality*. Albany: State University of New York Press, 2009.

Naipaul, V. S. *An Area of Darkness*. New York: Macmillan, 1964.

———. *The Middle Passage*. New York: Vintage Books, 2002.

———. "Two Worlds: The 2001 Nobel Lecture." *World Literature Today* 76.2 (Spring 2002): 4–10.

Nelson, William Javier. "Racial Definition: Background for Divergence." *Phylon* 47.4 (1986): 318–26.

Nesbitt, Nick. *Voicing Memory: History and Subjectivity in French Caribbean Literature.* Charlottesville: University of Virginia Press, 2003.

Noxolo, Patricia, and Marika Preziuso. "Postcolonial Imaginations: Approaching a 'Fictional' World through the Novels of Maryse Condé and Wilson Harris." *Annals of the Association of American Geographers* 103.1 (2013): 163–79.

O'Brien, Conor Cruise, Edward Said, and John Lukacs. "The Intellectual in the Post-Colonial World." *Salmagundi 70/71, Intellectuals* (Spring–Summer 1986): 65–81.

Onwuchekwa, Jemie, ed. *Yo' Mama!: New Raps, Toasts, Dozens, Jokes, and Children's Rhymes from Urban Black America.* Philadelphia: Temple University Press, 2003.

Page, Kezia. "What If He Did Not Have a Sister [Who Lived in the United States]? Jamaica Kincaid's *My Brother* as Remittance Text." *Small Axe* 21 (October 2006): 37–53.

Paré, François. "Edouard Glissant: A Poetics of Shorelines." *Sites: The Journal of Twentieth-Century/Contemporary Studies revue d'études françaises* 7.2 (2003): 267–76.

———. *Exiguity: Reflections on the Margins of Literature.* Translated by Linn Burman. Waterloo: Wilfrid Laurier University Press, 1997.

Pépin, Ernest. *Cantique des tourterelles.* Paris: Écriture, 2004.

Pfaff, Françoise. *Entretiens avec Maryse Condé.* Paris: Karthala, 1993.

Phillips, Caryl. *Dancing in the Dark.* New York: Vintage Books, 2005.

Pineau, Gisèle. *L'exil selon Julia.* Paris: Librairie Générale Française, 2010.

Prasad, Pratima. "Intimate Strangers: Interracial Encounters in Romantic Narratives of Slavery." *L'Esprit Créateur* 47 (2007): 71–85.

Price, Richard. *Maroon Societies: Rebel Slave Communities in the Americas.* Baltimore: Johns Hopkins University Press, 1979.

Retamar, Roberto Fernàndez. *Caliban and Other Essays.* Minneapolis: University of Minnesota Press, 1989.

Rhys, Jean. *Wide Sargasso Sea.* New York: Norton, 1966.

Ricoeur, Paul. *Histoire et vérité.* Paris: Seuil, 1955.

Rosello, Mireille. *Postcolonial Hospitality: The Immigrant as Guest.* Stanford, CA: Stanford University Press, 2001.

———. "Post-Cannibalism in *Histoire de la femme cannibale.*" *Feasting on Words: Maryse Condé, Cannibalism, and the Caribbean Text.* Edited by Kathryn Lachman, Nicole Simek, and Vera Broichhagen. Princeton, N.J.: PLAS Program in Latin American Studies, Princeton University, 2006: 29–47.

Roth, Philip. *The Human Stain.* New York: Vintage International, 2000.

Rowe-Evans, Adrian. "V. S. Naipaul: A Transition (Interview)." *Transition* 40 (December 1971): 56–62.

Rushdie, Salman. "The Empire Writes Back with a Vengeance." *The Times of London*, July 3, 1982: 7–8.

Saïd, Edward. "The Intellectual in the Post-Colonial World." *Salmagundi 70/71, Intellectuals* (Spring–Summer 1986): 44–64.

Saint-Eloi, Rodney. *Haïti: Kenbé la!* Paris: Michel Lafon, 2010.

Sansavior, Eva. "Entretien avec Maryse Condé." *Francophone Postcolonial Studies* 2.2 (2004): 7–33.

Sartre, Jean-Paul. *Huis clos, suivi de Les Mouches*. Paris: Gallimard, 1947.

———. *L'être et le néant: essai d'onthologie phénoménologique*. Paris: Gallimard, 1976.

———. "Orphée noir." *Anthologie de la nouvelle poésie nègre et malgache*. Edited by Léopold Senghor. Paris: Presses Universitaires de France, 1948.

Scharfman, Ronnie. "Créolité Is/As Resistance: Raphaël Confiant's *Le nègre et l'amiral*." *Penser la Créolité*. Paris: Karthala, 1995: 125–34.

Schneebaum, Tobias. *Keep the River on Your Right*. New York: Grove Press, 1969.

Schwarz-Bart, Simone. *La Mulâtresse Solitude*. Paris: Seuil, 1972.

———. *Pluie et vent sur Télumée Miracle*. Paris: Seuil, 1995.

Segalen, Victor. *Essay on Exoticism: An Aesthetics of Diversity*. Translated by Yaël Rachel Schlick. Durham, NC: Duke University Press, 2002.

Serres, Michel. *Le parasite*. Paris: Hachette, 1997.

Shakespeare, William. *The Tempest*. New York: Folger Shakespeare Library, 1994.

Sontag, Susan. *Illness as Metaphor and AIDS and Its Metaphors*. New York: Picador USA, 1977.

Spear, Thomas C. "Carnivalesque jouissance: Representations of Sexuality in the Francophone West Indian Novel." Translated by Richard D. Reitsma. *Jouvert: A Journal of Postcolonial Studies* 2.1 (1998).

———. "Point of View." *Haiti Rising: Essays on Haitian History, Culture and the Earthquake of 2010*. Edited by Martin Munro. Liverpool: Liverpool University Press, 2010: 35–42.

Surya, Michel. *Georges Bataille: An Intellectual Biography*. Translated by Krzysztof Fijalkowski and Michael Richardson. London: Verso, 2010.

Taylor, Lucien. "Créolité Bites: A Conversation with Patrick Chamoiseau, Raphaël Confiant, and Jean Bernabé." *Transitions* 74 (1997): 124–61.

———. "Mediating Martinique: 'The Paradoxical Trajectory' of Raphaël Confiant." *Cultural Producers in Perilous States: Editing Events, Documenting Change*. Edited by George E. Marcus. Chicago: University of Chicago Press, 1997: 259–329.

Thomas, Dominic. "Fashion Matters: La Sape and Vestimentary Codes in Transnational Contexts and Urban Diasporas." *MLN* 18.4 (September 2003): 947–73.

Trouillot, Michel-Rolph. *Silencing the Past: Power and the Production of History*. Boston: Beacon Press, 1997.

Vaughan, Alden T., and Virginia Mason Vaughan. *Shakespeare's Caliban: A Cultural History*. Cambridge: Cambridge University Press, 1991.

Vaughan, Virginia Mason. "'Something Rich and Strange': Caliban's Theatrical Metamorphoses." *Shakespeare Quarterly* 36.4 (Winter 1985): 390–405.

Vian, Boris. *J'irai cracher sur vos tombes*. Paris: Livre de Poche, 1997.

Walcott, Derek. *What the Twilight Says*. New York: Farrar, Straus and Giroux, 1998.

Winokur, Scott. "The Unsparing Vision of V. S. Naipaul." *Conversations with V. S. Naipaul*. Edited by Feroza Jussawa. Jackson: University Press of Mississippi, 1997: 114–29.

# Index

Bénédicte Boisseron is professor of Afroamerican and African studies at the University of Michigan, Ann Arbor.

CPSIA information can be obtained
at www.ICGtesting.com
Printed in the USA
LVHW110344140422
715649LV00005B/16